MEDITA

FOOD *For The* HUNGRY HEART

Daily Devotions for Overeaters

Cynthia Rowland McClure

❖ *A Janet Thoma Book* ❖

Thomas Nelson Publishers
Nashville

❖ *A Janet Thoma Book* ❖

Copyright © 1991 by Cynthia Rowland McClure

Published in Nashville, Tennessee, by Thomas Nelson, Inc., and distributed in Canada by Lawson Falle, Ltd., Cambridge, Ontario.

Scripture quotations are from the NEW KING JAMES VERSION of the Bible. Copyright © 1979, 1980, 1982, Thomas Nelson, Inc., Publishers.

Library of Congress Cataloging-in-Publication Data

McClure, Cynthia Rowland.
    Food for the hungry heart / Cynthia
    Rowland McClure.
       p. cm. — (Serenity meditation series)
    ISBN 0-8407-3222-8
    1. Eating disorders—Patients—Prayer-
books and devotions—English.
2. Devotional calendars. I. Title.
BV4910.35.M24 1991
242'.4—dc20   90–49395
                    CIP

Printed in the United States of America
5 6 7 — 96 95 94 93 92

To Ann McMurray,
who believes in my dreams

To the Lisas who have left us

To the loved ones left behind
to wonder why

To those living with an eating disorder—
I wish you courage and faith
to fight your monsters

To Father God, who has the answers
and holds us all in His loving hands

For those of you struggling with a weight obsession—bulimia, anorexia, dieting, exercising—I want you to know that I have been there. More than anything, I want you to know there is hope to overcome. You can be normal and love life and love God in a wonderful way.

For twelve years of my life I lived with an eating disorder called bulimia. The "monster" controlled my life until it nearly ended. When I was twenty-eight years old I entered the Minirth-Meier Clinic, barely alive because of bulimia. There the professionals taught me how to slay my "monsters." After fighting, reliving, and confronting my pain and past, I had to let go and forgive.

The journey to overcoming and reaching a point of wholeness can be long and painful, but the result is worth the effort. As you go on your journey to understand the whys behind your struuggles with food, I hope *Food for the Hungry Heart* will encourage you, spark new insight, give you some answers. I pray that the stories you will read about will help you to know you are not alone, no matter what you are struggling with.

God bless you.

Cynthia Rowland McClure

PLEASE ROCK ME, DADDY – *January 1*

In God is my salvation and my glory;
The rock of my strength,
And my refuge, is in God.

—PS. 62:7

Laura had struggled with her weight most of her life. It was painful being the only one in her family of six who did, and they chastised her to lose weight. In college she felt greater pressure. Her brother was a lawyer; one sister was going to be a doctor. Laura became bulimic, at first to lose weight. She later realized it was not just the weight the bulimia was "helping her to lose," but the pain inside of her as well. Eventually she found that what she was doing was self-destructive.

With the help of a caring therapist, Laura found answers. She learned she was the "lost child" of the family. Never a burden to her parents, she did not get the touching and loving she needed. She *knew* her dad loved her, but she did not *feel* it. Laura took a trip home. She asked her dad to go to the basement with her, down the stairs, to where an old rocking chair sat.

"Dad," Laura said shakily. "You know, you never rocked me as a child. Dad, I know this sounds weird, but I need to be just your little girl again for a few minutes."

Lovingly, Laura's father held and rocked her.

Tears fell from her soul. The little girl inside grieved over all the times she longed to hear "I believe in you. I accept you, fat or thin."

Today, imagine our Father of all fathers saying to you, "Do you need to be rocked and hugged, my child? I'm always in the rocking chair for you."

> *For I was hungry and you gave Me food;*
> *I was thirsty and you gave Me drink;*
> *I was a stranger and you took Me in.*
> —MATT. 25:35

When I was a child, my parents had a lot of burdens I did not understand. My dad traveled because of his job. My mom lived with depression. I never wanted to bother my parents, and when I felt lonely, I would go next door to see Grandma Hamstreet. We were not blood relatives, but she was my grandma. When I would knock on her door, her smile and the twinkle in her eyes let me know I was truly loved. She always gave me cookies and milk or a piece of candy. She would look in my eyes and say, "How is my Cyndi doing today?"

When I was near death because of my bulimia, Grandma Hamstreet was ninety-one years old. She wrote me when she found out.

My Sweet Cyndi,

How I wish I could be there to help you. Please know I pray for you every day. And I just know God will use this for his purpose. He'll probably use you like the apostle Paul when you overcome this.

How I love you, my precious Cyndi.

Grandma Hamstreet

Do you have a Grandma Hamstreet? If you don't, please find one. The love will fill up the places that cookies and candy never can.

Father God, thank You for the Grandma Hamstreets of this world.

*And you shall know the truth, and the truth
shall make you free.* —JOHN 8:32

What is *your* truth?

I believe with all my heart that Jesus wants us to know Him as the true answer for eternal life, but the "truth" goes beyond that. He wants us to be truthful with ourselves. When I had bulimia, I was obsessed with food, my weight, and my looks. I will never forget the pain I felt when I ate anything because it meant I would get fat. But the real truth was: I was not dealing with my life. The bulimia was numbing the pain. I did not want to look at all the pain inside, much less feel it. I was angry and sad and felt abandoned as a child. My past was haunting me and the food simply pushed my feelings down a little farther until one day my subconscious was filled to the brim. My heart and body said, "If you don't get these feelings out, you're going to die."

I had to find the truth, and ultimately it set me free. What is your truth?

Were you sexually abused as a child and you have never told anyone? Do you feel ashamed and your fat protects you from intimacy? Does your bulimia prove you are a bad person? Do you tell yourself that no one would like you if they really knew what you did?

Facing the truth is scary, but I have learned that Jesus' words are right. Know the truth.

Jesus, help us to be strong to face the truth of our past. Help us remember how it felt and deal with the painful memories so we can be set free!

> *And Jesus said to them, "I am*
> *the bread of life. He who comes*
> *to Me shall never hunger"*
> —JOHN 6:35

You go to the refrigerator. You want to eat that apple pie. Not just a piece, but the whole thing. And nobody is going to stop you. In fact, you feel as if you would knock somebody out of your way if they tried to stop you. But wait a minute. Maybe it is not physical hunger at all. Maybe it is the hunger of an empty heart or unresolved anger. Did you have an argument with your husband or wife and did not take the chance to tell your feelings?

When I was nineteen years old, my husband left me and I went through a devastating divorce. I thought my bulimia was just a great way to lose weight. What I did not realize was that it was helping me hide from my feelings. It took me a while to start dating again, and when I did I felt horrible. I remember going out with a guy and realizing he was not someone I enjoyed. As soon as I got home, I headed for the refrigerator, where I proceeded to eat an entire pecan pie. I did not stop and say, "Cynthia, what's really going on here?" I just plunged ahead, then purged.

As I look back now, I know I was filling an emptiness—filling up the hole left by my feelings of failure. I was not physically hungry for that pecan pie. I was hungry for my life to be normal. I did not need food. I needed someone to say, "Hang on, Cynthia."

Father, fill us up when we're hungry. Help us to stop and ask, "What am I really hungry for?"

Man looks at the outward appearance,
but the LORD looks at the heart.
—1 SAM. 16:7

As a television news reporter, I knew Mother Teresa was a Nobel Peace Prize winner. But as a self-reliant correspondent who wanted to look good on the nightly news, confident and ready to tell the story of the hour, I did not understand the uproar over Mother Teresa.

I was given the story assignment when she came to town. When my cameraman and I arrived at the airport, hundreds of people were crowded around the gate. In my arrogance, I thought, What's the big deal?

Mother Teresa was tiny, stooped, her face covered with wrinkles. She wore a simple white robe and sandals. I thought, Why do all these people want to touch this woman? Mother Teresa spoke in a packed football stadium. "We have such hunger in India. So many die of starvation, but I have learned that you here in America have so much food, yet you are hungry in the spirit. I see loneliness, despair, divorce, lack of prayer."

This beautiful wrinkled old woman was talking about me. I could eat twenty-five dollars worth of food and afford it, but after my self-destruction I was still empty.

Mother Teresa knew about my real hunger, and she filled me up.

Precious God, fill me with the food of love. Help me not to judge someone's appearance but to see the spiritual food they have to offer me.

> *"Be angry, and do not sin."* Do not
> let the sun go down on your wrath.
> —EPH. 4:26

Nice Christian girls don't get angry, I heard as a child. *Christians* don't get angry. So if I felt angry, I locked it away. I remember once, on the job, my news photographer did not get enough footage for my six o'clock story. I was furious. Did I tell him, "I feel really upset, and in the future I'd appreciate it if you would get more than enough footage without my asking. I'll try to remind you, but I feel upset because my story won't be as good as it could be"?

No. Instead, I got my purse, took out five quarters, and hurriedly took myself to the candy machine where I stuffed five candy bars down my throat.

I was dealing with anger by bingeing and purging, but this only intensified my anger toward myself. I felt so guilty for being out of control. I have learned since that anger is a God-given emotion. If I am angry, I need to voice it and then let go of it.

The Bible does not say, "Don't get angry." It says, "Be angry, and do not sin." In other words, do not hide it. Deal with it and get some sleep.

Nice girls *do* get angry.

How do you deal with day-to-day anger? If you feel the emotion, talk about it. Confront it.

Lord, help me to say, "I feel angry because. . . ." Give me the power to admit it, work through it, and get on with my life.

They . . . came to Jesus, and found the
man . . . sitting at the feet of Jesus,
clothed, and in his right mind.
—LUKE 8:35

Normal. How I longed to be normal. Within me there was so much jealousy and rage when I saw that others were normal and I wasn't. I once had a colleague who loved Snickers candy bars. Each day she would bring one to work, leave it on her desk, and when she was ready she would eat that candy bar. She enjoyed it savored it. When I watched her do this, I felt such remorse and anger. You see, she was normal It is normal to eat one candy bar. It is normal to have a candy bar available, and not have to eat it just because it is there.

When I was bulimic, I could never eat one Snickers. It had to be six, or ten, and I would stuff them down my throat in five minutes. I never tasted the chocolate and caramel and nuts. I just felt as if I had to rush and get the food to my stomach. Fill myself up. I could never take the time to savor the taste.

While I longed to be normal, I could not be because first I had to deal with what I was really trying to fill up. For so long, I tried to fill up my inadequacies, my fears, my lack of perfection, my ugliness. If I filled myself up with food, then I did not have to deal with my fears. But the problems were still there.

Do you desire to be normal? Then what is it you are really trying to fill up?

God, help me find out what I am trying to avoid, and find normalcy.

> *Be anxious for nothing, but in*
> *everything by prayer and sup-*
> *plication, with thanksgiving,*
> *let your requests be made known*
> *to God; and the peace of God,*
> *which surpasses all understand-*
> *ing, will guard your hearts and*
> *minds through Christ Jesus.*
> —PHIL. 4:6–7

> *Sadness is a silent cry or scream.*
> *A rain that never stops pouring.*
> *A long lost pet,*
> *Chilling in the rain that never stops.*

My friend, Maggie, wrote this poem when she was sixteen years old. Yet, when I met her, she looked like she was seventy. She weighed sixty-eight pounds. Maggie was starving herself to death by anorexia.

Why would a beautiful girl destroy herself like this? I was in the same psychiatric ward as Maggie, fighting for my life because of bulimia. We became friends.

Maggie's father constantly said, "Unless you have something to say, don't say anything at all." So she literally shut her mouth. Turning her anger inward, she got her dad's attention by starving herself.

Maggie learned she could not change her dad. She also found out her heavenly Father is not like her earthly father. He never says, "I don't want to hear what you have to say." Instead, our Creator, our true Father, longs for us to talk to Him.

Father, I need Your love. I need You to listen to my many needs.

*Bear one another's burdens, and so
fulfill the law of Christ.* —GAL. 6:2

When I was a little girl, I had a playroom that was my place of secrets. I could close the door of that room and escape from the world. In this room, I could be anything my heart desired. As a school teacher, I would imagine all my pupils listening to my every word. Or I would open the box of old Halloween costumes and clothes and dress myself as an elegant lady, to have tea with an imaginary friend. In this secret room I learned to be an actress. I desperately wanted to be somebody else instead of me.

As I grew up I always wore a smile on my face, fearing that if I did not people would not want to be with me. At age twenty-eight, no one knew I was living with an addiction that was killing me physically, emotionally, and spiritually. After all, what would people think if they really knew the real me?

Through intense therapy and growth, I have learned that it is OK to take off my mask and say, "I'm really hurting. I don't feel like smiling today. I feel like crying." God gave us people to help ease our pain.

Are you acting out the part you think is expected of you, yet inside you are miserable and thinking, What would people think if they knew the real me? God encourages us to bear one another's burdens. Take off the mask. Find people who will love you for you, and not because you are a great actor.

Father God, help us to unmask ourselves and help others to do the same.

> *Confess your trespasses to one*
> *another, and pray for one another,*
> *that you may be healed.*
> —JAMES 5:16

Bingeing and purging were all that mattered. My life was out of control. I no longer wanted to live. When I admitted myself into the Minirth-Meier Clinic it was a matter of life and death. There I slowly found the reasons why I was self-destructive. One night, I became very suicidal. A nurse stayed up with me all night. The first thing the next morning, my therapist, Mike, took me to a room and said, "Start talking."

I sobbed, "Mike, why didn't anybody ask how sick I was? Why didn't anyone know I was dying? Why didn't anyone do anything?"

He looked at me for a moment, then asked, "Did you ever tell them, Cynthia? Did you ever tell anyone how desperate you were?"

I had to say, "No, not really. I tried, but I couldn't say I felt like putting a gun to my head." There were many reasons why: fear of rejection, fear of disbelief.

Mike was letting me know it was time to be honest and say how bad it really was.

Today, are you desperate? Have you told someone who could help you understand why, or pray for you, or hug you?

It is OK to tell a caring someone how bad it really is.

Father, honesty is so hard—reaching out for help, revealing myself is scary. God, help me to be open. Give me courage.

*The devil . . . does not stand
in the truth, because there is
no truth in him.*
—JOHN 8:44

Ann had been in three different hospitals trying to find the answer to why she wanted to die. She would switch from being bulimic to anorexic. She had been near death many times. After years in therapy, a locked-up memory emerged: from the time she was four until she was eight, her stepfather sexually abused her. Each time he came into her room, he threatened her, "Don't ever tell your mother! If you do, she won't believe you, and she'll give you away!"

The very act of abuse from someone she trusted was so confusing she had blocked the memories. Once she remembered, she confronted her stepfather. His response was, "You're crazy! I never did that!" She knew it was true, but the little child within her questioned, Did it really happen?

After much prayer and continued therapy, she called her stepfather and said, "You have a problem. You need help. You have hurt me deeply and I'm sorry for you, but until you admit your sickness and seek help, I can't have a relationship with you. I'll be praying for you, but I refuse to ever protect you again."

Ann had to quit questioning and say, "Yes, it did happen." It was not easy, but she has gone on.

Are you protecting your abuser? Stop. Confront. Relive it and deal with the pain.

God, help me to confront and forgive the hurts in my past.

> *Be of good courage,*
> *And He shall strengthen your heart,*
> *All you who hope in the LORD.*
> —PS. 31:24

So many people are caught up in the lies, "I have this eating problem because I have no discipline." "I'm a bad person," or "I just don't have enough faith." It takes courage to say, "I'm sick and I need help."

If you have the flu, you go to your doctor. If you break your arm, you get to an emergency room. If you suffer from eating disorder, whether it is compulsive overeating or bulimia or anorexia, you need help.

With all my heart, I do not believe an emotionally unhealthy Christian is a glory to God. If you are obsessed to the point where nothing really matters but food or purging or starving, have the courage to say, "I need help." God needs you to be healthy and whole to overcome your eating disorder. It is never too late to admit you need help.

God wants you to be a glory to Him. It takes courage and the rewards of that courage are abundant.

God, give me courage to say, "Help me," to someone. God, help me to reach out for help.

*He has filled the hungry
with good things.*
—LUKE 1:53

Friend, I can't go away with you for the weekend because I've got the flu."

Translation: What I am really saying is, I have made myself sick with my bingeing and purging so I can avoid being with you. You might see the real me, and you would hate me.

"I'm just too busy to go to lunch with you."

Translation: If I eat, I might lose control.

"I can't go to the party. I have other plans."

Translation: My plan is to binge and purge and have my own party. I just can not handle being around people who will look at me and think I am fat and ugly. So I will prove them right by self-destructing.

I used to make so many excuses to avoid interacting with other people. There were always so many reasons to avoid loving and being loved. Food was my *friend*. Food was my party. Food was *safe*. And while it filled me up physically, I was so empty emotionally.

What is your excuse today to avoid being with friends? Today, with God's help, I challenge you to invite someone to lunch. Think of them. Ask them questions. Taste and savor the moments of friendship. You will be filled up in a heavenly way.

Father, thank You for the precious gift of friends. Help me to trust them.

> *For with God nothing will*
> *be impossible.*
> —LUKE 1:37

The urge would come. I couldn't stop myself; I would eat and eat and eat, without tasting one bite. What had I eaten? Seven candy bars, a pizza, a half gallon of ice cream, peanuts, another candy bar, a hamburger. Why? *Dear God, why?* As I stuffed all this food down my throat, I never even tasted it. This is what people enjoy. But why such huge quantities, and why couldn't I *taste* it? Why?

I was not eating for the taste. Food in great abundance was my medication. It was the medicine I needed to numb whatever was wrong in my life. Whatever I thought I could not handle I would bury with food. Instead of dealing with all my feelings of inadequacy I would run away. But I still did not feel worthy. The food did not really help.

Today, *taste* your food. You do not have to deaden your frustrations. Handle your situations before you run to the candy machine or to the refrigerator.

God, help me to realize that no matter what comes today—frustration, feelings of "I can't do it"—You and I will do it together. I don't need food, God. I need You.

*But we have renounced the hidden
things of shame.*   —2 COR. 4:2

It had been a hard day in the news room. I had written and reported on four stories. Weary and lonely but not knowing it, I headed to the convenience store to buy whatever caught my eye. The clerk, who recognized me as a local news reporter and because I was a regular customer, asked, "Hey, Cynthia, are you having a party down at the station?" I lied. "Yeah, yeah, we're having a party." I was too embarrassed to say, "Nope, a party in my car."

After my lie, I left with my two bags filled with party food. I pulled into the store parking lot and started shoving the food down my throat.

It was not until I was in a safe therapeutic place that I could understand why I lied. I was too ashamed to say, I need help. I was too numb to say, This is sick behavior.

Are you lying to yourself today? Do you say:

"Tomorrow I'll start my diet."

"Oh, I'm really just hungry."

"Only crazy people seek professional help."

Please, today, face the truth. If your eating is out of control, find out *why*. Lying to ourselves and others only makes us feel more guilty.

Father, forgive our lies. Forgive us when we don't face the truth. Help us today to be more honest.

> *I can do all things through*
> *Christ who strengthens me.*
> —PHIL. 4:13

Reporting the news is a stressful job. It is thrilling, but to tell an important event in one minute's time is not only a challenge but also a heart-pumping experience.

All reporters want the lead story, and there were many times when I was the lead reporter. Every time this happened, deep inside I always chastised myself, What makes you think you can do this well? Who do you think you are? And before I could actually sit down and write the story, I would run to the candy machine, get three or four candy bars, and eat them quickly. I believed I could not do anything if I had not binged.

I always got my stories done, but deep within, I did not feel I deserved the job. Hurting myself with food protected me from feeling good about myself.

I am sure you may know how I felt. You have a job you can do, but deep inside you don't *really* believe you can do it. Today, examine the real reasons *why*. First ask yourself, Who told me I couldn't do this? Recall your childhood. Did someone close to you say, "Just because you think you can doesn't mean you can!"

I have learned I do not need food to get the job done. I need to deal with why I feel so inadequate and to *quit* punishing myself for my God-given talents.

God, today, help me find out why I don't feel I deserve my talents.

> *This is the message which we have*
> *heard from Him and declare to you,*
> *that God is light and in Him is no*
> *darkness at all.*   —1 JOHN 1:5

Fashion experts say black is slenderizing. Wear dark colors. Dark colors hide the bumps and lumps of my body. That is good, is it not? Besides, if I wear red or hot pink, it will expose the *real* me. And I can not allow that. So my black will just have to do.

Dark colors go with how I feel about myself. If I wear bright colors, I would seem happy, and I am not. No, dark colors will have to do.

Wait a minute! I am hiding, am I not? Wearing black is just another way of saying, "I don't really care about me. If I wear black, no one will see me." Black is OK sometimes, but every day? What am I trying to hide— my body? If I wear bright colors I might be noticed, and I can not have that, can I? If I wear colors, I will have to be colorful, and I can not take that risk.

I am tired of feeling so dark inside.

As I entered therapy, my dark feelings about myself slowly turned to light. I learned it was OK to be me. I began wearing bright colors—hot pinks and blues and reds. Color returned to my life.

God! Help me! You are the father of colors, and I am Your daughter. I long to show that You live in my heart by wearing red and pink and baby blue and white. Help me, God, please help me to show colors today!

> *And the LORD God said,*
> *"It is not good that man*
> *should be alone."*
> —GEN. 2:18

I feel so different. I feel like I do not belong. Who would *ever* believe I do what I do? I starve for three days drinking only water, then the madness overpowers me and I eat and eat and eat, and then get rid of it. And I feel so badly when I hurt myself. I can not let anyone know. I must isolate myself. When I am alone, away from people, my work, my friends, I do not have to pretend It is so much easier to just hurt myself and be alone.

I hate being isolated. I hate being alone. I hate being "different." So *why* do I do this?

I waited for God to answer. After twelve years, a door opened. My walls broke down in a safe place, with a therapist who could help me rebuild my life. He helped me find out why I felt "different." My childhood had a lot to do with it. Some of those hurts I still carried around as an adult.

You, too, may be waiting for an answer. If you're lonely, find out why. Then let God show you a better way.

———————————

God, You say, "It is not good that man should be alone." And I know You mean woman too. God, help me when I desire to be alone and I shouldn't be. Take away this isolation from the world. The starving and purging is just another reason to protect myself, isn't it?

God, help me through my loneliness.

*The wisdom of the prudent is to
understand his way.*
—PROV. 14:8

A story on the news tonight touched my heart. An obese woman and her husband were on their way to the Bahamas for a vacation, and they were given seats in the back of the plane. The plane tried to take off twice but both times the pilot had to abort the attempts. Realizing what the problem was, the pilot went back to this couple and said, "Ma'am, I'm sorry, but your weight is causing an imbalance in the back of this plane, and you're going to have to move to the front."

The lady and her husband hurriedly moved to the front. She told the reporter, "You would have thought that embarrassing, humiliating incident would have started me on a diet, but it didn't. I ate the whole time I was on that plane, and even more on vacation. I even gained weight."

The story is familiar: God gives us a situation that leads us to change and to get help, but instead of facing it, we just continue to suppress our feelings. This woman finally admitted she needed help. She lost weight and now she helps others to do the same.

God, today, shake me if I need to be shaken. You are my Father who wants me to face my problems and be healthy.

Help me Father, to face me.

It is not in man who walks to direct his own steps.
—JER. 10:23

Sometimes we are wounded, helpless, out of control. We do not know where to turn and sometimes we turn the wrong way. After twelve years of bulimia, my body was breaking down and my emotions were scaring me. I felt suicidal. I felt as if I were going to lose me.

I was at work one day in the television newsroom, feeling despair, and I saw a friend in the recording booth. I went to her, closing the door behind me. I was shaking and weeping as I told this friend, "I don't know what's wrong. I feel like I'm going to die."

I hoped this person could help me. Instead, she put her hands on my shoulders, shook me, and firmly said, "Get yourself together! Snap out of it!" Devastation filled my soul. She did not understand that my addiction was killing me, that my past was haunting me, that I really wanted to die.

I have forgiven this friend. I rejoice that I have a God and a Savior who will never shake me and yell, "Snap out of it!"

No, I have a God who would ask instead, "Where does it hurt, Cynthia?"

God, I'm so grateful You're not like us. Thank You for Your tenderness. Thank You for not abandoning us.

The Spirit Himself bears witness with our spirit that
we are children of God.
—ROM. 8:16

My senior year in high school was a hard year. My Dad got a new job away from the city and the friends I grew up with. In my new school I was a little fish in a big pond. I was lonely. I felt like a nobody. I "stuffed" food because it made me feel better, or so I thought. I gained weight. My Dad did not like my weight gain, and one day he said, "Honey, you've gained weight and I want you to be thin for college, so if you lose ten pounds, I'll pay you three hundred dollars."

What a great deal. The three hundred dollars was a great bonus. And I not only lost ten pounds, I lost sixteen. It sounded good, but it was not. This deal started me on the road to bulimia. I did not realize it at the time, but the little girl inside was thinking, Daddy won't love me unless I'm thin. And I desperately want Dad to love me, so I better lose my weight.

You see, I did not feel accepted by my dad. The condition for acceptance was that I look thin, so I began a self-destructive pattern of behavior to stay thin.

In your life, who has given you the message, "I'll love you, *if* . . ." Examine your feelings. Accept yourself for who you are, God's child.

Father God, I am so glad You accept me right where I am. Fat or skinny, medium or hefty. You love me for me. Thank You, God.

> *Do not let your beauty be that outward adorning of*
> *arranging the hair, of wearing gold, or of putting*
> *on fine apparel; but let it be the hidden person of*
> *the heart.*
> —1 PETER 3:3–4

I was out of college, out on my own. Yet I still needed my parents' assurance and acceptance.

I felt pressure every time I visited my mom and dad because the survey would start. My dad's very first comment to me would be, "Hi, Honey! Hey, you look great! How much weight have you lost?" Or Mom would say, "Hello, Honey . . . your face looks a little full. Have you gained weight?"

The pressure of being thin and looking good was so overwhelming. In therapy years later, I would confront my parents. "I want you to quit talking about my weight. Accept me for me, whether I'm Two-ton Tilly or Skinny Minny. My weight is no longer going to be a topic of discussion."

I realize my parents thought they were doing the right thing. But their worry about my looks contributed to my addiction. It caused too much pressure.

Are others' visions of what you *should* be causing you to self-destruct? Look at this possibility, and stop. Take care of yourself.

———————

God, thanks for not putting pressure on me. Thanks for loving me as I am.

A soft answer turns away wrath,
But a harsh word stirs up anger.
—PROV. 15:1

Tab was so skinny. Her bones protruded out of her body. When she sat, she rested on her hands because the bones popping out of her bottom hurt her. Tab was going to die unless she started to eat.

In therapy, Tab learned she was the "son" of the family. She certainly looked like a boy. Tab was trying to be the son of the family because her dad had told her over and over again, "When you were born, I didn't want a girl. I wanted a son." To fulfill her dad's wishes, a dad who did not nurture and accept her, she starved herself so she would not look so much like a girl. Tab had no breasts, no hips.

She almost died. In therapy, Tab spoke of her pain. She grieved for what never was. Her anorexia was numbing her anger and sorrow at not being accepted.

Has someone in your life ridiculed you? Have you heard the message, "I don't really love you"? Don't turn those feelings inward. Talk about the pain. God created Tab, He created *you,* and He is never disappointed with His creations.

God, others may reject us. When they are people who should accept us, love us, and nurture us, it hurts so deeply. Help us remember that You are our true Father.

Help me, today, to deal with my pain.

> *When I was a child . . . I thought as a child; but*
> *when I became a man, I put away childish things.*
> —1 COR. 13:11

Eat all your food!"

"Clean your plate!"

"You know, there are starving children in Africa!"

That is what Mom always said, and you have to do what mother says. The problem is, you are twenty-eight, or thirty, or thirty-five, or forty-five years old, and you are overweight. Does doing what your mother said give you an excuse to eat? After all, we are supposed to obey our mothers, right? *Stop. Think.* Why are you allowing your Mom's rules to hurt you? Mothers are not always right. Sometimes we have to make our own rules. If cleaning your plate means gaining weight, is that healthy, or wise?

Maybe it is time to let go of Mother's rules. You are an adult. It is time to grow up and take charge. Take care of *you.*

_____

God, I need to examine some of my childhood rules, and I need to let go of some of them. Help me to let go. Help me do what is best to be healthy.

These things I have spoken to you, that in Me you
may have peace. In the world you will have
tribulation; but be of good cheer, I have
overcome the world.   —JOHN 16:33

So many letters come to my office from people who
are losing hope. "The professionals say I'll never be rid
of this addiction," the letters say, or, "Even if I don't
binge, the feeling will be lurking around the corner."

I do not believe these statements have to be true. Of
course, there will be days when we *feel* like bingeing
or starving, but we must ask ourselves why? What am I
not dealing with? Why do I feel a need to go to food?
Frank Minirth and Paul Meier have written a book,
Happiness Is a Choice. We may choose bingeing and
purging yet once we have understood why we have
behaved self-destructively, we must consciously say, "I
don't need food. I need _____" (fill in your
blank).

Sometimes people confuse *needing* with being *self-*
ish. God created us to *need* food, water, shelter. In the
same way, we need to feel loved and nurtured. Studies
have found that newborns who aren't touched and
held can actually die from lack of attention. We *need*
love and compassion.

Today, give yourself permission to ask "What do I
really need?"

God helps people *overcome*. He is the God of hope.

Father, help me today to choose to deal with my life.

*Then He took a little child and set him in the midst
of them. And when He had taken him in His arms,
He said to them, "Whoever receives one of these
little children in My name receives me."*
—MARK 9:36–37

I loved candy when I was a child. My favorites were
cinnamon-flavored Hot Tamales, Red Hots, Sour Lem-
ons, and Slow Pokes. Candy was soothing. It filled up
my emptiness. It replaced a hug.

My parents' worries led me to believe that I needed
to keep out of their way. Many times Mom gave me a
quarter and I ran to the local store and bought five five-
cent candy packages. I never bought just one, but *five*.
Then I would hurry home, go into my "make believe"
room in our basement, sit in the corner, and enjoy my
feast.

The candy was my best friend. It took the place of
my mother. The sugary taste helped me escape what
was going on around me.

As an adult, candy was still my refuge until I realized my life was falling apart. Candy was not going to
take away my problems. I had to *feel* what was going
on, then deal with it. Candy still tastes good to me, but I
have learned I do not need it to overcome a problem.

I encourage you to recall your childhood. Close your
eyes. Relive what you felt. I have learned that as a
child, I wanted someone to assure me everything was
all right, but I did not feel safe to ask. Candy made me
feel safe.

*Father, today, I ask You to fill me up. Help me to look to You to fill me
up. Help me to see why I* need *canay to soothe my broken heart.*

*Do not judge according to appearance, but judge
with righteous judgment.* —JOHN 7:24

I have a friend whom I admire greatly because she
knows who she is, and she does not really care what
people think about her. (I think deep down she does
care, but she never reveals it.) This friend is a well-
known professional woman in the city where she lives.
Everyone knows her. She has a beautiful face, a great
bubbly personality, and a good figure. Her one physical
flaw is her "behind" is unusually large. People would
talk about her "behind." Yet this friend would hold her
head up high, smile her beautiful smile, and walk on
by. You see, she knew her worth was not based on her
behind. She did not like the fact that she had a problem
back there but she knew who she was and she knew
she had talents, despite what others thought.

I used to wish I could be more like her. Consumed
with the shape of my body, I covered it up with suits.
My friend would wear dresses that showed off her
small waist. I asked her once why her big behind did
not seem to matter. She just smiled and said, "This is
me, and I have to make the most of what is good and
attractive."

We all have flaws. Today, instead of focusing on
them, let us focus on what is wonderful and pretty
about our bodies.

———————

*God, You created us in Your image. Help us rejoice in who we are,
not how we look.*

> *And you, fathers, do not provoke your children to*
> *wrath, but bring them up in the training and*
> *admonition of the Lord.*
> —EPH. 6:4

I entered my room in the psychiatric ward at 1:10 A.M., near death, not understanding why I was so self-destructive. I was so scared. I tried to be quiet because my roommate was sleeping. Her knees were pulled up, and I could clearly see her legs. She had no meat on her bones at all. I learned the next day that Elizabeth was anorexic.

I found out Elizabeth was fourteen years old and her parents hospitalized her because she was near death. During therapy, she found out that she used anorexia to control her parents. Her mom and dad were heavy-handed disciplinarians. There were a lot of rules and regulations. Punishment resulted if the rules were broken. Elizabeth felt so controlled that she took back control by starving herself. Subconsciously she was saying, I'm angry at you, Mom and Dad, for controlling me, so I'll show you! I'll get you! I'll stop eating! She did not know she was angry.

In family therapy, Elizabeth had to express her need to be set free a little bit more. She needed to be free to express what she felt instead of Mom and Dad always telling her what she should feel and do.

Are you allowing someone to control you? Are you trying to take back that control by hurting yourself and others by starving, or bingeing, or purging? Examine who is in control. Free yourself.

God, help me give up control and give it to You.

*If we confess our sin, He is faithful and
just to forgive us our sins and to cleanse us
from all unrighteousness.* —1 JOHN 1:9

It's your problem, not mine," a father said to his daughter, dying from bulimia. When she was growing up, this father was critical and strict; the daughter could never do anything right. Her self-esteem was so low. She numbed her emotions by eating and then using huge quantities of laxatives. In family therapy, her father would not admit that he had a part in his daughter's addiction. She was hurt. The bulimia protected her from her pain.

She had to face the fact that her dad would not admit he had hurt her. Alone, she then had to face the *truth* with a caring therapist. Eating disorders do not exist without reason. There are many, many reasons. Family dynamics and childhood experiences may be principal reasons.

This woman had to face the fact that her dad was in denial, and that he would not take any responsibility or feel sorry for his daughter's condition. It was his way *out* of the situation.

Slowly, she overcame her food addiction. And she realized that our Father in heaven never says, "It's your problem, not mine!" No, Father God says, "Any problem you have is Mine and I will be with you every moment of the day and night to work it out."

Thank You, God, for being such a true father.

> *Fear not, for I am with you;*
> *Be not dismayed, for I am your God.*
> —ISA. 41:10

I am amazed how childhood memories play such roles in who we are. A memory just flashed into my head this week, which confirmed again how much candy soothed my fears and pain. I was about eight years old. My mom was in the hospital about three miles from where we lived. I had an old, little bike with no brakes, and after school I would jump on that bike and ride over to the hospital. But before I got to the hospital, I stopped at a grocery store where they sold a lime-flavored candy called *Grasshoppers*. I would buy ten, stuff them in my pocket, and proceed on my little bike to the hospital. What overwhelms me with sadness is I do not remember the visits with my mother. All I remember is the Grasshopper candy.

As an adult, I still have that little girl inside me. She still takes that three-mile ride on an old brakeless bike. She feels the loneliness of having to take care of herself. Today I allow her to feel sorrow because no one was there to help her through the absence of her mother.

It is OK to relive the past and grieve. Do you remember a time in your childhood when food filled the emptiness in your heart? God understands, and I have realized that I wasn't alone; He was with me riding alongside me on His old, little bicycle.

Father, You love Your children deeply. Thank You for being there wherever I go.

But I would speak to the Almighty,
And I desire to reason with God.
But you forgers of lies,
You are all worthless physicians.
—JOB 13:3–4

Who could possibly understand why I eat, lose control, get rid of the food, and then starve myself? Who would believe I eat seven candy bars in one sitting, and then self-induce vomiting or take a handful of laxatives? I used to ask myself these questions. When I got enough courage, I went to one doctor and told him, "I lose control. I can't stop. I eat all I can in one sitting, and then I get rid of it." The doctor looked at me with unbelieving eyes.

"You do what?" he asked, "Well, stop it! Don't you know it's bad for you?"

Yes, I knew that but I just could not *stop it*. I felt so stupid, so weak, as I left that doctor's office. After all, I told myself, don't doctors have *all* the answers?

After I told psychiatrist Paul Meier this story, he said there are a lot of "M.D.-ieties" in this world. He is so right. I think that doctor who said "stop it" did not understand the complexity of the emotional problems that caused my eating disorder. So, instead of saying, "I'm not sure how to help you but I'll find someone who can," he took the easy way out.

Maybe you have doctors whom you trust, only to be put down. Forgive them. Educate them.

Father, help me forgive those who have failed me. Help me to see that, through the rejection, You may teach me some valuable truths.

> *I have no greater joy than to hear that my children*
> *walk in truth.*
> —3 JOHN 1:4

Shelley was overweight most of her life. She kept thirty pounds surrounding the 'thin" Shelley most of her adult life. One day Shelley got depressed, severely depressed. She sought professional help and her therapist helped her to recall the issues of her past. Shelley's dad had sexually abused her as a child. This thirty-eight-year-old woman had to work through her guilt and pain from childhood and come to say, "It wasn't my fault." She had to yell, "My dad was a sick man! The abuse was not my fault!"

Those extra pounds of Shelley's were protecting her from being sexually intimate with her husband. She would say to herself, I'm fat. This gives my husband good reason not to be attracted to me. The truth was her fat made her feel bad about herself, so she never felt like being intimate. Being overweight helped her avoid good friendships. During therapy, she decided to take care of Shelley. Along with understanding why food protected her, she started a healthy diet plan and lost the thirty pounds. It has been six years now, and she has not gained any of her weight back.

Shelley has a new respect for herself. She is open and honest now.

Are the extra pounds you are carrying protecting you from intimacy? Ask yourself, Why do I need to protect myself? Why do I make excuses to avoid intimacy?

God, expose what we're protecting. Expose what we're afraid of.

Wrath is cruel and anger a torrent,
But who is able to stand before jealousy?
—PROV. 27:4

It is really mysterious how people respond to someone who loses weight. After I bragged on Shelley's accomplishment, a friend would say to me, "Oh, I bet she'll gain that weight back in a month. It will never stay off." I responded to this lady with a smile, and said, "Oh, I don't know. I believe in her, and I think she'll keep it off."

It baffled me why anyone would put someone down who was obviously working so hard, someone who was committed to giving up old eating behavior and dealing with her life. But as I looked at the woman who made these comments behind Shelley's back, I could not help but think that perhaps this woman was somehow threatened, maybe even jealous. She had about forty-five pounds of extra weight on her body that she needed to lose.

Shelley proved the woman's theory wrong. After six years, she is still at a healthy weight. She is happy and getting on with her life, while the other woman still has forty-five unhealthy pounds on her body.

Do you struggle with jealousy, or with being threatened by others overcoming their weight problem? Take a deep look into your heart and examine why. Be proud of your friends, and allow them to be an example in your life.

_____

God, rid us of jealousy. Rid our hearts of feeling threatened. Help us to understand our feelings and take care of them.

> *That which has been is what will be,*
> *That which is done is what will be done,*
> *And there is nothing new under the sun.*
> —ECCL. 1:9

Every time the newspaper or television or magazine advertised a new "quick loss" diet plan, my eyes were hungry to see what new miracle was out there.

"Lose twenty pounds in a week!" the ads would scream.

And then I would invest twenty to forty dollars and get some awful-tasting powder to mix with water, or some fig leaf tea, or some horrid-tasting cookies. I used to be a sucker for such ads. Then I realized that my preoccupation with diet plans simply meant I was focused on my body and not on what was really going on inside of me: sadness, loneliness, anger, fear of being abandoned.

The bottom line, the awareness that came about the hard way, is I do not need a miracle pill or miracle diet to lose weight. My weight is normal. My eating is normal when I am dealing with my emotions. And as the majority of doctors around the world say, the only really healthy way to lose weight is to eat less fat, to eat nutritiously, and to exercise more. I believe if we can combine that with understanding why we overeat, then we in turn can giggle and shake our heads at the next ad that reads, "Lose thirty pounds in five days!" Right!

God, give us wisdom when it comes to our diet and our emotions.

He who guards his mouth preserves his life,
But he who opens wide his lips shall have
destruction. —PROV. 13:3

I don't think I want to know what's wrong." So says a wonderful woman I love and admire. I worry about her, because she is two hundred pounds overweight. My heart breaks every time I hear her say that because it is just another sad reason, another excuse not to deal with her past, her mom and dad, and her husband.

This friend did try therapy but she quit after the third session. Her husband was threatened. He told her he did not want her "wasting" money. The truth is, this husband wants his wife fat. She is vivacious and very loved, and he feels threatened every time she seeks professional help. He fears he will lose her if she identifies the reasons she is obese.

I grieve for my friend. It is not that I do not accept her right now at three hundred pounds. I know she hates how she looks. And she may not live a long life. Already at age thirty-two, she has had numerous surgeries because of her weight. But until *she* is ready to find out what is *really* wrong, and why her husband is so afraid, she will remain in bondage.

If someone close to you is encouraging you not to get professional help, I encourage you to examine why, and take responsibility for you.

God, too many times we don't live for You. We do what we want or what someone else wants. Help us, God, to take responsibility. Please examine our hearts, God.

> *You who preach that a man should not steal,*
> *do you steal?*
> —ROM. 2:21

From age sixteen to twenty-three, I thought starving and bingeing and purging was just a great way to lose weight, until one day I went shopping.

Being bulimic is like being an addict. One Saturday I was on a "high" and I went happily to the grocery store. While stacking all the food I desired in my cart, I took a jar of peanuts from the shelf. I opened and consumed three-fourths of the jar and put it back on the shelf. Going farther, I came across a package of hot dogs. I took two hot dogs out, ate them, and put the *rest of the package back in the refrigerator.* Happy as a clam, I went on.

Out of nowhere, a man approached me. He was an undercover cop. "Lady, I saw what you did with the peanuts." I was thinking, *But what about the hot dogs?*

I said nothing. He repeated, "Lady, I saw what you did with the peanuts!"

"I don't know what you're talking about. I didn't steal any peanuts."

"Lady, I saw what you did. . . . It's called shoplifting, and I'm going to let you off this time, but if you *ever* come into this store again and steal and I catch you, I'll arrest you and put you in jail!"

I walked out of that store shaking all over, and my heart said, *Cynthia, you are sick. Get help.* It was my day of reckoning.

Jesus, help me to admit I need healing.

For the LORD does not see as man sees;
for man looks at the outward appearance,
but the LORD looks at the heart.
—1 SAM. 16:7

Julie struggles all the time with alcoholism, bulimia, life and death. She recently got into intense therapy and her counselor is slowly cracking her hard shell of pain. Julie visited me last week, and she was so down on herself. She told me she hated her "saddlebags."

"Julie," I assured her, "they're not that bad. Quit putting yourself down. I think you're beautiful." But Julie did not want to hear my compliment; she wanted to hang on to a negative comment someone had made that day. Julie works with mentally handicapped people, and she had taken her group to an amusement park. Because it was a hot day, she wore walking shorts. One of her clients said, "Boy, Julie, you've got big thighs!" It embarrassed her and made her feel bad. She said her "special" clients are "so honest and notice everything!" Again I assured her she was OK. But she refused to listen. She savored the negative.

I hurt for Julie because truly she is a lovely girl inside and out, but she did not believe it. It will take time for her to focus on the good instead of the bad.

Isn't it wonderful to know God does not look at our "saddlebags" and say, "You need to do something about your fat thighs!" No, our God looks at our hearts and yearns for us to be honest and deal with why we are so obsessed with our bodies.

Thank You for accepting me for me.

How beautiful upon the mountains
Are the feet of him who brings good news,
Who proclaims peace,
Who brings glad tidings of good things;
Who proclaims salvation. —ISA. 52:7

Once my boss took me into his office and said, "Cynthia, I've got some good news and some bad news. First the bad news." He proceeded gently to tell me I performed well in some areas of my job but there was room for improvement. I wanted to cry. I felt so bad that I was not doing my job "perfectly."

After his constructive criticism, he said with a smile, "Now, the good news. I'm giving you a raise." I should have been joyful but I was not. I went to the bathroom and cried my eyes out. My heart cried out, "You're such a failure, Cynthia!"

After work, I stopped at three McDonald's and binged on Big Macs and hot fudge sundaes. I was devastated. I had been criticized. I felt like a failure.

Looking back I wonder, Why didn't I hear the good news? My boss did not have to give me a raise. But he did, which meant he valued my talents. But I only heard the negative and not the positive.

It makes me question, How many times does God bless us or open a door for us to get help and we just say, "I'm not worthy of any blessings." I wonder if God shakes his head when we refuse to see the good in our lives.

God, help me savor the positive in my life and improve the negative.

Be still, and know that I am God.
—PS. 46:10

Nothing in my life really satisfied me. I strived to be perfect and ultimately I always set myself up to fail, because no one can reach perfection.

Food filled me up physically, but it left me feeling sick and empty emotionally. I strived to do my best on the job. Once I competed in and won an award for producing "The Best Television News Documentary," and I thought, Now I'm perfect. But about thirty minutes after receiving the award, I thought, OK, what's next, Cynthia? What can you achieve next?

I strove to keep winning but I still wasn't happy and fulfilled. Looking back on my twelve years of living with bulimia, I was always busy. I had to run around, go to movies, binge, exercise, fast. I never stopped to listen to the words, "Be still, and know that I am God." If I did, I would have to face me and my pain. So I strived for perfection and always failed. But I did not quit trying until I reached the point of suicide.

Think. Are you running from God? Are you so busy you cannot stop and be still? Today, let's stop. Talk to God. Feel His presence and get honest with why we need to be perfect. Let's give our true reasons to God, and listen.

> *Whatever things are true . . . meditate*
> *on these things.*   —PHIL. 4:8

If people don't like me as I am, well, it's just tough!
They either accept me or they don't accept me!"

Lisa is 230 pounds overweight. She admits she is
obese. But she says she does not care. I know differently. I have seen her cry. She does care but she would
rather suffer than do something. Yet silently she
screams, Accept me!

She is beautiful inside, so talented, so sweet. People
should accept her. Many do but some do not. They are
turned off by her obesity. They wonder, How could a
woman as precious as Lisa get so out of control? Lisa
tried therapy for a while but it hurt too much. She admitted that she had problems to solve, but she did not
want to go through the pain. She even shared once that
her obesity is an outward sign of anger toward her
mother, who has always urged her to lose weight. Lisa
feels she has never been accepted by her mom. It
breaks my heart because her health is at stake and in
reality Lisa is playing games with herself.

I know God accepts Lisa, but I am sure He feels hurt
and sorrow for Lisa because she has so much to give.
Her obesity holds her back with anger, insecurity, and
heartache.

We are all guilty of playing games. We all are guilty
of hiding behind our fat.

---

*Today, Lord, may we quit making excuses and may we accept the
truth that we need help to overcome our true pain.*

He who gets wisdom loves his own soul;
He who keeps understanding will find good
—PROV. 19:8

My eating disorder started so innocently. At sixteen I thought taking a laxative was such a great way to lose weight. And then one laxative a week turned into one a day, then three a day, and twelve years later, I took sixty to one hundred laxatives a day. The "monster" would lie to me and say, *But, Cynthia, if five work just think how much more weight you'll lose by taking ten more!* At age twenty-eight I was an over-the-counter drug addict and I did not even realize it until I nearly had a heart attack. I realized I no longer wanted to live anymore.

You see, I lied to myself: *I can handle this bulimia. If I want to stop, I will.* But I never stopped until the reality hit me: *I am going to die if I do not get help!*

How often do we say to God, "Don't worry about it, God. I can take care of my problems myself." And then we end up despondent. We lose our self-respect and we do not want to face tomorrow. And it is even harder to turn to God because we feel so guilty.

No matter where you are—the top, the middle, or in the pit—your Creator needs you to know He is there to pick you up. He is there to hold you. He is there to get you back to the top. It usually does not happen overnight. But He is there to get you through no matter how long it takes.

———

Father, I want to depend on You, but it's so hard. Teach us to lean on You every day.

He shall regard the prayer of the destitute,
And shall not despise their prayer.
—PS. 102:17

God, are you there?" Silence. "Oh, never mind, God. I'll handle it myself. I know you're probably too busy."

So many times I whispered a prayer like this when I needed God to help me. I did not understand at the time, but I viewed God like my earthly father. My dad was always too busy taking care of business. He was gone a lot, and when he was home it seemed he was always dealing with my rebellious brother.

I never wanted to bother my father. He was just too busy to notice me. So in turn I thought my Creator and heavenly Father surely did not have time for me either. I reasoned, Look at all the zillions of people praying to Him, needing help. Why would He want to hear from me?

During my hospitalization, the child within me had to grieve over growing up with a demanding father, and rejoice that my heavenly Father is not like him. God always has time for me. I came to terms with the truth that He is the Father of all fathers and will never be too busy for me.

Today, are you overeating to smother the painful truth that Daddy did not have time to notice you? Are you confusing him with God, our perfect Father?

Examine your feelings and your fear and draw near to Father God—or Abba—which means, your Daddy.

Abba, Father, thank You for being my perfect Daddy. Thank You for making me Your child.

For your Maker is your husband,
The LORD of hosts is His name.
—ISA. 54:5

If I could just get married, then I know I'll lose my weight," my friend said so earnestly. Janice is one hundred pounds overweight. She has a great career, is so talented, but she, like so many of us, uses the old excuse, "If only this or that would happen . . . then I'd be happy!" At age thirty-four, Janice did get married to a wonderful man who loved *all* of her.

Six months after they married and moved away, Janice called me and said, "You remember when I said I'd lose the weight after I married? Well, I haven't lost a pound."

While there is nothing wrong with hope and believing that love can be a healing force, Janice has to be the one to decide to deal with why she has one hundred extra pounds. Only then can she slowly but surely be determined to lose her weight in a healthy way. Her husband can love her like no other but until Janice loves herself the weight will stay put.

Too often I, like Janice, waste my time and health with the "if onlys." Let's you and I focus on today, not tomorrow. And learn to love ourselves *today*.

God, thank You for the gift of having this day. Help me not to dwell on "if onlys," but instead to be grateful and trust in You.

> *Let each of you look out not only for his own*
> *interests, but also for the interests of others.*
> —PHIL. 2:4

My friend Janice is the sort of girl who everyone says would be such a pretty girl if only she would lose that weight. Still I admire Janice so much because she knows she needs to lose her one hundred pounds but she does not give up. She works hard. She is very active in her church. Everyone loves and admires her. Her clothes are always bright, and as slenderizing as they can be. She admits she needs help, but she is not quite ready yet. I know with all my heart that when Janice is ready she will succeed. Until then I know Janice will serve God as best she can, and when she decides to deal with what she is hiding, she will be victorious. Until then I have to keep loving her, accepting her, and encouraging her.

Do you have a friend like Janice? Encourage her today. Pray with her and for her.

Are you a Janice? Don't give up. Wear bright, attractive clothes, and ask yourself, *Is today the day I'll be ready to get help?*

_____

Lord, thank You for accepting me no matter where I am in this life.
Help me to accept myself and others as completely.

*Therefore do not worry about tomorrow, for
tomorrow will worry about its own things.*
—MATT. 6:34

Tomorrow I'll start my diet."

"Next week, after the wedding, that's when I'll eat right."

"After vacation, I've got to lose these extra ten pounds."

But then tomorrow comes. The wedding was over last week, and it has been a month since that vacation. The promises you made never evolved, and the extra baggage is still there.

It is so easy to *say*, "I'm going to do it tomorrow." But tomorrow is today, and it *is* looking at us right in the face. Today is a gift from God. Today we can start eating right. Today we can start our exercising by walking around the block.

Today, we can say, "I need help."

Today is ours. Let us not take another day for granted.

Tomorrow is tomorrow, but today is here.

Father, thank You for the gift of today. Thank You for being the same perfect God yesterday, today, and tomorrow.

> *You, O LORD, are our Father;*
> *Our Redeemer from Everlasting*
> *is Your name.* —ISA. 63:16

My bad relationships with men confirmed that I was no good. It gave me reason for stuffing my face with food, and then numbing myself further with purging, starving, exercising excessively. Because deep inside I never felt worthy of my father's love, I never felt worthy of dating "good" guys. I always got involved with men who really did not care about me. And when the relationship never worked out I could say, "See, I'm no good."

But the truth is my unhealthy relationships formed a self-destructive pattern. I had to find out *why* I thought I deserved "damaged" men. In therapy, I examined my behavior with men and confronted my father about how I felt. I slowly learned I did not need bad relationships. I did not need to overeat. What I needed was to deal with the hurt of a father who was away from me too often. I came to terms with the true reason why I felt so undeserving of good relationships.

Our Father in heaven is never away on trips. He is always home. He longs to have a healthy relationship with us. If you are struggling with unhealthy relationships, examine why you feel that is what you deserve. The answers may hurt, but the hurt will get you closer to health.

God, relationships can be so complicated! Help me to understand my negative patterns and find the strength to change.

Have we not all one Father?
Has not one God created us?
—MAL. 2:10

There was a movie on television recently that told the story of a woman with ninety-two different personalities. She had been sadistically abused—sexually, emotionally, and physically—by her stepfather. The multiple personalities protected her from dealing with all of the horrors she had suffered. After the movie aired, I got a call from a friend who struggles with obesity. The movie struck a chord in her heart and soul because she had been abused as a child by her stepfather. Feelings surfaced that hurt deeply. My friend told me that her obesity was her protection. She said she grieved for the little child within her. This woman's husband had not watched the movie, and was sound asleep as she suffered alone. But as her tears fell, she felt God gently stroking her head. And He softly whispered, "My child, I'm here. Bring it to me."

My friend could have gone straight to the refrigerator and avoided her deep childhood problems but instead she dealt with her pain. She grieved and allowed God to grant her peace.

Today, may we turn to God and not to food for true peace.

Prince of Peace, enter my heart and soul as I walk through the valley of sorrow.

> *God will hear, and afflict them, . . .*
> *Because they do not change,*
> *Therefore they do not fear God.*
> —PS. 55:19

It's too late to change." I heard this reason so many times. I have heard it from people who are twenty-five to seventy years old. I wonder if underneath that statement they are really saying, "I'm too afraid to change. I'm too scared to risk losing this weight or finding professional help for my bulimia or anorexia because if I change it won't be safe anymore. I won't be able to hide behind my food addiction. I'll have to deal with the locked-up reasons why I'm out of control."

Believe me, it is never too late to change. Yes, it is a risk to change. It is a risk to confront problems. It is a risk to get therapy or join a support group because it will hurt to face truth, but I would rather *feel* hurt and face the pain than destroy myself with food. I've seen forty-five-year-old, even sixty-five-year-old men and women change. First, it takes courage to say, "I'm going to make changes." Then we must admit we cannot change without God's strength, and love, and grace.

Surely God is proud of us when we change our self-destructive patterns. It is not that He loves us more, but He knows we will be better able to serve Him as we grow.

_____

My Father, thank You for never giving up on me, for turning around my failures and helping me change.

*Let all bitterness, wrath, anger, clamor, and evil
speaking be put away from you.* —EPH. 4:31

She was a beautiful college coed on a tennis scholarship. She had everything going for her, but she was depressed, bulimic. There was rage inside of her. She did not understand it but her rage was directed toward her mom and dad because they always expected so much of her. "We want you to make it to the pros," they told her. They never said, "We love you." Her parents never said, "If you want to quit tennis, that's OK with us." The parents gave their daughter a lot of *conditional love* messages. As a result, this girl was frustrated and angry, and her rage turned inward. She was hurting herself, damaging her body and her potential.

As she shared her feelings with me, I said, "So, when are you going to grow up?" My question startled her. There was silence.

"You see, you're angry but you're afraid to express that feeling to your parents because if you do, they may totally reject you."

This girl took my question to heart. She went to her parents and poured her heart out. Her mom understood. Her dad had a hard time with her feelings. But she felt more free. She learned she could not be their little girl anymore. She needed to grow up.

Are you holding on to being your parents' little girl? Afraid to stand up for what is best for you? Recently I got a letter from this beautiful girl. She wrote, "It's fun being grown up!"

Lord, help me never stop growing, no matter how painful it seems.

> *"For my thoughts are not your thoughts,*
> *nor are your ways My ways," says the LORD.*
> —ISA. 55:8

If all we know is abuse when we are children, we see abuse as normal. We do not know any different.

Darcie was abused as a child. She became anorexic as a teenager and nearly died at age twenty-four. Her therapist probed, and tried to get her to relive some painful memories. She remembered once having fallen off her bike. She was eight years old, and when she fell her head hit a mailbox, cutting her forehead. Blood poured out of her scalp. In a daze, she walked home. Her dad saw her wound and instead of comforting her and taking her to the hospital to get stitches, he yelled at her, "You're such a stupid little girl! It's your fault you're bleeding, and I ain't gonna do nothing for you!"

Darcie laid on the couch and waited three hours. Her mother came home. Fortunately, her mother saw the seriousness of the cut and took her to get stitches, but she, too, blamed Darcie for being so "stupid." After Darcie told this painful story, the therapist asked, "Do you think it was abusive of your parents to react the way they did?"

At first she said, "No." But then the tears flowed and she admitted, "Yes! It was abusive! Why was it my fault?"

Darcie, it was not your fault.

Father God, hold on to the Darcies of this world! Help us to understand the pain of our abuse and how eating disorders protect us from that pain. Free us, God, from our abusive past.

*Behold what manner of love the Father has bestowed
on us, that we should be called children of God!*
—1 JOHN 3:1

When Darcie was in the depths of her anorexia there
was no denying she was sick. She was so skinny she did
not look normal. Outsiders did not understand her eating disorder. Many people avoided her; some even con-
demned her.

At church one day, Darcie went to the bathroom,
and as she was leaving a woman took her arm and angrily said, "You are evil, Darcie! What you're doing to
your body is evil and you'd better stop it!"

Maybe she thought she was doing the right thing but
it was the worse way, a cruel way, to try to help Darcie.
Darcie already hated herself. Her abusive background
made her feel as if she must be evil. This woman confirmed those feelings.

"Am I evil, Cynthia?" Darcie asked me.

"No, Darcie, you're not evil," I assured her. "You
have a heart that is empty. The abuse was not your
fault. You are a child of God."

*Father God, wrap Your arms around those who feel so bad. Help us
to be wise with our words. Help us today to know that our abusive
childhood is not our fault.*

And I say to you, ask, and it will be given to you; seek, and you will find; knock, and it will be opened to you.

—LUKE 11:9

My eating disorder was not working anymore. I was desperate for help. I found a magazine article about bulimia and I could not believe it. It described me to a T. That article told me I was not alone.

After reading it, I made a decision. I was scared but I felt my parents should know what I was living with. First I gave it to my dad. After reading the article, he looked at me and said, "You don't do this."

I was stunned. Here I had finally revealed my secret to my dad and he did not believe me. Doctors did not believe me when I told them how much I ate and how I purged, and now my own father did not believe me. Was I really crazy?

A year later when I was near death in the hospital, we had our first therapy session together. I confronted my dad. "Why didn't you believe me when I told you I had bulimia?"

"I denied it," he said. "I couldn't believe that my perfect, beautiful daughter did such a thing. So instead of believing it, I denied it."

Denial is such a destructive thing. In denial we refuse to believe.

Today, let us commit to seek truth and to admit we have a problem, no matter how many of those we love are in denial.

***

God, help me not to deny truth, but to expose and deal with it.

My grace is sufficient for you.
—2 COR. 12:9

I would know that southern drawl anywhere. It was Sandy calling. Bulimic one day, then anorexic the next.

"I have to go back into the hospital, Cynthia," she told me.

"Why, Sandy?"

"I'm taking too many laxatives again." I listened as she told me all the reasons. Finally I stopped her. "Sandy, I'm not going to talk to you about your laxative abuse."

Silence. "Well," she said, "if I could just stop taking laxatives, everything would be all right."

"No, Sandy, everything will not be all right until you deal with why you have an addiction. Sandy, it goes back to your childhood."

"Oh, I don't think so, because I can't remember anything about my childhood."

"That's because it's too painful to remember."

"Well . . . I have to go."

Sandy knows there have been severe abuse and problems in her family life. Her mother has been married four times, with many men in between. Abandoned as a child, Sandy cannot seem to connect her past with who she is today. It will be hard for her, but I pray to God that her therapist will guide her to her locked-up memories.

God, thank You for protecting us from our pain, but when we are self-destructive, help us to understand how our past pain affects us today.

For now we see in a mirror, dimly, but then face to face. Now I know in part, but then I shall know just as I also am known. —1 COR. 13:12

One day I loved mirrors and the next day I would not allow myself to look into one. Mirrors told the truth about how I really looked. If I was thin, great. If not, my reflection would throw me into a severe state of depression. Defeated, I ate and ate and ate, then purged the damage. Sometimes when I looked in the mirror I could see my face growing, becoming fat as I watched. I would scream at my fat face, "You are so ugly!" I felt so ugly, inside and out.

Mirrors told the truth about the outside but not the truth of my heart. It did not show how my heart was lonely and hurting. The mirror did not reveal that my family's expectations controlled what I thought of myself.

After working through the real ugliness inside of myself, and after healing came, then I could see the real me in the mirror, a beautiful child of God.

Today, look at yourself in the mirror. What do you see? Ugliness? Sorrow? Pain? Or do you see a beautiful child of God? If you do not, maybe you are looking through the wrong mirror. Look through the mirror of God's love.

God, help me today to reflect Your love.

*For everyone who asks receives, and he who seeks
finds, and to him who knocks it will be opened.*
—LUKE 11:10

Now I will tell you about Mom's denial. My eating disorder was extreme some days and mild other days, but
as years ten through twelve wore on with the bulimia, I
was becoming more and more suicidal. I was losing
hope and wanted to die.

Usually I would never have revealed this pain, but I
was getting scared. During a particularly desperate
time I was visiting my parents, and Mom and I went
out for a walk. I blurted out, "I want to kill myself."

Mom's reaction was, "Oh, Cynthia, please don't talk
that way. Don't you know if you did that you'd hurt
your dad and me?"

The old denial button was pushed. What my mother
really was saying was, I'm going to pretend this didn't
happen. My perfect daughter does not feel this way.

I felt more alone than ever before. If your parents
cannot understand and respond to your cry for help,
who can? It would take a while for me to take responsibility for getting help myself. But I will never forget the
added despair when I revealed my feelings and got
nothing back.

Can you relate to my story? Don't despair! If someone does not understand your pain, keep searching.
God will not abandon you.

---

*God, sometimes I think You allow doors to be closed in our faces so
we will open Your door for answers. Help us to forgive those who
don't understand. Help us to keep knocking on doors for help.*

*Praying always with all prayer and supplication
in the Spirit, being watchful to this end
with all perserverance.*
—EPH. 6:18

My search for a therapist who knew how to help me was a discouraging journey. I went to more than eighteen until I found the ones who could save my life. I shudder when I think of some of the things I was told. "Just stop it," was the most common reaction.

"But if I could just stop it, I would," I would reply.

"Just trust in God and everything will be all right," I was told by Christian therapists. Well, I was trying to trust in God and nothing was right.

The real zinger came from two different psychiatrists in two different cities. When I told them, "I eat and eat, I lose total control, and then I get rid of what I've eaten," they both said, "What you need is a man."

I could not believe it. In fact, one of them said, "You need a sugar daddy, Cynthia." They thought a man could cure my bulimia. I could not give love much less receive love. A man was not the answer. I knew deep inside there were reasons I was bulimic.

I wanted to give up because all of the professionals I encountered hurt me rather than helped me. But for whatever reason, I kept searching.

Are you receiving band-aid answers? Keep searching. Keep knocking on doors. God will open a door for you.

---

*Father, give me the faith to keep "knocking" till I find the good things
You have for me.*

*Therefore, my beloved brethren, let
every man be swift to hear, slow to
speak, slow to wrath.*
—JAMES 1:19

I was so lonely. No one knew about my eating disorder. At times I really did make an effort to find support and love. One weekend I went to a seminar at a nearby church. The speakers were a married couple who had many wonderful things to say about the Christian family. I learned this couple lived near me, and after hearing them, I decided to introduce myself and get to know them. We exchanged some small talk, and then I said, "I'd really enjoy getting to know your family. I'm single and my family lives far away."

I expected a warm response. The man said, "Oh, don't worry. You're pretty. Someday a guy will come into your life and you'll get married." I am sure my mouth dropped open. I felt like crying. After he said this, he just walked away.

I wanted to scream, "Hey! Wait a minute! I didn't say I was looking for a husband. I said I needed a Christian family to know and love!"

After I said the risky, "I'm lonely," this prominent Christian man could not hear my words. I never took a risk like that again for a long time. It has taken time for me to forgive that brother in Christ. I learned to listen to what people are saying.

God, even though someone doesn't understand me, help me not to give up. It hurts, God. But help me to keep on searching for a listening ear and a loving family. Thank You for being my family.

> *God is faithful, who will not allow you*
> *to be tempted beyond what you are able, but*
> *with the temptation will also make the way*
> *of escape, that you may be able to bear it.*
> —1 COR. 10:13

It is right there. In 1 Corinthians 10:13, Paul said God will not give me more than I can handle. He promises me that. But today I just do not think I can handle much more. I am so out of control. I have left work and have come to an all-you-can-eat restaurant. I have eaten until I cannot move. There is a monster within me saying, "Do it, Cynthia! Destroy yourself!" What is going on?

Sometimes I wish someone would chain me to my desk or to my bedpost so I cannot move. Maybe I need a straight jacket. Yes, that would do the trick, wouldn't it? Yet I think the force that drives me to eat and self-destruct would be able to escape from anything.

That's just how I feel. God promises to be faithful. His Word says so, and I must hang on and believe.

Dear God, You promise that You will not give me more than I can handle. So right now, help me forgive myself and begin again. But God, please help me find out what is wrong.

*The end of all things is at hand; therefore
be serious and watchful in your prayers.*
—1 PETER 4:7

Are you like me? I can not seem to pray, or even want to pray, when I do not eat right. I am unable to pray if I am bingeing or if I do not exercise because I feel bad about myself.

I believe you must be self-controlled to pray. If I am out of control, whether it be with food or anger, it is hard to pray. I hope you are reading this page in the morning. When my eyes first open I find it best to say, "God, thank you for another day. May I glorify Your name today by what I eat, and by how I eat. May I praise you by how I love me with the love You have given me, so I can love others."

Today, let's be self-controlled with our eating and with our emotions.

Father, I need You when I feel out of control. Please be with me as I struggle to have self-control. Be near me.

I was naked and you clothed Me.
—MATT. 25:36

My closet was filled with skinny clothes, just-right clothes, and fat clothes. How I longed to always be able to wear my skinny clothes. Yet even when I was wearing them, a voice inside would whisper, Cynthia, you don't deserve to look good. So I would eat and eat and wear my fat clothes. Soon I would get tired of covering up myself with my fat clothes, so I would exercise excessively and get into my just-right clothes, working my way back into my skinny clothes. It was one big vicious circle, fraying my emotions and my health.

In many ways having three different sets of clothes gave me more excuses to slip out of control. I could tell myself, Well, I can binge today. I've got just the outfit to hide that extra five pounds.

May God give us today a state of mind that will enable us to determine what our healthy size and weight should be. May He help us strive to quit making excuses.

———————

Father, help me not to hide from myself or You. Shelter me with Your love.

The wise shall inherit glory,
But shame shall be the legacy of fools.
—PROV. 3:35

I was so smart. When I knew I'd be bingeing during the day, I wore a suit to work, a suit with a big jacket to hide my bulging stomach. No belts, mind you, nothing snug-fitting, but dark skirts and draping jackets to conceal my body. Nobody could see me, nobody.

I felt so superior. I would think, Ha! I'm fooling everyone. They think I'm thin, but if they only knew! After work, of course, I would have to take that suit off and look at what it was covering up. Tears would fall because what was under that suit was not a pretty sight.

We may fool the people around us, but we cannot fool ourselves or God. God commands us to be honest. Today, let us look through our closets and really think about our clothes choices. Let us make a commitment to quit hiding. The only person we are really fooling is ourself.

God, I get so tired of hiding. Please help me be honest with myself. Give me strength to be open.

> *But You, O Lord, are a God full of*
> *compassion, and gracious,*
> *Longsuffering and abundant*
> *in mercy and truth.*—PS. 86:15

You're fat, Cynthia. You've gained so much weight!"
My dad said these words after not seeing me for two
months. I felt so ashamed. My dad was embarrassed at
the sight of me. Now that I know what was going on
inside me, I have often wondered why my dad didn't
comfort me, and try to find out why I had gained so
much weight so quickly?

I was just twenty years old and my heart was broken
over a marriage that had lasted just eight months. I had
lost a college scholarship because all I wanted to do
was run away from the humiliation of that marriage
and everyone who knew about it.

After my divorce my family and friends encouraged
me to try another Christian college. So I went to a
strange city and college. It was one of the biggest mistakes I have ever made. I felt rejected and had no one
to run to, so I ran to food. I could not get enough to fill
me up. So I got fat.

I was devastated when my dad reacted with disdain.
I needed his help and love, not his disapproval. It has
taken time for us to talk about it, and for me to forgive
him. But I feel secure now in the belief that our God
who made us never looks at us with disdain, but rather
with compassion and empathy.

God, I know You feel much sorrow for our suffering and our pain.
Thank You for loving us unconditionally.

The Lord gives strength to His people;
The Lord blesses His people with peace.
—PS. 29:11

My friend Kathy has a beautiful spirit and she is also pretty on the outside. Like a lot of us, she struggles with gaining that five or ten extra pounds. She will lose it, then gain it back only to lose it again. Some days Kathy panics about it. She feels hysterical and says, "I don't want to be fat and ugly!" Her panic causes her to eat more.

On other days, she asks God to resolve it. She gives her panic feelings to God so He can take care of them.

Kathy is like so many of us. We panic, fret, and worry about five pounds. When we do this, we focus on what is wrong and not what is right.

Today, let us take time to give our panic to God. He will give us peace if we allow Him to.

God, right now we give our extra five pounds to You. Take away our panic. Help us to focus on You, God.

> *Rest in the LORD, and wait patiently for Him . . .*
> *Do not fret—it only causes harm.*
>
> —PS. 37:7–8

A year ago Kathy had a baby, and like many women she gained extra weight. Kathy gained fifty pounds while pregnant. She did not like it at all. As soon as her baby boy was born, she told me with a panicked tone, "I'm getting on a strict diet next week." She joined a weight loss organization the next week but instead of feeling good about it, now she felt even more pressure.

When she called me she said, "It's just too much pressure. I'm tired. The baby is so wondrous but he takes every minute of my day and I've got to take care of my home and husband and job. I just can't focus on a diet plan right now."

You know what? That is OK. I know Kathy, and when she is ready she will lose her weight. For now, for today, she has decided to relax, to take one minute at a time, and to focus on her child and husband.

Sometimes we need to just relax. We need to stop panicking over having to lose the weight *now*. It only makes matters worse when we keep putting so much undue pressure on ourselves.

Today, relax in God's grace and love.

God, take away my fretting today. I want to depend completely on You, the God of peace and rest.

When He, the Spirit of truth, has come,
He will guide you into all truth.
—JOHN 16:13

Ten months after Kathy's baby came, she had lost her extra fifty pounds. She lives far away from me so we catch up on the phone, and after talking about the baby and her husband and work and church, I asked about her diet.

"So, how's your weight, Kath?"

"Oh, I lost it all!"

"Kathy, that's wonderful," I said. "How did you do it?"

"Well, along with the diet group I attend, I continued going to my Adult Children of Alcoholics group. Cynthia, as you know, my weight was just the symptom of deeper issues. I had to keep dealing with the past."

Kathy grew up with an alcoholic father and a mom who was too young to know how to care, love, and nurture her child. Kathy was abused emotionally and has experienced a lot of hurts in her life. Her constant five-pound weight variations before the baby and the fifty pounds after his birth were symptoms. She had to dig deep to uncover what was really wrong.

Kathy is such an example to me. She could have used the excuse of having a baby to justify her weight. Instead she faced her past. She focused on feelings instead of food.

God, help me dig underneath that five or fifty pounds, and face the issues.

Indeed we count them blessed who endure.
—JAMES 5:11

Kathy has now lost all her "baby fat" and feels so good physically. She revealed to me, "I always wanted to be thin and I thought it would be a big deal when I was. Now that I am I really don't feel any different. I mean, I'm glad I've lost the weight. I needed to for my health and appearance but it doesn't mean everything is going to change."

Kathy envisioned life would somehow be a little more special if she got thin. The reality is she still has to change diapers, work out conflicts on her job, and deal with frustration and fear and worries.

For many people this anticipation of an ideal thin life is a very dangerous way to feel. We set ourselves up to fail. In other words, when our mind says, If I lose weight then my life will be perfect, or, I'll meet my mate, or, People will love me more, we are having unreal expectations. The truth is we have to keep on dealing with our life. Chances are we may not meet the man of our dreams just because we are thin. As the saying goes, "Beauty is only skin deep."

Sometimes, God, it's disappointing when we think life will be different. But help us to change what we can and accept what we can't change.

A friend loves at all times.
—PROV. 17:17

Cynthia, I know you're really struggling. Come over and spend the night."

Friends are such gifts from God. When my friend Pearl called me and invited me to come over, she did not realize I was drowning in bulimia. I wanted to give up but I could not tell her. But I did go and spend the night at her house. It was a real haven for me. She rescued me from one night of complete despair. I have learned that I need friends.

Those of us struggling with extra weight or bulimia or anorexia need friends. If we are not at the point of talking to our friends, we need support. Please, join a group of people struggling with the same problem.

So often we feel alone. We do not have to be alone. Find a friend who will encourage you every day you are on that diet. Find a local support group that will help you through the issues you need to face. Or start a group in your church or in your home. We all need friends and we all need encouragement.

God, I thank You for giving us people who love us and who sometimes save us from despair and loneliness. Friends are gifts. Thank You for knowing our need by providing us with friends.

> *It is more blessed to give than to receive.*
> —ACTS 20:35

Lisa is desperate to be loved. She wants to be accepted for who she is, all two hundred fifty pounds of her. The problem is she is *too* needy. She is a real giver, which is good, but Lisa gives so much she is a turnoff to many people. When she wants someone to be her friend, she will call twice a day, send a card every day, or buy lots of gifts. She wants to go out and do things all of the time.

It is tough being Lisa's friend. If you do not give back to Lisa in the same way she is giving to you, she cries, "Nobody loves or cares about me! I'm such a good friend; why isn't anyone else?" Then she eats everything in her refrigerator.

Lisa expects so much that she keeps failing in friendship. She takes out her anger and hurt on herself by eating. Lisa needs to stop and examine why she turns people off, why she needs so much and gives so much, and why she is so hurt when she does not receive back what she gave. Perhaps she could back off a little, and not try so hard. It is fine to give, but if she did it a little at a time and did not expect the same back in return, maybe then she would gain friends instead of lose them.

God, sometimes we feel too needy. We're too clingy and we lose friendships instead of gaining them. It's so easy to blame everyone else instead of examining what we're doing wrong. Help us, Lord, to learn about ourselves and about how to love in a healthy way.

Do you want to be made well?
—JOHN 5:6

The man had been an invalid for thirty-eight years. Jesus knew he had been in that condition for a long time yet He asked him, "Do you want to be made well?" Jesus, why did you ask such a question? Of course he wanted to get well!

As I question Jesus' question, my heartstrings are being tugged. I hear, Cynthia, do you want to get well?

I have to wait for my answer. I have been sick for so long. What does "getting well" really mean? I am afraid if I start eating normally I will get fat, and I cannot have that, now can I? Besides, it is easier being sick. If I recover it means I will have to deal with the real reasons why I binge and self-destruct. I am not sure I want to go through that fire.

"So, Cynthia," Jesus asks again, "Do you want to get well?"

———————————

Father, those words are so scary. It's a gut-wrenching challenge to face my monster, and I'm not sure if I can do it. I do know that being sick and unhappy is not a glory to You. So, I ask that You keep asking me the question. Probe my heart and spirit to answer, "Yes," and seek help.

For everyone who asks receives, and he who seeks finds, and to him who knocks it will be opened.
—MATT. 7:8

I had fasted for three days. The monster told me to take laxatives because I would lose even more weight. I did. Now I cannot move my right side. I cannot hear and see out of my right ear and eye. My heart is beating so hard it feels as if it is going to pop through my chest.

"Dear God, I've done it this time. I'm going to die? But, God, I don't really want to die."

I called a friend. She rushed right over. When she saw me she said, "Cynthia, your fingers and lips are blue. We've got to get you to a doctor."

By the time we arrived at the hospital the feeling in my right side had returned. I had drunk half a gallon of Gatorade and was feeling a little better. "Doctor," my friend said, "Cynthia is addicted to bingeing and purging, then she starves herself." The doctor listened to her while I longed for him to give me the magic words that would make me stop.

"Well, I think it's just nerves," he finally said. Then he handed me a prescription for Valium and sent me home. I was devastated.

I think God sometimes needs us to keep knocking on doors. He allows us to be tested so we can depend totally on Him. When He hears our prayers uttered in desperation, He listens.

Lord, help me to believe that one day a door will open, though they may all slam in my face at times.

For what I am doing, I do not understand.
For what I will to do, that I do not
practice; but what I hate, that I do.
—ROM. 7:15

You might think the fact that I could die from the madness of bulimia would make me stop. It did not. Even after turning blue and numb, unable to move my right side, I woke up the next day and started bingeing and purging all over again. I knew then I had reached the point where I simply could not go on living this lie. Ending my life seemed to be the only answer.

I wrote in my journal, "Death, yes, death seems to be the only answer for peace." The strange thing is part of me wanted to die, yet part of me desperately wanted to live. Part of me cried out to be normal. The other part yelled, "You deserve to die! Look at your lack of control!

I saw myself being put in a strait jacket, and making myself live in it for a month. Maybe then I would be free. A strait jacket was not the answer though. My answer lay within that part of me that wanted to die. "God," I cried out. "Are You there? I can't take this much longer. Please, please, be there for me!"

Do you struggle with wanting to be well, but wanting to give up at the same time? Take heart. God is listening to you today and He will not give up on you.

Are You there, God? I must believe You are. Yes, even in Your silence I will believe.

> *Out of the depths I have cried to You, O LORD;*
> *Lord, hear my voice!*
> *Let Your ears be attentive*
> *To the voice of my supplications.*
> —PS. 130:1

I will never forget the day. It was a Sunday. The sun was shining, the birds were singing, and I did not know why because this was the day I was going to die. My phone never rang anymore. I had alienated myself from my family and friends. I had stopped going to church. The thought kept going over and over in my head, Get a gun. Take your life. You're no good, Cynthia.

I called my neighbors to borrow a gun. Fortunately they were not home. I laid on my couch hoping they would return soon so I could end my madness. I surveyed my house. There were food cartons everywhere, left over from my "last night of bingeing." I wanted to cry but tears would not come. I battled and screamed at this person called God who I had always heard loved me.

"Where are you, God? God, if you're there, you'd better please help me now or there's not going to be a Cynthia Rowland around after today!"

If you are crying out prayers as I did, please know that God is near and He is listening.

God, be near me and hear me when I cry out in desperation. Give me a sense of Your love for me.

*The Lord said, . . . "Satan has asked for you, that
he may sift you as wheat. But I have prayed
for you, that your faith should not fail."*
—LUKE 22:31–32

Silence. An hour passed. The phone rang. It was my
friend Joan, who had taken me to the doctor who prescribed Valium.

"Cynthia, this morning at my church a woman
named Jan told how she nearly died of bulimia, and
she went to a clinic near Dallas. She said the Minirth-
Meier Clinic saved her life. Here's her number."

After I hung up two feelings fought inside me. One
side said, You're no good, Cynthia. Take your life! The
other side said, No, Cynthia, this is hope. You hang on
and call Jan!

On this day I knew with all my heart that there was a
God in the world, and there was a Satan too. Good and
evil, and both fighting for my life. I prayed, "God, I
want You to win this battle. Please don't let me die.
Please help me through today and tomorrow and the
days to come."

You, too, may feel that a battle rages within you.
Today, be assured. It may feel as if Satan is winning but
Satan has lost the battle already. Jesus Christ won the
war by dying for you and me.

*Lord, I know that sometimes I must wait for You, but thank You for
saying yes to my needs.*

Those who are well have no need of a physician.
—MATT. 9:12

Jan, my name is Cynthia Rowland and I have bulimia. I feel like I'm going to kill myself if I don't get help. . . ."

Jan told me to run, not walk, to the Minirth-Meier Clinic. I had to take the first step. I had to say, "I'm powerless. I'm sick and if I don't get help I'm going to die."

It took a week before I was ready to go to the clinic. They needed to verify my insurance and have a bed available for me. I hung on by my fingertips. I needed to take a leave of absence from my job, so I had to tell my boss. He was shocked when I told him what was wrong. Gary said, "Cynthia, lately I knew something was wrong but I had no idea what. Go and get well."

Go and get well. I grasped his words and would tell myself driving from Little Rock to Dallas: Cynthia, go and get well.

Jesus, you are the Great Physician. Please may I find help and healing at the Minirth-Meier Clinic.

Today, may you not wait or walk or ponder or question; may you *run*. Go and get well.

God, thank You for the people who helped me. Thank You for being my Great Physician.

Your right hand has held me up . . .
You enlarged my path under me;
So that my feet did not slip.
—PS. 18:35–36

As I drove the five hours to Richardson, Texas, outside of Dallas, I saw an exit every once in a while and I wanted to turn my car around. I wanted to go back to my home and my job and my addiction. But I told myself, "No, Cynthia. This is hope."

But then I panicked, But Cynthia, you'd better binge because this may be your last time! So I stopped at every fast food restaurant I could find and I ate and ate. When I arrived at the hospital, it was midnight. For a long time I just sat in my car. Cynthia, I said to myself, either you find the answers to your self-destructiveness or you'll die. After saying this, I downed a big box of laxatives. I knew this would be the last time. Now was the time to "go and get well."

I entered the hospital not even realizing what was ahead. "God," I prayed. "You've brought me this far. I beg You, see me through."

Today God will see you through. Trust Him to keep your hands on the wheel. Go forward and do not turn back. Trust Him.

Jesus, thank You for Your example of going to the Cross. Thank You for not turning back. Help me to trust You and Your love for me.

Wait for the LORD, and He will save you.
—PROV. 20:22

The lady in admitting was not busy. After all, it was past midnight and not many patients were in line to enter the psychiatric ward. She asked all the necessary questions then she said, "Now, you're admitting yourself so you must stay for ten days. The maximum stay is usually sixty days, but heaven forbid you'll have to stay that long."

I thought to myself, Lady, if getting over this addiction means I have to stay here the rest of my life, I'll do it!

I signed all the paperwork. It was time to start my journey. A nurse came and took me to the fifth floor. On the way we came to a locked door. She pushed a button and a buzzer sounded, signaling the door was now unlocked. I went through and the door shut behind me. I was now behind locked doors. I wanted to scream, "Let me out!" But I could not turn around.

My life and my body needed help desperately. There could be no turning back for me.

"Dear God," I prayed, "another step has been taken. Please be with me each step of the way."

We have a Father who loves us, whose desire it is to be with us each step of our journey, no matter where that journey might lead us. He promises to be with us always. God is ready and willing to take your journey with you.

———————

Father, take my hand and lead me where I need to go.

A man's heart plans his way,
But the LORD directs his steps.
—PROV. 16:9

Whenever I went crazy with food, spending money that I did not have and going so out of control, I used to wish I had a brain tumor. I wanted an excuse for my behavior, anything but the real reason.

Upon entering the psychiatric unit, I was given a battery of tests: brain scan (no brain tumors), blood test, and physical exam. I was weighed and I shut my eyes tight so I would not have to see what the scales read. I was asked a bunch of questions.

"Describe your binges." (Oh, wow. Do you have a week?)

"Do you exercise excessively?" (Do you want me to start with the time I ran four miles in ninety-eight-degree heat?)

"How many laxatives, diuretics, and diet pills have you taken?" (Does anyone here have a calculator?)

I gulped every time I answered a question. I already felt self-conscious because I was naked underneath my hospital gown. Now I felt my soul was being exposed too.

I had the choice to lie, deny, or tell the truth. I told the truth.

Lord God, exposing the truth is so hard. Yet it's just the first step, isn't it? Hold my hand each step of the way.

> *Do you not know that your body is the temple*
> *of the Holy Spirit who is in you?*
> —1 COR. 6:19

My body had been so abused. I would lose weight, gain weight, feed it junk, damage it with laxatives, fast, and binge some more. Dr. Frank Minirth was amazed I was even alive. How my body made it through twelve years of the destruction was a miracle in itself. He told me my brain scan was normal. My electrolytes were way out of line though. He explained that the abuse was so severe I was on my way to having a heart attack. He and the nurses would be closely monitoring me for the next couple of weeks.

"My body is supposed to be the temple of God. Why, why, why do I hurt myself so?"

After eighteen other doctors, Dr. Minirth gave me the words I had longed to hear: "Give yourself time, Cynthia," he reassured me. "We'll help you find the reasons to the whys."

Perhaps today you can pray as I did.

God, I'm sorry. I haven't treated my body as the temple of the Holy Spirit. I know I need help. I admit that and ask You to bear with me as I search my heart so I can make my temple livable for You.

You have been My God.
Be not far from Me,
For trouble is near;
For there is none to help.
—PS. 22:10–11

Give up the control, Cynthia." I sat down to eat in the psychiatric ward. I did not want to eat. I was afraid. If I ate, I would get fat. The staff would not let me get rid of all this food. I could not leave to buy my laxatives. I had to sit in the lunch room for thirty minutes after I ate. I wanted to leave. I was going to get fat. Anger choked me. They're making me eat, I screamed to myself. I don't want to eat!

"Give up the control, Cynthia," the staff would say.

"What are you talking about?" I told them angrily.

"It's not the food, Cynthia. It's not the bulimia you're angry about. Who are you really angry at? Give it up."

I did not know it at the time but "give up the control" meant quit numbing, quit avoiding truth, and deal with what is really wrong. The bulimia controlled my emotions. It was time to let go.

I got angry with God. "God, if I let go and allow You to take over I don't know what's going to happen!"

Do you share my fear of losing control? Does it frighten you to think of God taking over? If it does, you must give your fear over to God. He understands. He also knows what is best for you. Trust Him to show you what is best.

God, help us to give You the control over our lives.

The wise in heart will receive commands,
But a prating fool will fall.

—PROV. 10:8

When you admit yourself into a hospital, you are saying, "I'm out of control. Help me." One of the first things the professionals have to do is take away anything that could hurt you. The staff checked through all of my belongings, searching for anything sharp or breakable. They confiscated all drugs, even aspirin. They locked all of that potentially harmful stuff away.

I did not like being invaded. I did not want anyone to take control over me. I did not like someone else telling me what I could or could not do, what I could or could not have, what I should or should not eat. But while I did not like it, I also felt safe knowing these people cared enough to protect me.

Maybe you need protection. Perhaps you need someone to sift through who you are and point out the dangers. Maybe you need someone to encourage you, to confirm the good in you, to give you a hug. Do not be afraid to find someone to help, someone you can open up to.

_____

God, it is hard giving the control away. It is hard obeying rules that will not allow me to hurt myself. So, God, help me as I allow someone to help me. Most of all, help me allow You to help me, God.

For the Lord God will help Me;
Therefore I will not be disgraced . . .
And I know I will not be ashamed.
—ISA. 50:7

In the hospital I had such feelings of guilt and embarrassment. I kept hearing what my dad had said to me over and over again. When I told him I was going to take off from work and check myself into a clinic, he said, "You don't need to do that. You don't need to leave your job. Just buck up, and if you have to get help, find it locally so you can keep working." Now I found myself in a strange city, away from my job, disobeying my father. I felt guilty.

Wait a minute. I'm twenty-eight years old and I'm worried about making my dad mad, I thought. Why am I here? Because I'm dying, that's why! Could it be that my dad isn't always right?

That was a difficult thought for me. I went to my heavenly Father for comfort and assurance. "God, I'm not a little girl but I feel like I am. Why do I feel like that, God? You want me, don't you? Please, God, say 'Yes.' Please say you are glad I'm here! Give me peace. Help me to grow up."

Are you struggling with what people will think if you get help and invest money to overcome your serious eating disorder? Let go and take care of you. If you had cancer or a broken leg you would seek help. Do not be ashamed to get help for the struggles you face.

God, I know You want me to be whole physically, spiritually, and emotionally. Help me never to be ashamed to ask for help.

> *Blessed are those who hunger and*
> *thirst for righteousness,*
> *For they shall be filled.*
> —MATT. 5:6

I cannot remember a day in my twenties when I felt happy, a day when I liked me and my life. Depression was an unwanted friend who followed me around wherever I went. When I visited my parents they could see I was depressed yet they felt helpless.

One day a letter came from my dad. I was glad to receive it but as I opened it I saw it was not a letter but a picture cut out of a magazine. The picture showed a starving African child, all bones, with a huge protruding stomach, and flies crawling all over his face and shoulders. My dad had written a question on the bottom of the picture: "And I feel sorry for myself?"

Dad's message was: Why should you be depressed? There's always someone worse than *you*. After this I felt even more guilt, and I increased my pain by asking myself, Yea, Cynthia, what do you have to feel sorry about?

While that starving child had pain and hunger, so did I. The problem was my dad refused to validate my pain and anger. I know he was trying to help but he did not.

Is it not wonderful to know that God validates our hurts and struggles? He wants us to express our pain. He wants to help us just like He wants to help the starving children. He understands there are many ways to starve.

Do not judge according to appearance,
but judge with righteous judgment.
—JOHN 7:24

My first thought when I saw my therapist, Mike, was, He's fat! No way can he help me. In my arrogance and self-reliance I judged Mike by how he looked. Can someone overweight help someone who is scared to death of getting fat? I did not know it then, but Mike would be the person who would help me find my monsters and slay them. I learned to trust him and to feel safe in his presence. Mike understood that underneath my defenses was locked-up pain and sorrow. I had judged Mike like a book, by the cover and not what was inside.

People do this all the time, do they not? It does not matter if they are thin or fat. Fat people do not like thin people because they feel so fat around them and they are afraid they will be judged. Thin people judge fat people because they are afraid of getting fat themselves. But the truth is no matter what size we are—small, medium, or large—we all have a heart and soul and joy and pain. We are really not that different, are we?

Today, look beyond the exterior packaging and into the heart, just as God does.

God, thank You for looking at my heart instead of my outward appearance. Help me to do the same with others.

March 25 – THE CRUELTY OF CHILDREN

Therefore let us not judge one another anymore.
—ROM. 14:13

My eleven-year-old buddy Lavinia told me a sad story today. I asked her if kids made fun of other kids who were not thin and she said, "Yes. There's a girl who is really fat and at lunchtime when she walks by certain kids say, 'Watch out. Mary's coming and she's going to cause an earthquake!' They duck under their table and pretend an earthquake is happening."

My heart hurt for Mary. She's eleven years old and she is not accepted. Some people ignore her and others make fun of her. Lavinia told me Mary is always alone. I encouraged Lavinia to befriend Mary.

How many of you can remember when people made fun of you? Does it still hurt? Talk to a friend about it. Write your thoughts down and know that God will never make fun of you. Jesus died for Mary, and He also died for the kids that humiliate her.

Today, remember and forgive.

God, thank You for accepting me, flaws and all. Comfort the "Marys" of the world and show them they are truly loved by You.

Be merciful to me, O God . . .
For my soul trusts in You;
And in the shadow of Your wings
I will make my refuge,
Until these calamities have passed by.
—PS. 57:1

Today is a precious gift from God.

Today I commit to cherish the gift and not to take a moment for granted.

Today, instead of dwelling on what I am going to eat, I will first thank God for calling me His child.

Today I will ask for His strength and for courage to focus on the gift of life instead of my weight.

Today I will feel His presence.

Today I will depend on Him and not on myself.

Today I will be honest.

Today I will show His love to someone else.

Today, just for today, I will trust in Him, because I know today will prepare me for tomorrow.

Father, today I give You my life. Today I look to You for answers.

> *Jesus Christ is the same yesterday,*
> *today, and forever.*
>
> —HEB. 13:8

Do television commercials frustrate you sometimes? They do me. One commercial shows just how great you look if you drink a certain diet soda. What bugs me about this commercial is, just once, I would like to see someone with big hips drinking that one-calorie soda. Why do advertisements always feature thin, beautiful people with no hips?

This commercial is followed by another for a luscious chocolate cake you can microwave in three minutes. Right after that is a pitch for a diet pill and then thirty more seconds of someone flipping mouth-watering hamburgers.

These messages in our society are so confusing. On the one hand, we are told we need to be thin. On the other hand, we are told to go out and eat a greasy hamburger. Food is constantly being presented to us in all forms, especially at meal times, and the rest of the time we see diet pills, diet candy, diet soda, and diet programs. We are tossed one way, then the next.

God is consistent. He never wavers. He never goes back on His Word. He is the same yesterday and today and tomorrow. It helps to know that while the world is so inconsistent and confusing with its messages, God's message is always the same. He loved me yesterday. He loves me today. And no matter what I do, He will still love me tomorrow.

Thank You, God, for being a consistent father.

Do not worry about your life, what
you will eat or what you will drink . . .
Look at the birds of the air, for they
neither sow nor reap nor gather into barns . . .
Are you not of more value than they?
—MATT. 6:25–26

So much precious time is wasted worrying about diets and food. I can remember driving in my car, and I never took the time to look at the blue sky or the trees or people. I would look instead at this or that restaurant or fast food place or this candy store or that ice cream parlor.

I never stopped to savor the real beauty around me. I never grasped the beauty of the wrinkled face of a wise old woman or stopped to enjoy the laughter of a child. I was in too big a hurry to satisfy *me*.

God must do a lot of sighing when He sees us focusing on destructive things instead of on the free gifts He offers us.

Today, may we stop looking at the restaurants. May we stop concentrating on what can fill us up physically. Take hold of all the beauty of God, which can fill you up in a way food never can.

Father God, I waste so much time worrying. Fill me with peace to believe we can handle together whatever life brings.

> *But let patience have its perfect work,*
> *that you may be perfect and complete,*
> *lacking nothing.*
>
> —JAMES 1:4

To lose two pounds or sixty-five pounds we must have patience. In a world of "fast relief" and television shows where life's problems are solved in an hour, we get the false sense that our problems should be over quickly too. But the truth is our extra pounds did not happen overnight. It took us time to gain them, maybe even years. It will take time to lose them.

One definition of patience says it all: Patience is the ability or willingness to suppress annoyance when confronted with delay. In other words, it is hard. It is annoying to cut back on calories, to avoid food high in fat and sugar, to take a walk for a mile or two instead of eating those cookies. But if we are patient, the reward of a healthy body is right around the corner.

God, if I want to give up on my diet today, help me to endure. Help me to keep on taking care of myself.

Fear not, for I am with you;
Be not dismayed, for I am your God.
I will strengthen you.

—ISA. 41:10

It has been a hard day at work. I deserve a hot fudge sundae.

The kids were fighting all day. I need a candy bar to settle my nerves.

I got a promotion. Let's celebrate by going to that all-you-can-eat restaurant.

My husband hurt my feelings so I am going to show him by eating the rest of the pie.

Why is it so easy to justify our reasons for eating when life does or does not go our way? It would do all of us good to change our way of thinking when it comes to food. Instead of running to food when life is troublesome or victorious, let us exchange food for a healthy outlet.

Take a bubble bath instead of indulging in that hot fudge sundae.

Go for a walk to settle our nerves.

Go out to a restaurant that has a select menu.

Talk to our spouses about our hurt feelings.

Father, the need to turn to food is so much easier than doing something healthy. Today, God, may I turn to You for answers.

> *Mercy and truth have met together.*
> —PS. 85:10

So, Cynthia, tell me about your mom and dad," my therapist said point-blank.

"What do my parents have to do with my eating disorder?" I asked defensively. "It's my problem, Mike. I'm undisciplined and if you'd just put me on a good diet, my bulimia would be gone." Mike gently laughed at me.

Mike knew that my parents and my upbringing had a lot to do with my eating disorder. I was just too blind to see it that day. Mike wanted me to get honest and to quit protecting my "perfect" parents. The truth was that there were many conflicts in my family and my bingeing and purging shielded me from remembering my painful memories.

My biggest problem was putting my parents on a pedestal. It was time to see that they were human beings who made some serious mistakes that were affecting me as an adult.

Perhaps you place the blame for your extra weight or your eating disorder on your lack of discipline. We could all be more disciplined but sometimes we need to go to the *root* of the problem. Sometimes it starts with our childhood.

God, help us unravel the hurt we have created in our lives. Help us to look deep inside and to deal with how our upbringing might affect us today.

For He does not afflict willingly,
Nor grieve the children of men.
—LAM. 3:33

I can't believe you don't get it! It's so simple! Put your thinking cap on." My dad tried to teach me math but I just did not understand. He yelled at me, "It's so simple! Now figure it out!" His words made me feel so stupid, and he got so mad at me I could not think. When I cried he became even angrier.

"Go wash your face and come back and do it right!"

In the hospital during a group session, I relived that memory. As an adult I could hear the many times the message went straight to my heart, "You're not good enough." I tried so hard to be perfect and not to disappoint anyone. Bingeing and purging confirmed that my dad was right. I am not very smart.

My salty tears poured as I relived the pain. My therapist listened and gently pointed to an empty chair. "Put your dad in this chair and tell him, 'I'm not dumb, Dad. If you couldn't be patient with me, maybe you should have hired a tutor.'"

After I had done that, Mike said, "Cynthia, now close your eyes and picture God teaching you math. What would He do?"

I pictured God being gentle, taking time to understand my fears of multiplication and division. He did not yell.

Can you remember a painful memory and a message that may be controlling you today?

God, thank You for being a Father who is truly patient.

> *Be kindly affectionate to one another*
> *with brotherly love.* —ROM. 12:10

In the psychiatric ward I lived with people who struggled with all kinds of different symptoms: depression, obesity, anorexia, bulimia, drug addiction, alcoholism. I was so blind before I entered the hospital; I did not know why people hurt or why people want to die or why people have addictions. I left my ignorance at the door.

I came to realize in the hospital that people may look different, and they may have a different addiction or a different symptom from mine, but we all have reasons for our addictions. I think that is why God created His church. He knew we needed each other. He wanted all walks of life to know Him and His Son. He wanted the church to worship Him. I also believe He wants all of us from all walks of life, with different sets of problems and struggles, to relate to each other, to encourage each other, and to love one another.

So many churches today are giving God glory by loving people in need. If you do not usually go to church, today think about finding a loving, supportive church home. We really do need each other.

Jesus, You taught us the meaning of love. May we look to You to help us truly love each other.

*Bear one another's burdens, and so fulfill
the law of Christ.*
                                    —GAL. 6:2

One definition for support: "to provide a person with the means of sustaining life." Isn't that inspiring? To provide the means of sustaining life!

People who are committed to going to a support meeting do so because they know they need encouragement. A person struggling needs to know they are not the only one going through that problem. Having a group cheer you on because you are on your way to losing your ten pounds, or congratulate you because you have reached your goal weight, or help you when you have blown it and need to start over, really does sustain you.

Some people are too embarrassed to "weigh in" with a group, or to admit they have a problem. They are embarrassed to be part of a group because to them that means they will have to let go and allow others to help out.

If you need help or support or friendship, find a group that can cheer you along the way. It is a great feeling to know we do not have to go through our struggles alone.

_____

Father, thanks for always bearing my burdens. Help me to reach out to others to help them with their burdens too.

> *When you have eaten and are full, then you*
> *shall bless the LORD your God for the good*
> *land which He has given you.*
> —DEUT. 8:10

My Uncle Rick's motto is "Eat to live; don't live to eat." He abides by it. A former swimming coach, Uncle Rick swims every day, eats right, and at age fifty-four looks trim and healthy. His motto is a good one to live by. God made our bodies to need food for energy. Too much food causes us to gain weight.

I know there was a time when what I was going to eat was the priority of the day. Food was all I thought about. I needed to stop and say, "I need to eat nutritious meals to help me do what I need to do today. I need to eat to live, not live to eat."

When I was obsessed with food, I could not take the time to enjoy life, to help someone, to listen, to laugh, or to pray, because I was too busy thinking about food.

Today, let us stop and really take care of ourselves by eating right. Let us live our lives in a healthy way and love God.

God, help me to eat to live and not live to eat. Help me to live for You. Help me to focus on Your love and the love that is within me.

He who loves his brother abides in the light.
—1 JOHN 2:10

Group therapy can be an overwhelming experience when you are on the road to healing. You sit in a circle. Two therapists are usually in the group to help start everyone talking. Anyone can share whatever he or she is feeling. What is amazing is when one person talks about a memory or a hurt or a feeling, everyone can identify. The memories are not identical, but somewhere along the way you find you have been in the same place, under different circumstances but with similar feelings. One person shares, another confronts, and another remembers something that clicks into his or her head.

During one group session, a man named Clint relived that he had been physically abused by his grandfather. Our therapist asked us to stand up, surround Clint, and put our hands on his head, shoulders, and back. Then each of us said to him, "Clint, we care. We're supporting you, Clint. Your grandfather was wrong to abuse you. We care." Clint began to cry, mourning the lack of support and love he had experienced as a child.

In a group that shares problems and love, healing can come. God can work through the sharing of pain.

God, help us to seek a group that understands us, whether our problem with our weight is big or small. Help us find a safe group so that we may overcome.

> *Behold, the fear of the Lord, that is*
> *wisdom,*
> *And to depart from evil is*
> *understanding.* —JOB 28:28

I want to prove I can do it myself. I can stop today!"

Self-reliance. Relying on one's own power is a course that is usually doomed to failure. Every day that I binged, the next day I would say, "I don't need help. I can stop." I would try, but the monster was still inside, controlling me.

So many of us fear that people will think we are weak or lack faith if we reveal our struggle, if we seek professional help. Our pride takes over and we try to solve the problem ourselves. Relying on ourselves usually leads to isolation and loneliness. When the guilt that comes from our inability to solve our own problem takes over, it is very difficult, if not impossible, to glorify God. We find it hard to even pray to Him.

It is true that no one can make the decision for us to start that diet or to walk into that therapist's office. We decide we need help. I guess there are two sides to self-reliance: one can be destructive when we say, "I can do it myself! I don't need help!" The other side says, "I must decide to seek help!"

God, I am tired of relying on myself. Today I desire to rely on You. I pray for wisdom, God.

Therefore do not let sin reign in your mortal
body, that you should obey it in its lust.
—ROM. 6:12

Here are ten reasons we should not get on that good, healthy diet plan:

1. The chocolate industry would go broke.
2. I need to support the people who make control-top pantyhose.
3. Baggy clothes are in style.
4. My friends would not recognize me.
5. Who would be the official ice cream inspector?
6. Mother always said I looked good with meat on my bones.
7. My extra weight keeps me warm in the winter.
8. People will mistake me for Cher.
9. In some cultures fat is sexy.
10. Big thighs just run in my family.

Father, You must laugh at the silly reasons we have for staying unhealthy. Help us to get rid of our unhealthy excuses.

> *Let everything that has breath*
> *praise the Lord.*
> —PS. 150:6

Here are ten reasons why we should get on a healthy, well-balanced diet plan:

1. Because God needs me healthy.
2. Because what people see is their first glimpse of Christ living in me.
3. Because I will feel good about me.
4. Because self-control inspires me to do more for the glory of God.
5. Because I am commanded to love myself.
6. Because I am tired of excuses.
7. Because I will have fewer health problems later on.
8. Because it will make my spouse proud of me.
9. Because my children will be proud of me.
10. Because I need to do it, and I know I can if I allow God to help me.

God, these are a few reasons I give You to lose my extra weight. There are so many more. You know what they are, God. Help me to know them too.

So it was, when the king saw Queen Esther,
standing in the court, that she found
favor in his sight. . . .
—EST. 5:2

When we look good, we feel good." The saying is so true. Whenever I have extra pounds on my body I feel tired. I do not feel motivated. I look in the mirror and say, "Ugh. I am so fat and ugly." It is hard to do something about it because I feel defeated before I even start.

But then I start walking. I eat vegetables and protein and fruit and grains. When I am hungry I drink water. I call a friend instead of heading for the refrigerator. I ask for a hug from someone who loves me instead of eating something sweet.

Consider Esther. On her way to becoming a queen, she had to complete twelve months of beauty treatments. I bet they had a form of aerobics and a good diet plan to keep in shape. When the king saw her after those twelve months, he was more attracted to her than to all the other women. Esther won the favor of the king, allowing her to save her people when they were in need.

Esther had a goal: to save her people. She won the king's heart. It is so true that when we look good, we feel good, and we accomplish so much more for God's kingdom.

_____

Lord, I know I am not as beautiful as Esther. But God, I do want to take care of myself and look good so I can do more in Your name. God, help me as I strive to be healthy.

> *And Jesus said to them, "I am the*
> *bread of life.*　　—JOHN 6:35

Tab was in the hospital with me. She weighed next to nothing. One day she stopped eating altogether. She was put in seclusion for days to give her special medical attention. She had to be fed intravenously to give her nutrients. When she came out of seclusion she had to start eating on her own. There she sat at the table, a full food tray in front of her—apple, meat, vegetable, dessert. The pile of food on that tray looked larger than Tab's stomach.

The hospital staff made her sit down and start eating. She took one bite and wanted to stop. She started crying. It terrified her to eat. She wanted to starve. I watched all of this, frustrated because they were forcing her to eat. I finally spoke up to one of the staff, "She doesn't want to eat all that food. It's too much! Don't make her eat it."

A nurse took me aside and said, "If Tab doesn't eat that food, she'll die." It changed my way of thinking. "Please eat, Tab," I said. "I don't want you to die."

Jesus said, "I am the bread of life. He who comes to Me shall never hunger, and he who believes in Me shall never thirst." Not only did Tab need physical food, but also she needed to know Jesus Christ, her Savior, would give her the bread of life, hope, peace, and love.

Today, may we partake of the living bread of Christ.

For God has not given us a spirit of fear, but of power and of love and of a sound mind.
—2 TIM. 1:7

Over the next several days I will explore statements made to therapists by people seeking their help. Sometimes those of us dealing with eating disorders want to get help but we want it on our own terms. If a counselor or therapist is competent they will be able to see through these statements.

Jessie battled with weight all of her life. Depression was hitting her hard so her husband encouraged her to get help. Her first words to the therapist were, "This is just the way I am. I don't think anyone can really help me." Her therapist knew what she was really saying was, "I'm stuck. Being overweight is the way I am." Together, they began to probe into Jessie's past and learned that she was using her weight to avoid dealing with the pain of growing up with an alcoholic father. Being fat was less painful than dealing with a lonely, hurtful childhood, when she never knew whether Dad would be angry, loving, or drunk on the floor.

Jessie had to let go of "this is just the way I am," and really open her heart to see what she was and what she could become. She had to move on and create a new identity.

It is good to know God takes me as I am, but it is even more wonderful to know His Spirit creates a new spirit in us each day.

> *The wisdom of this world is foolishness.*
> —1 COR. 3:19

If willpower can't change it, nothing can."

Sometimes we are fed quotations—words that sound good but don't help us at all.

Louise did not want professional help. She would not go to a support group because her parents always said, "You just have to have willpower!" She began to lose hope and gained more weight. She hated herself so much she did not want to live. When she finally let go and allowed God to work through a therapist, she felt all she needed was discipline. "Would you help me be more disciplined?" she asked.

"Louise, what you're really saying," her therapist lovingly told her, "is stop me from bingeing, but don't make me look underneath." Before when she asked for help, all too often Louise had been advised, "Just pray and read the Bible." She took the advice to heart and thought that was all she needed.

While prayer and Scripture is vital to helping us through our struggles, Louise needed more. She needed to get in touch with why she craved food, why she was numbing herself. She needed to open up her wounds and find out why food was so important.

When we say, "All I need is willpower," we think we should be perfect. God wants us to strive to be our best for His glory, but He needs us to quit putting Band-Aids on our infected, unhealed wounds. He wants us to clean them out.

———————

God, help us to know You want us to expose our pain, not cover it up.

*If any of you lacks wisdom, let him ask of God,
who gives to all liberally. . . . But let him ask
in faith.*
—JAMES 1:5–6

What if you can't help me?"

This question is one of real fear. When we have been obsessed with our weight and food and diets all our lives, we get to the point that it is all we know. Have you ever heard someone say, "I've lost 999 pounds over my life, and gained 1,000!" It seems as if everyone we know is on a diet. Those who have a serious eating disorder or weight problem get so caught up in the vicious cycle that they experience a panicky fear that they really will not ever be able to stop. They think, If I do seek professional help for this, what will happen if they can't help me?

When we assume no one can help us, we are allowing pride to prevent us from being healed. We are refusing to consider that our pride does not allow us to look at the underlying reasons. Pride overpowers us, preventing us from gaining the strength to repair the damage inside.

When we let go of our pride we can say, "I can't do this alone anymore. I need help." Scripture reveals that God longs for us to say, "Father, I can't do this alone."

Today, God wants to help, and He has given the gift of insight and wisdom to many waiting to help you. You can be helped. Push pride out of the way.

> *For this my son was dead and is alive again;*
> *he was lost and is found.*
>
> —LUKE 15:24

John told his therapist, "It's better to be fat than to feel." This man hated being obese. He was determined to get help but his therapist started pushing buttons. They talked about how he felt being ridiculed as a child for being fat. John began to relive what it was like to be different from everyone else. He began to relive the loneliness and isolation and he began to feel. It did not feel very good. He quit going to the therapist because it was easier to eat and stay fat. Facing the truth was just too painful.

As I write this, I think of the prodigal son. He did things his own way and ended up in a pigsty. It must have hurt to face the truth that he had blown it. Yet he faced that truth and went to confess to his father, expecting no more than to be one of his servants for the rest of his life. When he returned home, his father rejoiced and said, "He was lost and is found."

Like John, we are lost and need to be found.

Today, like the prodigal son, may we not give up. Let us admit our pain, sin and guilt before God, face the truth, and be found by God. Let us not quit seeking and feeling.

*For with the heart one believes to righteousness,
and with the mouth confession is made to
salvation.*
—ROM. 10:10

Confession is good for the soul.

I was a good little girl, except for the time I walked in the store and saw bright, colorful candy staring at me. Since the candy was just laying there, I honestly thought it was free. I took some lollipops and some bubble gum.

"Where did you get that candy?" my mom asked, upset. I told her. "Well, you just take that candy back to that store this minute," she demanded. "You confess to the store manager that you stole that candy!"

Going back to that store was really hard to do, but I did as my mom said. I went to the store manager and began to cry. "I'm sorry I took your candy," I said.

I remember feeling so bad because I took the candy. Yet after I repented I felt cleansed. I felt like a good little girl again.

Whenever we confess to God that we are out of control, we are saying, "I can't handle this anymore. Help me!" When we confess to a loving friend, we are saying, "I need to be cleansed. I need to repent. I need your help and love."

Confession is a way to begin to fill up the real hunger.

God, today I confess I am a sinner. I need Your help in all areas of my life. Please cleanse my heart and help me as I start over.

> *If we confess our sins, He is faithful*
> *and just to forgive us our sins and to*
> *cleanse us from all unrighteousness.*
> —1 JOHN 1:9

Confession means we take risks to talk about the truth: the truth of overeating, the truth of "stuffing" our feelings instead of expressing them. When we confess we are exposing ourselves.

It is good to walk to the front of a church and talk about sin in our lives and ask for prayers for forgiveness. Many of us are not that bold. It may be more comfortable for us to be alone with a trusting friend or therapist and confess all our pain and sorrow. When we confess to people who love us there is an assurance of forgiveness. When we feel forgiven, it is as if the slate has been wiped clean and we can start over.

Sometimes we may think, If I tell God who I really am and what I really do, He will not listen. He will not love me. But He promises that "if we confess our sins" and say, "God, I did this," or, "I feel so bad it's hard to tell you," we will be forgiven. God says to us, "My child, I'm listening. I want to take your pain away. I love you. That's why I sent my Son to die for you."

Confession is facing the reality of self. We may not like what we have to say, but it is another step to wholeness.

Father, help me to open myself up to You, to confess myself to You, and accept the love You have for me.

Where can I go from Your Spirit?
Or where can I flee from Your
presence? —PS. 139:7

One day as I sat in group therapy I found out a suicidal teenage boy was leaving the hospital because his insurance had run out. It made me cry. Mike, my therapist, asked me why I was crying. "Because the boy is so lonely," I said through my tears.

"Loneliness. Now that's a good word," Mike replied. "Tell us about loneliness, Cynthia."

Suddenly a memory came flooding back. I was four years old. I was laying in a hospital bed, wrapped up in bandages from my waist down to my toes. I had been critically burned when a pan of boiling water fell on me. I was so scared. I thought I had been a bad little girl. I thought the accident was my fault. Mommy and Daddy must be angry with me, I concluded, because they were not here to help me.

At twenty-eight years old I learned I had a locked-up little four-year-old inside of me. The trauma of being burned and not understanding what was happening was too much for that four-year-old. I had pushed my confusion down deep inside of me. It was one of the secrets my bulimia was guarding. In order for me to stop the symptoms of my eating disorder, I had to deal with my locked-up grief. Like confession, grieving cleanses our hearts and soul.

God, if there is locked-up grief inside of me, please expose it. Help me through my pain of loneliness. Help me find a safe place to grieve.

> *If I say, "Surely the darkness shall*
> *fall on me,"*
> *Even the night shall be light about*
> *me . . .*
> *The darkness and the light are both*
> *alike to You."* —PS. 139:11–12

We have a safe little world as children. But when trauma invades, we develop ways to protect ourselves. When I was in the burn unit as a child, my roommate's name was Susie. Susie looked so scary to me. She was wrapped in bandages from the top of her head to the tips of her toes. She looked like a mummy. I remember asking Susie, "Why are you in the hospital?"

Susie's answer was muffled through her bandages. She told me. "My mommy threw me in the oven." I was so afraid I could not move. I thought, "Mom and Dad never come to see me and Susie's mom never comes to see her. I must be a horrible little girl!

I did not know how to say, "I demand to see my mom and dad." No one ever asked me what I was feeling. I again promised myself I would do whatever it took to be a good little girl. I decided I would not be a bother to anyone. I isolated myself from others. Food became my friend.

Blocking our memories can mean safety for a while, but we end up hurting ourselves more. We need to stop and examine where our self-hatred comes from.

God, as adults our childhood pain needs to come out. Help us as we deal with our pain.

Hear my prayer, O Lord,
And let my cry come to You.
　　　　　—PS. 102:1

So, Cynthia, when did you become damaged freight?"
Mike, my therapist, would ask this question repeatedly
during therapy. My monster would rattle its chain, bit
by bit, as I relived memories as a child. One day after
another patient shared a traumatic memory, I flashed
back to that hospital room as a burned four-year-old. I
was trying to sleep. Suddenly the door to my room
opened and six of the biggest people I had ever seen
came in wearing white coats and masks. I could not
see their faces. They circled my bed, put me on my
back, and taking off my covers and bandages, began to
rip the burned skin off my body.

I screamed, "Please, please leave me alone. I'll be a
good girl!"

"You feel like you were raped, don't you, Cynthia?"
Mike asked. "Yes," I screamed. "What were they doing
to me?" One of the nurses there explained, "You were
burned, Cynthia, and probably they were doing something to protect you from infection."

The problem was no one told me. I felt like damaged
freight, scarred both inside and out by that verbal and
emotional abuse.

Do you feel damaged by something that has happened to you? God is ready and willing to deal with our
damaged hearts.

God, open my heart to know that it is Your desire to restore me, to
touch me, and to heal my pain.

Save me, O God!
For the waters have come up to my
neck.
—PS. 69:1

There were many reasons why I was bulimic. In the clinic, I learned that the family plays a large role in addictive behavior. When someone finally takes that step to get help and family issues surface, there can be great healing when the parents are involved in the therapy. I thank God that my parents were willing to come into therapy with me.

The first question I asked my dad and mom was "Where were you when I was four years old and in the hospital?" I was angry and wanted to know what had happened.

"They wouldn't let us in to see you, but we were there, in the waiting room, practically the whole time you were in the hospital," they told me. They had no idea I had suffered as much as I did.

I learned that back when I was burned, they did not let people go in because of the risk of infection. But no one told me my parents were there. I felt abandoned. I felt as if Mommy and Daddy did not love me. No one told me the truth. And thinking I already had the truth—that I was a bad little girl—I never asked.

Children were rarely given the total perspective on what was happening around them back then, especially in a crisis situation.

Are you still looking at events in your life with the incomplete understanding of a child? Maybe it is time to take that child out and look at what has happened to you from an adult point of view.

*How often I wanted to gather your
children together, as a hen gathers
her chicks under her wings, but you
were not willing.*

—MATT. 23:37

My parents will tell you that after I was burned I never wanted to cuddle. I did not want to be touched. I did not like being hugged. The truth was that deep inside I felt as if I were a bad little girl. I felt my parents did not love me, so I decided I really should not bother them. I hoped that if I could just be a perfect little girl, maybe they would love me.

When I finally explained to Mom and Dad how I had felt all those years, they took me in their arms and held and rocked me. Dad said, "I never knew what to do. I always wanted to hug you but you always resisted."

There was wonderful healing in knowing that my parents really did love me. It was of great value to know why I was afraid to be hugged or touched. I was reconciling, in my adulthood, the pain from my past.

As I write this I think of how God is saying constantly, "I want to hug you, but you resist My love." It is not God who hurts us. Life and people hurt us. Sometimes we get God confused with human frailities and sin. We need to learn the difference so we can embrace our Father as He wishes.

Today, God is saying to you, "Be willing to come under My wings."

*Father, embrace me, even when I can't hug You. Let me be aware of
Your love for me.*

April 22 – SMILE FOR THE CAMERA!

O God, You know my foolishness;
And my sins are not hidden from You.
—PS. 69:5

Picture time! It's time for family pictures!" Oh, joy.

Don't you dread it every time there is a get-together and you hear those words? Do you try to duck out to the bathroom? Are you the one who is always hiding behind Uncle Harold? Do you stand at the back with the children in front of you, hiding your tummy that is bulging from too many hot dogs, chips, and cookies?

Why do we think we can hide from ourselves just because we hide in a picture? We know how much we have really eaten. God knows how much we have really eaten. And He knows we know. Today, let us not be ashamed. Let us be proud of who we are and to Whom we belong.

For a change, be bold and get in the front of the line for that picture. Stand tall and quit hiding. Take pride in yourself.

Eat right.

———————

God, You know all about me. You know when I want to hide. Help me not to hide behind food or other people. Help me to accept me for me.

I will never leave you nor forsake you.
—HEB. 13:5

Carla was overweight most of her life. Her mother liked her that way. Carla's dad had abandoned the family when Carla was six. Her mom did not want to lose Carla, so she encouraged her to eat, and Carla did. Carla did not have many friends because her mother needed her and took all of her time. She did not go to college because her mom said she really did not need to. So Carla settled for a minimum wage job.

Carla would say, "Oh well, after all, I'm fat. Who would want to hire me for a really good job?" Because Carla was overweight, and because her mother did not want to lose her, Carla always settled for less: less activity, less love, fewer friends. As long as she was fat, she did not have to really try.

At age twenty-six Carla found out she had cancer. She died a few months later. People who knew her said, "She rejoiced in dying." Isn't that sad? Carla basically gave up when the cancer came. She did not fight it. She settled for less.

Do you settle for less? Or are you striving to go for the gold? God does not want us to settle for less. He wants us to strive for the perfection of His Son. He does not demand that we be perfect but that we strive for it. Today, let's examine why we settle for less and strive for more.

God, it's so easy to just give up. It's easier to not try. But You don't give us a spirit of timidity. Today, give us Your power to help us to endure.

> *I press toward the goal for the prize of*
> *the upward call of God in Christ Jesus.*
> —PHIL. 3:14

Strive. It is a strong word to plant in our hearts today. Today, will you strive to love yourself more? Will you strive to take care of yourself today? Will you share your love with others, just for today? Today, strive to touch God with your words and to depend on Him to meet your every need.

To strive is to exert yourself vigorously; to try hard; to contend in any conflict. In other words, to strive means to keep on keeping on. It means to look at that goal you have set and stick with it, to not get sidetracked along the way.

Today, let us eat right, and if we do not, let's forgive ourselves and get back on track. Let us focus on what is good and right, and not on what is wrong and negative. Like the apostle Paul, let's strive for the prize! Along the way we will have the reward of feeling successful and of feeling healthy pride in our accomplishments.

God, help us as we strive today to be Your children, children about whom people say, "I want to be like that."

*You shall love the LORD your God with
all your heart, with all your soul,
with all your strength, and with all
your mind.*   —LUKE 10:27

I'll start on Monday." How many times have we said that? We are tempted with lots of food at a friend's house over the weekend. We say, "I've been so good all week so I'll splurge today and start my diet on Monday." Then Monday comes and we say, "My stomach is stretched now so it's just too hard to diet today. I'll start tomorrow."

Next thing we know, we are trying to play these games with God. "God, You'll still be around when I decide to do Your will, won't You?" "God, I just don't have time for You today. Maybe tomorrow."

God longs for us to do His will today. He knows what sin does to us. He wants us to love Him today because true happiness comes through trusting Him.

"I'll start on Monday," needs to be changed to, "I'll start right now." When we take care of the body God has given us, we feel good about ourselves. When we feel good we can serve God and glorify His name.

Today, let's accept the challenge of starting today, not tomorrow or Monday or never. Tell yourself, "Today is a better day to start than Monday. Today is here now, and Monday may never come.

Father, forgive us for overindulging. When we do, we don't feel good afterwards. Lord, help us to serve You today. Help us to quit thinking about tomorrow and start working on today.

Our days on earth are as a shadow.
1 CHRON. 29:15

Susan visits her seventy-three-year-old mother who lives in a retirement home as much as she can. Susan loves her mom, and everyone else enjoys her too. She is a spunky, warm, loving woman. Last week as Susan was saying goodbye, her mom said, "Susan, I'll pray for you if you'll pray that I'll lose my weight."

Susan wanted to scream, "Mom, it doesn't matter. You're seventy-three years old. You don't need to worry about your weight!"

Her mom is in her twilight years and she is worried about how much she weighs. Susan says her mom dwells too much on her weight. She is not that over-weight to begin with. Yet instead of enjoying her life to the fullest, she focuses on her weight.

Does this sound like you? Maybe you are only thirty or forty-two or fifty-five but you can still relate to Susan's seventy-three-year-old mother. It is time to say to ourselves, I don't need to focus my life around what I weigh. I need to focus on life and enjoy just being alive.

Father God, help me to enjoy life and being Your child. Fill up my insecurities.

He makes His sun rise on the evil and
on the good, and sends rain on the just
and the unjust. —MATT. 5:45

Thin people aren't lonely," says one lady struggling with her weight. "Fat people are lonely because the world doesn't like fat people."

This lady imagines that if people do not struggle with dieting, they must have lots of friends, a great job, and they simply must not have time for loneliness. How sad that we think, just because someone looks as if they have it all together, they never feel lonely or have problems. The truth is all of us experience the same feelings at one time or another, no matter what size we are. Some people wallow in their problems, complaining all the time. Others suppress their problems and never discuss them. Still others look at their struggles face-to-face and do something about them.

There are a lot of lonely fat people, and in truth there are a lot of lonely thin people. Perhaps it is time that we recognize each other beyond our looks. We need to understand that all of us need love and to get love we must seek it, give it, and nourish it.

Today, do not dwell on how much someone weighs. Let's realize they have a heart just like us, and at one time or another they will feel alone.

_____

God, help us not to think that others have a better life than us. Help us to be friends and give of ourselves, no matter what the scales say.

Love never fails.
—1 COR. 13:8

I know someone that everyone loves and admires. She is a servant. She is joyful, even though she has experienced some pain in her life. She needs to lose a lot of weight for health reasons but she is just not ready to deal with that yet.

When you meet this girl the first thing you notice is she is obese. Then she smiles and talks and shares her warmth and love for God, and you go beyond her size. She is so beautiful inside. Her clothes are always bright and beautiful.

Although she is a giver, she finds it hard to accept herself. On Sunday morning at church, people will say to her, "You look so beautiful today," or, "My, what a beautiful dress." She finds it really hard to say, "Thank you." Inside, she thinks, "Liar! I'm obese and I'm not pretty!"

She does not say what she would like to, of course. But what is sad is people really mean it when they say those things to her. She does not love herself the way she is and cannot understand that other people can.

We are this way with God sometimes, are we not? We will say, "God, you can't possibly love me as I am!" Yet God does. His Son died a cruel death to set us free.

Thank You, God, for setting me free. Thank You for accepting me. Help me believe You really do love me.

I will sing to the LORD,
For He has triumphed gloriously.
—EX. 15:1

Do you do this? You have completed a job, or had a hard day at work, or are to be congratulated on a job well done, and you say to yourself, Because I've done this, I deserve a pizza, and a hot fudge sundae. You indulge and then get sick because you ate too much. Stop and ask yourself why you make yourself sick after accomplishing something wonderful.

It could be that underneath the success, there is another voice inside: You don't deserve to be successful. You're really a phony. Sure, you won this award, but it was just a fluke.

If you hear these messages, explore where those thoughts are coming from. Maybe it was from a demanding father or a negative teacher or a mom who felt inferior and in turn took it out on you. If you find those messages are coming from past voices, think about how you felt. Talk to a friend. You may even have to go back to those people who first said those words and tell them they were wrong. You may need to tell them that you are not a phony. Tell them that God has given you talents and you are special no matter what anyone thinks or says.

Then, believe it. You are special. The next time you feel like celebrating over rich food, buy yourself a bunch of flowers instead. You are special.

God, thank You for believing that I'm special. Thank You for loving me, and knowing me, and calling me Your child.

> *And the LORD called yet again, "Samuel!"*
> —1 SAM. 3:6

When God needed to speak to Samuel, He specifically called his name. God knew his name. If God knew Samuel, He must know yours and mine. God is on a first name basis with us all. He does not call us Ms. or Miss or Mr. or Mrs. He lovingly knows our name.

To "know" someone is to perceive or understand them clearly. One translation of the Greek word *to know* is *to be intimate with*. God calls us by our first name. He understands all our struggles and He wants to be intimate with us. He wants us to be intimate with Him, sharing our questions and problems and joys with Him.

The next time you pray, dwell on the fact that He knows you by your name and, like Samuel who became a great prophet, He has plans for you.

Father, thank You for knowing my name and my heart. Use my life to glorify Your name.

I have fought the good fight, I have finished the race, I have kept the faith.   2 TIM. 4:7

I see her every day in my neighborhood. She is walking very fast, always wearing black. It is obvious she is trying to work off those extra pounds she has gained over the winter months. As I watch her walk, she looks so determined. Her whole body, soul, and mind are into her mode of burning off calories.

I do not know her. She does not know me; she does not even know I am watching. But one of these days I am going to tell her what an example she is in my life. She is determined and dedicated and I bet within six months she will be slimmed down and will not have to wear black anymore, but pink and white and blue.

I admire this lady from afar because she is trying to finish the race. Even when the race is finished, I have a feeling she will keep on going.

How do people see you? Do they admire you because you keep on going, because you try to take care of yourself? Are you doing something to make yourself feel healthier every day? Walking is a free gift. Take that gift and finish the race!

Father, starting the race is easy. Finishing it is what's hard. Give me the determination to finish my race.

> *Then God saw everything that He had made,*
> *and indeed it was very good.* —GEN. 1:31

Our bodies are so amazing. When we have a cut, we clean it and it heals. When we get sick, our bodies produce antibodies to fight off the sickness. When we eat, the food nourishes our bodies.

Our bodies are made to walk, run, bend, reach, and stretch. Don't you think God must have had a wonderful time designing us? He must enjoy it when we exercise the ability of movement He made into us. When we are running, walking, jumping, bending, reaching, and stretching, God must be happy because we are using the special features He put into our bodies.

God made our bodies to use food for energy to do all those things. He meant for food to be a blessing to us, not a curse. He did not make us to need food just so we would have to exercise it off, but for energy to use the body He made in the way He intended.

Take a look at your own body. Is it out of shape? Then start moving it a little bit. Start by stretching, then go for a walk around the block. Join a health club. Ask your spouse to hold your feet down while you do sit-ups.

God made us to move. Enjoy that gift. Be thankful to God for the way you were made.

God, we marvel at Your creations. Thank You for making us the way You did.

*Let us draw near with a true heart
in full assurance of faith.*
—HEB. 10:22

My cousin, Diana, had just had her house blown away by a tornado. She and her two children were in the house at the time. Their lives were spared but Diana was in critical condition for a long time. As soon as I could, I drove to where she lived and visited her in the hospital.

We held each other, grieving over what had happened, and I cried out, "Why you? Why couldn't it have been me?" I was single, bulimic. I did not care about myself or about life.

Diana could not believe I felt the way I did. I was the cousin who was a television news reporter, who seemed to have everything going for her.

Diana has struggled with her weight most of her adult life. She has always been a little self-conscious around her "thin" cousin. In that hospital room, we drew closer together. She thought my life was perfect and was shocked to find out it was not.

How many times do we assume things about other people based on how they look? We are blind to the real truth about those around us. Sometimes we even blind ourselves to our own truth. We think if we are thin then everything must be all right.

It is time we are honest with each other and with ourselves.

_____

God, help me not hesitate to permit others to come near to me. Most of all, may I come closer to You, God.

> *To everything there is a season,*
> *A time for every purpose under heaven . . .*
> *A time to weep,*
> *And a time to laugh.*
>
> —ECCL. 3:1, 4

There is a woman at church the children call the jolly fat woman. Always friendly, this lady is full of life. In fact, she is so jolly everyone thinks she does not need anyone. When someone asks her, "How are you doing?" she answers, "Oh, everything is just great!"

When she comes home after church, she is not so jolly anymore. She cries by herself because she feels so miserable. She grieves over a husband who died early in their marriage. She cries because her daughter never comes to see her. She turns to food for solace.

This woman thinks she has to be jolly to show everyone how well she is doing. But what she really needs is for someone to ask her, "No, how are you *really?*"

This woman hides behind her false identify, and then goes home and eats and eats and eats, gaining more weight and adding to the facade.

Being a happy person is wonderful, but when it hides the true person, happiness is self-destructive. It is OK not to be jolly all the time. Sometimes we need to admit to others that we are sad or lonely or just not feeling so hot. We need to be able to talk about it, grieve over it, and then walk on.

Father, it's so easy not to reveal what we really feel. Thank You for letting me be "me" with You.

*When you have eaten and are full, then you
shall bless the LORD your God for the good
land which He has given you.*
                                   —DEUT. 8:10

Don't you admire people who do not always worry
about dieting? One woman I know has this philosophy
about eating: "Eat and enjoy what God has set before
you." Eat and enjoy. She knows that God has given her
this food for the nourishment of her body, to provide
her with the energy she will need to battle the problems of the day. She does not worry about calories. She
knows there is a need for food and she enjoys the blessing of eating. She does not overindulge; rather she eats
what her body needs.

I do not know many people struggling with dieting
or with food who really stop and enjoy it. They may
eat a lot of food, but they do not enjoy it. They are too
busy counting up all the calories and figuring out what
they will have to do to work it off. It is no wonder they
do not enjoy it—they are working too hard. Whew.
How I admire those who can say, "Eat and enjoy what
God has set before you."

*God, food is a blessing. Help us to remember all good things come
from You. Thank You for supplying a banquet of constant love!*

Is not life more than food?
—MATT. 6:25

It is a gift to have a grandmother who takes time to love and nurture her grandchildren. I know of a grandma who takes her four grandchildren to church every Sunday. During the service she touches the children's hair, smiles at them. It is obvious she is in love with them.

One night during a class at church the question was asked, "How do you feel about diets?"

Her response to this was, "People are too preoccupied with weight and not with health. I struggle with weight, but I have more important things to worry about." Her "important things" are loving grandchildren whose parents are divorced and teaching God's love and grace to them.

God loves her in spite of her weight. Praise God for that. This grandma does not wallow in self-pity because of a few extra pounds. She goes on, focusing on giving love to those around her, and cherishing the love she has from God.

———————

Father, forgive us when we are too preoccupied with our weight. Put our minds on other things. Teach us to accept and love ourselves and to share our love.

This hope we have as an anchor of
the soul, both sure and steadfast.
— HEB. 6:19

Hang in there!" That is what God would say to me as I diet.

Shirley is determined to lose the weight she picked up on her vacation. She is on a good diet plan, watching what she eats and exercising moderately. Sometimes she is tempted to give it all up but she asks herself, "What would God say to me right now?"

"Hang in there!" That is what God would say to Shirley.

Shirley knows that God is not going to take the pounds off miraculously. She knows she is going to have to be self-controlled and determined, that she will have to burn those extra pounds off herself. When things get tough and she gets tempted, she reminds herself that God is saying to her, "Hang in there, Shirley!" So she does because she trusts Him.

God says to all of us, every day, as we bumble and fumble, succeed and fail, laugh and cry, "Hang in there! I'm right here and I'm rooting for you all the way!"

> *Blessed are those who mourn,*
> *For they shall be comforted.*
> —MATT. 5:4

Jesus never promised us a life without sorrow. He warned His disciples of trials and tribulations. He even said people would want to kill whomever believed in His name. He knew life would hold uncertainties.

Life is still a challenge and sometimes problems are thrust into our lives and we feel despair and hopelessness.

Jesus' words spoken on that mountain a long time ago give me great comfort. He said, "Blessed are those who mourn, for they shall be comforted." Jesus gave us permission to grieve, to let our locked-up tears flow freely. He told us He understands for He, too, has grieved, and He has been comforted by His heavenly Father.

Some doctors say that if we do not grieve after a traumatic experience, the suppression of those emotions can lead to sickness. Our immune systems weaken because our bodies cannot handle all that we are holding inside.

Do you need to grieve over past mistakes, abusive situations, or memories of deep sorrow, which you may have blocked out? Today, maybe it is time to think of pain from the past that is stunting your growth, and ask God to help give you strength as you mourn. He promises you will be comforted.

God, there is so much inside me that hurts. Free those hurts, God. Wrap Your loving arms around me as I mourn.

Blessed are the merciful,
For they shall obtain mercy.
—MATT. 5:7

As we walk through why we overeat or struggle with obesity or have bulimia or anorexia, most of us will find key issues in our lives buried in our subconscious.

When I was in intense therapy, I experienced so much anger and even hostility over feelings of being emotionally and physically abandoned as a child. My feelings of anger increased as I examined serious mistakes my parents had made and how those mistakes had damaged me as a child. After I expressed my anger with my parents, healing eventually came. Mercy came too.

Some parents will not admit their mistakes. My parents did and I will never forget it. My dad said to me, "If you only knew how many times I've kicked myself for the mistakes I've made as a father! I need you to forgive me."

Mercy came after I understood my dad a little more. I needed that child's vision to comprehend what was happening to me as an adult, but once I understood, it was time to put that child to rest and start to see as the adult I was.

I have learned that sometimes people do things because that is all they know to do. Over time I have come to understand my dad even more. I realize I need to show mercy because I need mercy too.

Father, teach me to deal with my pain and anger, and teach me to have mercy on those who hurt me.

*And at the end of ten days their countenance
appeared better and fatter in flesh than all
the young men who ate the portion of the king's
delicacies . . .*
—DAN. 1:15

We live in a world of processed food, chemically forti-
fied food, and greasy fast food. If we want a quick bite
to eat, we open up a package, plop it in the microwave,
and a minute later, we are eating.

I think if Daniel lived with us today he would understand our plight. In Daniel's day the king wanted Daniel to eat a diet of delicacies and drink a lot of wine,
selections not in keeping with the Jewish diet.

Daniel asked to be allowed to eat only vegetables
and drink water for ten days. After ten days Daniel
looked healthier and better nourished than any of the
other men who had eaten from the king's table.

Daniel's story sounds familiar, doesn't it? Health offi-
cials are always stressing that we should eat more vegetables and fresh fruit instead of so much processed
food and sugar-laden sweets. Daniel could have given
in to the king's command, but instead he did it God's
way.

In a magazine recently were various tips for keeping
weight off and one of them was to commit one day a
week to eating only fruits, vegetables, and water. Another suggestion was to start the day with protein, and
eat vegetables for lunch and dinner. I wonder if the
author had ever read the first chapter of Daniel.

*God, forgive us when we always seem to choose the wrong food. Help
us to look to the good foods You give us to enjoy.*

Wisdom has built her house, . . .
She has slaughtered her meat,
She has mixed her wine;
She has also furnished her table.
—PROV. 9:1–2

Dorothy was sent to private schools most of her life. The meals she was served there were nutritious and small in size. She grew up in Africa, and in Africa dessert was a rarity.

When she came to America, she was amazed at how many candy, cookie, and ice cream stores she saw. Then she noticed how people here are always concerned about their weight. Dorothy made a decision not to go the "American way." She does not make it a habit to eat *our* way. If she is at a friend's house for dinner, she asks for a piece of fruit instead of the dessert that is being served. At her house recently a guest asked her for sugar for the coffee. Dorothy did not have any. We laughed over her "no sugar in the house" policy. But Dorothy is thin, beautiful, and disciplined.

She chose to hold on to the good habits of her childhood. Dorothy never leaves the table with that sick, bloated feeling from gorging.

All of us need to look to Dorothy as an example. We need to put down the sweets and pick up the fruit. We need to put down the fork and pick up our plate, saying, "That was great, but I've had enough."

Father, You made our bodies special, to eat and enjoy our food. Help us to know when to say enough is enough.

Come, eat of my bread
And drink of the wine which I have
    mixed.
Forsake foolishness and live,
And go in the way of
    understanding. —PROV. 9:5–6

Dorothy loves salads. We go to an all-you-can-eat salad bar restaurant sometimes. She picks out only fresh vegetables and a bowl of soup.

"Dorothy," I asked in frustration, "here are all these great things, pizza, muffins, garlic bread, cookies, and all you want are vegetables and soup?"

"Cynthia, I don't understand people who think that just because the food is there, you have to eat it. It's not as if all this food is going to run off! No, the same food will be here tomorrow. Today, I'm going to eat what my body needs. I don't live to eat."

Dorothy has something there, doesn't she? She has learned the wisdom of eating properly. She is proceeding "in the way of understanding." She has learned the hard truth that God made our bodies to run on just so many calories, and if we eat too much, we gain extra weight that is difficult to lose.

How often do we say to ourselves, "The food's right here in front of me. I might as well eat it." We really do not *have* to eat it. We can push our plate away after one serving and say, "I've had enough." Ask God for the wisdom to know when you have had enough.

Father, help me to be content with what You have given me.

*The heart of him who has
understanding seeks knowledge,
But the mouth of fools feeds on
foolishness.* —PROV. 15:14

Every once in a while I remember a particularly pain-ful time in my life. I was only nineteen years old, and I had gone back to college to start over after a rough divorce. I buried the guilt of the failed relationship in food. From that September to December my weight went from 130 to 185 pounds. I simply could not stop eating.

One weekend I went home for a visit, and my par-ents were shocked. I wanted to scream, "Help me!" but I could not. I did not understand why I was doing this. My parents did not understand either. They just knew I was unhappy.

I do not believe my weight will ever again get that out of control. I have learned to identify and work through the reasons I could not stop eating. But I still remember the embarrassment of going away thin and coming back fat. It hurts to think about what that meant about the shape of my life.

If you are struggling with a sudden or constant weight gain, take a break and look at what is happen-ing in your life. What hurts? What is broken?

God is here to mend your brokenness. He creates a new day for us in which to change and grow.

God, sometimes we dwell on the past too much and it stifles today. Help us to focus on today and to change if we need to.

*If we confess our sins, He is faithful
and just.* —1 JOHN 1:9

Ghosts from the past. Thinking back sometimes conjures them up, doesn't it? Sometimes I think of all the sins I committed years ago and they haunt me today. Even though I have asked for forgiveness and received it freely, sometimes I just cannot help doubting that forgiveness. I allow all the vivid memories of hurting myself, and Jesus, flood into my mind, and I feel so bad.

A famous author, Corrie ten Boom, said that God puts all our sins into a big fishing pond, and then posts a sign that says, "No Fishing." Instead of obeying the sign, we bait up our hooks and go fishing anyway. When we go back and fish out our past sins, it hampers our spirits and causes us to feel anew the turmoil of pain. Reliving the sins He has already died for and forgiven can isolate us from God.

Sometimes I share the pain that I am reliving with my best friend, and he will say to me, "Let go of it, Cynthia. God has."

God promises to faithfully and justly forgive us when we confess to Him. Today, let's take God at His word.

———————

Father, I know that You have forgiven me of my past. Help me to let go of it too.

Pleasant words are like a honeycomb,
Sweetness to the soul and health to
the bones.
—PROV. 16:24

You just need willpower!" Whoever says those words does not understand that it is not that simple. A lady who wants to lose a few pounds told me, "When I'm struggling to lose weight my willpower is no problem at all. My *won't* power causes me trouble."

I know a man whose wife says, "You're fat. Lose it. Get some willpower." With those insensitive words ringing in his ears, he will head straight for the pantry. As he is feeding his face he silently screams at his wife, I'll show you! I'll eat and get even fatter!

This man has excellent willpower, but he is using it to get back at his wife for the way she treats him. He is using "won't" power too. He is responding to his wife, I won't listen to you and I won't lose weight!

Anyone losing weight needs to know why they are doing it. Do you want to shed the pounds so you will feel better and your clothes will not be so tight? Or because of what other people might think?

Losing weight for other people and not for yourself is the wrong motivation, doomed to failure. Other people may benefit from your weight loss, but the first and foremost reason has got to be for yourself. No one else can do the work for you, so do it for *yourself*.

Father, help me to stop looking to others for my reasons for losing, or gaining, weight. Help me to take responsibility for my own body.

> *Nevertheless the solid foundation
> of God stands.* —2 TIM. 2:19

Nothing in this life offers us security except lives built on God's "solid foundation." Our houses can be ripped apart in a moment by a tornado. A fire can consume our prized possession in a flash. Our lives can be snuffed out in a second by a drunken driver. Nothing in this life is secure but the love of God.

My father once knew a man in Alaska who was very rich and powerful. He employed hundreds of people, and his signature on a piece of paper could move around millions of dollars. When my father went to see him the last time, he was weak, frail, and forgetful. He was dependent on others to bathe him, to dress and to feed him. He had a dozen pill bottles on his nightstand and someone had to be responsible for telling him what to take and when.

As my father watched this once powerful man reduced by the ravages of age, a verse of Scripture popped into his head. "Our days were numbered," he remembered.

We need to look around us and identify the fleeting things of this life and hold on to the solid foundation of the Lord. Our health is one of the most precious things we have, but it is not automatic. Today, let's commit to take care of ourselves, and to protect the health the Lord has given us.

Lord, help me build my life on a foundation that will stand up against the rain, the wind, and the storms of this life.

*For the good that I will to do, I do
not do; but the evil I will not to do,
that I practice.*   —ROM. 7:19

Life can be so frustrating at times. Just like the apostle Paul, I know what is right and what I should do. I also know what I should not be doing. When I get up in the morning I make a conscious decision, Today, I'm going to do what I should. But before the day is over, sometimes even before the morning is done, I have failed. I have broken my fast or I have cheated on my diet. I find that I have lost my temper, or failed to take advantage of an opportunity God has presented.

I know I am responsible for the choices I make. I get so frustrated when I cannot be perfect. Sometimes, after I have made a decision to just eat what is right, and I go ahead and have that cookie anyway, I want to give up and eat the whole bag. I have to stop and ask myself why I went to that cookie in the first place.

When I am frustrated with my failures, I have to remember that God does not expect me to be perfect. He understands when I fall. He is there to give me the strength to pick myself up again and strive to do better. Instead of kicking myself for eating that one cookie, I should congratulate myself for not eating the whole bag. And if I am hungry, I should look for something that is better for me.

Father, frustrations and failures are part of this life. Help me not to be surprised when they come and to claim victory over them.

> *She watches over the ways of her household,*
> *And does not eat the bread of idleness.* —PROV. 31:27

Boredom is the brother of idleness and it too can be the workplace of Satan," says my father, Robert H. Rowland. Boredom can cast a weight around our neck. It seems that sometimes we carry it around with us. Nothing is interesting. We get bored with life and its demands. We get caught up in our dull routine. We wind up with time to spare and nothing to do with it.

Why is it we always seem to turn to food when we are bored? We feel icky, and we want something to make us feel better.

We do not have to turn to food to make life seem more interesting. With a little imagination and force of will, we can fill up that extra time with something else besides food. We can go the library and check out a mystery novel. We can write a short story or a poem. We can take art classes at the local college. We can write a book of childhood stories. We can write down our dreams and aspirations.

There are so many other things to do out there than just eat. We can start a hobby, take an aerobics class, go swimming, or join a walking group. Start by getting out of the house, away from your refrigerator.

Lord, help me to find things to do to replace the emptiness I sometimes feel. Help me to know that there is something new to learn and experience every day!

*I am like a pelican of the
wilderness;
I am like an owl of the desert.
I lie awake,
And am like a sparrow alone on the
housetop.* —PS. 102:6, 7

It is so easy for some people to hide in the wilderness or in the desert or even escape to the housetop, away from others. We all need times when we can be alone, but being alone and being lonely are not the same.

I read a magazine article a few years ago about loneliness. It said that loneliness is one of the most prevalent diseases in the United States. The article described husbands and wives eating at the same table, sleeping in the same bed, and even going to church together, yet living in a lonely world of their own choice.

Why do children grow up in a house full of people and still feel the burden of loneliness? Children learn early to withdraw, some rejected by the people around them, while others feel vulnerable. Their self-esteem trampled, they retreat into their own safe little worlds.

Like the pelican, we can fill our bills with food. Like the owl, we can watch the world pass by us. Like the sparrow, we can escape to the rooftop where we do not bother anyone and others do not bother us.

Instead of reaching for food, maybe we should start reaching for the phone. Call someone with whom you feel safe. Tell them how much you love them. Allow them to express their love to you.

Lord, help me to take the first step in building a relationship.

*If you see the oppression of the poor, and
the violent perversion of justice and righteousness . . . do not marvel at the matter.*
—ECCL. 5:8

My older brother and I were three years apart and
when my brother was born my father had a supervisor
job at a large sawmill in Alaska. He could afford an
expensive movie camera and other luxuries when my
brother was a baby. But my father gave up his job and
went back to graduate school after I was born.

Whenever the family would all get together my dad
brought out the movies of life in Alaska. And there
would be my brother, big as life, all his wonderful
"firsts." I would hear the oohs and ahhs and the laughter over my brother's antics. I was not in a single reel. I
thought, That's not fair!

Later I learned that my father simply could not afford film for the camera on the part-time salary he
made while in graduate school and had sold it. It did
not mean that my youngest moments, not recorded,
were any less special than my brother's, but I just did
not understand that at the time. I had to let go of my
resentment and look at the reasons why I resented. I
was not missing from the pictures because I was loved
any less.

Do you have resentments in your life over being
treated unfairly? You need to look at the big picture
and determine why.

_____

Lord, help me to keep my balance when life is unfair.

They shall neither hunger nor thirst, . . .
for He who has mercy on them will
lead them. —ISA. 49:10

God made our bodies to seek just what we need to keep a normal weight and have the energy to work and play. Then why do we go back to the refrigerator or the pantry for one more helping, one more piece, one more can or bottle? What is the real hunger we are trying so hard to fill up? Will another piece of pie, or another sandwich, or another cookie, satisfy the real hunger?

God has promised that we shall never hunger or thirst. I think He was talking about our physical needs *and* also our spiritual needs. And aren't the spiritual and emotional needs contributing to our physical hunger? The closer we come to a satisfying relationship with God the more those needs are filled, and the less need we have to fill up our emptiness with the wrong kind of food.

Hunger can be a state of mind instead of a need of the body. Jesus said, "He who comes to Me shall never hunger" (John 6:35). Let food fill up the physical needs. Let God fill up the spiritual ones.

Lord, help me to understand where my real hunger lies. Help me to satisfy that hunger through You and not through food.

> *Behold, You desire truth in the*
> *inward parts,*
> *And in the hidden part You will*
> *make me to know wisdom.*
> —PS. 51:6

Remember when you were a kid and something was broken or misplaced and your mom lined all of you children up and asked, "OK, who did it?" One by one you all responded, "It wasn't me, Mommy!" Maybe one of you would even venture a guess as to who it really was, causing a shouting match of "Did not," and "Did too."

Just as in childhood, we all have that tendency to cover up our embarrassments, our mistakes, our sins. We tell white lies and outright falsehoods to maintain our innocence. We are always ready to say with convincing conviction, "It wasn't me!"

When we deny the truth of our actions we are actually denying ourselves. In doing so we must bear the burden of guilt, not only for the deed, but also for the lie to cover it up. We pile guilt upon guilt until we are buried under it. The first step in coming out from under our load of guilt is to tell the truth to ourselves and to others. Reality has a way of being forced on us regardless of the lies we tell.

The next time you are caught with your hand in the cookie jar, instead of shouting, "It isn't me," reduce your feelings of guilt by admitting what you have done. There is great freedom in truth.

Lord, help me to be more honest with others and myself.

*Every wise woman builds her
house,
But the foolish pulls it down with
her hands.* —PROV. 14:1

I once knew a woman who was filled with anger. It oozed from her pores. It dripped from her tongue. She was always angry with her husband, her children, her boss, her neighbors. No one could ever please her.

The parade of boys who mowed her lawn always left a row of grass uncut or a crooked edge somewhere. The man at the gas station could never get the corners of her windshield clean enough. At every restaurant she visited the service was poor or the price was too high. She never left a tip.

This woman walked around with a chip on her shoulder the size of Cleveland. She dared anyone to knock it off. She went to bed angry and woke up the same way. Anger defined her life.

I have always wondered why she was so angry. Perhaps she felt the world owed her something that she never got. Maybe she felt that all the people around her were there just to fulfill her every wish.

How do you express your anger? Do you keep it in or do you vent it on others? If you are angry with someone, even yourself, do you take it out by eating something sweet to make you feel better? Everyone will get angry. We need to express it in a way that is constructive, and not destructive.

*Lord, when anger enters my heart, please help me to understand it
and not be consumed by it.*

*Do not be deceived, God is not mocked; for
whatever a man sows, that he will also reap.*
—GAL. 6:7

A number of years ago, a magazine cover ran a very interesting picture. The first square showed a husband chewing out his wife. The second picture showed the wife chewing out her son. The third picture showed the son chewing out his little sister. She was then shown kicking her brother's dog, who bit the neighbor's cat, who scratched the neighbor's wife, who got mad at her husband, who reprimanded someone at work, who in turn bawled out the man in the first picture. Anger came full circle.

What would have happened if, instead of getting mad at his wife, the man in the first picture had taken time to compliment her on something she had done?

If someone responds to you in a negative way, think about how you respond. Do you react in anger toward the next person you meet, or do you run and grab a candy bar? The next person you meet has nothing to do with you being chewed out, and that candy bar is only going to make you feel worse. Neither solution takes care of how you are feeling. Instead, why don't you decide whether or not what was said was deserved? If it was, but the way it was delivered was wrong, accept the need to change but talk to the person about their delivery. If it was undeserved, let that person know. Deal with it; don't "stuff" it.

Lord, help me speak carefully. Help me to take the opportunity to say something nice instead of something negative.

*A false balance is an abomination
to the Lord,
But a just weight is His delight.*
—PROV. 11:1

The other day I was behind a large woman in an all-you-can-eat line at a restaurant. She had piled up two dinner size plates full of salads, entrees, and vegetables. The fried chicken was spilling over one plate onto her tray. When she got up to the cashier, she politely asked if they had any Sweet and Low.

I barely kept myself from laughing out loud. I mentioned the episode to my friend when I got to my table, and both of us laughed. Then he suggested that she might be diabetic. I was guilt-struck until I remembered the third plate filled with chocolate cake and pecan pie.

Isn't it a little ridiculous to attempt to feel better about our overeating by using a sweetener in our drink? It is the same as ordering a large hamburger, large fries, apple pie, and a diet soda. Who do we think we are kidding? Certainly not ourselves.

Being careful about the amount of sugar we eat is a good thing. But we also need to be aware of the *amount* of food we are eating and *what kind* of food we are eating. We need to slow down when we eat and enjoy our food. We need to be consistent in our eating and drinking choices.

Lord, help me to look honestly at the eating choices I make. Help me to eat those things that are good for me and not just those things that taste good.

Do not let the sun go down on your wrath.
—EPH. 4:26

Most of us have experienced situations so negative we could not get them out of our minds. We carried them home with us from wherever they happened—school, work, even church. We were so angry that we could not eat or sleep. We tossed and turned all night, unable to get what happened out of our thoughts.

When my mom and dad got married, one of the first things they promised each other was that they would never go to sleep with one of them angry. They agreed to settle their differences first. They told me the sun was nearly up before they hashed out some of their differences, but they have always gone to sleep in peace.

God knows it is important to solve our problems before going to bed. Chances are you will wake up feeling the same way.

How many times have you been angry with your spouse and you headed for the refrigerator? Sometimes food seems to give better answers than fighting with your mate. But the morning always comes.

It is better to settle your differences. You need to be able to let go. Too many times we carry around our anger with us for days, weeks, even years. That anger can lead to destructive behavior. Wrath eats away at our peace of mind.

Father God, help me to have the courage to face my anger, to settle my differences, and to forgive the wrongs done against me. Give me the peacefulness of a good night's sleep.

Whatever things are true, whatever things are noble, whatever things are just, whatever things are pure, whatever things are lovely, whatever things are of good report, if there is any virtue and if there is anything praiseworthy—meditate on these things.
—PHIL. 4:8

We often feel so joyless when we start a diet plan. We dread exercising and lowering our calories.

Fran decided to do things differently when she made up her mind to lose those five pounds she gained over the holidays. Every day she exercised thirty minutes to an hour, but she did not want to be tied to one set routine. There was a park near her and she chose to ride her bike there one day, walk another, and run and walk the next. She resolved not to dread the time spent exercising but to enjoy God's beauty. The park was filled with trees and had a small lake. She would look at her surroundings and praise God for His beautiful world.

On some days, Fran put on a headset and listened to contemporary Christian music while she exercised, strengthening herself physically and spiritually at the same time. While enjoying herself, Fran also lost those five pounds and even now savors her time in the park.

We need to stop dreading what we know we have to do and learn to enjoy it. We need to take advantage of the opportunities around us and to be creative in our answers to our weight problem.

Father, help us to stop dreading. Help us to start hoping and searching for the free things You give us to enjoy that truly are good for us.

*For nothing is secret that will not be revealed,
nor anything hidden that will not be known
and come to light.*
        —LUKE 8:17

The big family dinner is finished. All the relatives are sitting in the living room. Martha, the hostess, starts clearing the dishes off the table. She has eaten small amounts during dinner, but as she puts the food away she starts nibbling at the leftovers. She has another piece of turkey, a bite of potato salad, several large gulps of chocolate cake, eaten in a rush. Guilt does not come because no one is watching.

After everyone has gone, she wonders, Why did I eat so much? Everytime I have the family over I do this. As she thought back over the evening she remembered her mother had commented that she needed to discipline her children more. Her father had noticed that her carpets needed cleaning. Her husband had done nothing to help get the meal on the table.

Martha realized she had allowed all of those people who are close to her to get to her. In her frustration she turned to the solitude of her kitchen to eat and to forget about what was really bothering her. The next time the family came over, Martha resolved to take charge of her feelings.

Ask yourself, while you are nibbling away at food, What is nibbling away at my heart?

Father God, there are no secrets You do not know. Reveal mine to me.

> *Therefore I urge you to reaffirm your love to him.*
> —2 COR. 2:8

For the first time in twelve years I got in my car and honestly noticed the sky and the trees and listened to the wind blow. I did not look at all the flashing neon restaurant signs. It was as if I had been reborn. God opened many doors for me as I sought Him earnestly. After going to the clinic and confronting my past, I fell in love with God all over again. I saw His compassion and desire for me to serve Him.

I have learned we can lose sight of who God really is and what He is about when damaging events take place in our lives. I look back at all the times I could have died from my abuse but somehow He gave me strength to endure. I look back to that Sunday morning when I had decided to end my life and the phone call from a friend that stopped me. I know with all my heart that God was there fighting hard for my life.

I fell in love with God when I gave up the control, and when I said, "Help me find the truth! I can't do this alone!"

In Isaiah, King Hezekiah was dying. He did not want to die and he prayed to the Lord to deliver him. God replied, "Thus says the LORD, the God of David your father: 'I have heard your prayer, I have seen your tears; and I will add to your days fifteen years'" (Isa. 38:5).

God sees our tears. He loves us and will answer our pleas.

God, thank You for setting me free and giving me a new beginning.

> *O LORD, You have searched me and
> known me.
> You know my sitting down and my
> rising up;
> You understand my thought afar off.*
> —PS. 139:1-2

There is a poster of a little boy sneaking into the cookie jar and a voice from heaven saying, "I see you!" In Psalms, King David, the man after God's own heart, proclaimed that God sees us. He is looking at us, watching. David wrote that the Lord searches us and knows us. The Lord wants us to know He is near and He sees every step we make, every turn we take.

God knows when we sit down on our couches to watch television and when we sit in a chair next to a sick friend in the hospital. He knows what time we get up in the morning, what mood we are in, why we are getting up, and if we will be late for work or church.

He understands our thoughts from afar. He knows what we think and why we think it. He knows what we will do with those thoughts.

So many people who struggle with life's hurts ask the question, "Is God really alive? Does He really care about me?" The first two verses in Psalm 139 prove it loud and clear. He sees us. He knows us. He loves us.

Father, with all the people in this big world, it's hard to believe that You see me, that You know me. Thank You, Father, that I'm never alone. Help me when I want to cheat on my diet. Help me to know that You know and understand, and that You can give me the strength not to cheat.

Where can I go from Your Spirit?
Or where can I flee from Your
presence? —PS. 139:7

A husband abandons his wife and six children not even bothering to leave a note or call because it is easier to leave and not look back.

One out of three marriages will fail because couples decide it is easier to divorce than to change.

Millions of people spend money on weight loss plans and lose it only to gain it right back because it is simply easier to eat than to eat right.

Sometimes we go our own way and do our own thing instead of thinking about what God's plan is for our lives. We feel we can handle life. We think we can flee responsibility by pretending it does not exist. We do not think or care about how our bad example affects others. After all, it is just easier to walk away than to stay and endure.

It is true that we can walk away and eat away, sinning all we want. We can kid ourselves that God is too busy and will not see what we do, but the truth is we can never flee from God's presence. He is right here with us during the good times and the shameful times. He is there when we forsake responsibility. When we are kind or unkind, selfish or giving, we cannot flee from His presence. He is here for us, always.

God, it's easier to give up. It's easier to rely on ourselves and not on You. But, God, I thank You for not fleeing from me when I run away from You.

> *If I ascend into heaven, You are*
> *   there;*
> *If I make my bed in hell, behold,*
> *   You are there.*
> *If I take the wings of the morning,*
> *And dwell in the uttermost parts of*
> *   the sea,*
> *Even there Your hand shall lead me,*
> *And Your right hand shall hold me.*
> *   —PS. 139:8–10*

No matter what we have done, God loves us.

No matter who we have hurt, God loves us.

No matter how much we hurt, God loves us.

No matter how much we've eaten, God loves us.

No matter if we are fat or skinny, God loves us.

When we hide behind baggy clothes thinking no one will know we have gained weight, God knows and He loves us.

If we make ourselves sick from stuffing our faces to fill our empty spirits, God knows and He loves us.

When we are alone in our despair, barely fitting into our size sixteen dresses, God knows and He loves us.

When we are ready for healing and help and hope, God knows and He will lead us.

When we learn all the reasons why we are numbing ourselves and we go to battle with the locked-up monsters, God's hand will hold us. He will not let us go. Yes, even when we want to give up, God's hand will hold us.

Father, You are love. Thank You for loving and accepting me even though I do not deserve it.

Lest you ponder her path of life—
Her ways are unstable;
You do not know them.
—PROV. 5:6

Rebecca has always been overweight. As a result her health is not very good. She has a lot of wonderful gifts to offer others, yet every time you talk to her something is wrong. She does not feel good. She twisted her ankle. She has a kink in her neck. Her son was not nice to her. The preacher did not say hello to her last week at church. And after all her complaints, she talks about how unhappy she is with her weight.

Rebecca has a problem with responsibility. If she is sick or does not feel good, that is her way of not being responsible and taking charge of her life. She does not have to deal with conflict. She does not have to be accountable for her actions because, after all, there is something wrong with her and she just does not feel up to facing her problems.

There are different forms of escaping our fears and problems. Rebecca does so by focusing on how she feels. There are pieces of Rebecca in all of us.

When I think of taking responsibility I look to Jesus. He took all the responsibility for each one of our sins. He did not complain. He died on the rugged cross so our souls would be spared.

Today, let us look at the example of our Lord. Let's walk with Him and be responsible for our problems.

God, forgive us and help us to deal with the problems and hurts life gives us.

> *My grace is sufficient for you, for My*
> *strength is made perfect in weakness.*
> —2 COR. 12:9

The first few days in the psychiatric ward my fellow patients thought I was a doctor. I wore a mask that said, "I'm strong. I'm not going to break."

With time, my facade crumbled. My therapist, Mike, said I was like a gorilla. He would pound his chest like a gorilla and mock me by saying, "Me don't need anybody! Me take care of me!"

Eventually all my walls of pseudostrength fell down, and I allowed myself to feel weakness. I did not like that feeling at all. Mike tenderly said to me, "You know, strength can be a weakness." Gradually I learned that by being strong in yourself all the time you can lose your need for God and for others. I learned that I do not have to be strong all the time. It is OK to show my fear and failures to people who love me and say, "I can't handle this right now, God. Will You help me?"

I was always afraid that if I was not strong all the time, no one would like me. But God uses weakness for His glory. The apostle Paul had a "thorn" in his side that he asked God to remove three times. Each time God said no. Paul ended up understanding that strength from God can come from our weakness.

Today, remind yourself that it is OK to be weak. It is OK to say, "I'm struggling." It is OK to be real.

Father, in my weakness help me to depend on You.

*As You sent Me into the world, I also
have sent them into the world.*
—JOHN 17:18

My therapist told me I could leave the psychiatric ward and go out into the real world in two weeks. In the two months I had been in the Minirth-Meier Clinic I had gone back to my childhood trauma and unlocked painful memories I had been trying to numb. I understood better how my family had played a part in my bulimia. I knew I was on the way to complete healing, but I was still afraid. When Mike told me I would be leaving I felt a panic set in. I did not want to leave my safe cocoon. In my cocoon I could break down and expose my broken heart. I could confront my monsters in safety. Now it was time to get on with life.

I realized whether or not I was strong enough was not the point. God was and is strong enough. I realized my strength had to come from Him. Cocoons are nice and safe, but God has work for us to do in the world. There are times when all of us must retreat into our safe cocoons and renew ourselves, find answers, and gain strength and wisdom from God. But God does not expect us to stay there. He has sent us out into the world to make a difference and to give glory to Him.

The safety and comfort I felt in the cocoon were from God all along. He was perfectly willing to allow me to take that comfort with me when I went back into the world. I do not need a special place anymore to find comfort. God is my cocoon.

Lord God, You are my warmth when it is cold. Thank You.

I will praise You, for I am fearfully
and wonderfully made;
Marvelous are Your works,
and that my soul knows very well.
—PS. 139:14

It was one of the final days of group therapy before I was to leave the hospital. Ike, a wonderful guy who had been severely depressed, was going to be leaving soon too. He was a "good" guy, and good guys had always scared me. My therapist, Mike, knew I was intimidated by Ike, so during this group session he made me look straight at Ike and say, "Ike, getting burned was not my fault. The scars are not my fault. I'm not damaged freight!"

Good-looking, strong Ike got out of his chair, tenderly hugged me, and said, "You're right, Cynthia. You are not damaged freight."

Mike had each person in the group say to me, "You are not damaged freight. You're beautiful and we love you." I felt I was on the road to healing my broken heart.

We come into this world as innocent children, and God made the family to love and nurture and cherish one another. But the world and our sinful nature can take over. We are confronted with abuse, neglect, and abandonment.

Today, you may feel damaged. God is always trying to tell us, however, "I don't make junk. I made you My child and you are loved."

God, help us confront the damage that's been done in our lives. We praise You because we are wonderfully made.

*And the LORD God said, "It is not good
that man should be alone."*
—GEN. 2:18

"Cynthia, the next time you feel like bingeing, it means you need people, not food. From now on I want you to be a people binger." Those words came from the overweight person I thought could never help me, my beloved therapist, Mike. "You don't need food, Cynthia," he added, "you need people." Mike had found the lonely little girl underneath my strong career woman facade and set her free.

I felt free. I felt alive. I would be leaving the hospital soon and I knew I would have to start filling up my needs with people instead of food. I had learned to stop myself when I was heading for the refrigerator and say, Cynthia, you're not really hungry. What is it you really need? Was I lonely? Call a friend. Was I angry? Then I needed to go talk to the person I was angry with. I learned what I needed was to deal with my feelings and surround myself with people who loved me.

God is always saying to us, "What do you need? I'm here to provide it." Today, before you eat that bag of candy or potato chips, ask yourself, What do I really need?

Father God, You are a fulfiller of needs. You say to us, "Ask and it shall be given!" Sometimes, God, we don't know what we need. Help us to understand our needs and to allow You, and those You give us as friends, to fill us up.

> *But why do you judge your brother? Or why do*
> *you show contempt for your brother? For we*
> *shall all stand before the judgment seat of*
> *Christ.*
> —ROM. 14:10

We live in a world where news headlines tell only of the bad and the ugly. Positive stories are often relegated to the back pages or after the weather report. It was that way when I was a news reporter and it is still that way today.

We often complain about the lack of positive stories. We wonder why it is only the bad that gets told. Sometimes we even get disgusted with it all and turn it off.

We decry the negative focus in the news, yet turn around and do the very same thing in our own lives. We find ourselves talking about all the bad in our own lives and in the lives of others—weird behavior, overweight friends, kids on drugs, alcohol addiction, pregnant teenagers, divorces.

Not only are we guilty of the same things we condemn in the news, but also we can be even worse. We talk about each other and immediately think the worse, condemning the person without even knowing the circumstances. We pass judgment and usually make sure that judgment gets passed around.

Instead, we should try to see the good in our friends and neighbors. If we knew the pain and problems they were facing, maybe we could act out of sympathy and not judgment.

God, help me to look into a person's heart and love him because You love him too.

Every way of a man is right in his
own eyes,
But the LORD weighs the hearts.
—PROV. 21:2

Magazine, newspaper, and television ads offer us products which will tone our muscles, get rid of fat, rid us of wrinkles, grow hair, reclaim our youth—all for a modest sum of cash payable by check, money order or credit card.

Presto! Our package arrives. We use the weight sets or diet pills regularly for a while. But then something else catches our eye and we run after that rainbow.

My dad bought a new set of weights one year. While he was assembling them in the garage our next door neighbor came over.

"Why did you buy those?" she asked. "My husband has a complete set in our garage that have only been used a couple of times. We've had them for three years and I'd have given them to you just to get them out of the way. I'm always tripping over them whenever I go out to use the washer."

It has been said the road to hell is paved with good intentions. Our path through life is often littered with all the get-thin-quick gadgets we have bought.

Incidentally, I visited my folks recently and there were the weights, gathering dust and cobwebs in the corner of the garage. There is not even one scratch on the paint.

Lord, give me the will to follow through with my good intentions.

Repent.
—ACTS 2:38

It is never too late to change. As long as we know what we are doing and why, we can change. The Lord did not command the impossible. We can change our habits, lose our weight, and keep it off. We can eat less. We can exercise more. We can improve our health and our happiness.

Nothing is impossible with God. We simply have to recognize the possibilities and cooperate with Him. God is not going to zap those twenty or thirty extra pounds away, no matter how much we might want Him to. What He will do is enable us to do it ourselves.

Before He can do anything, we have to repent. By repent I mean we have to recognize what we are doing and that it is wrong and we need to change it. God will not do anything to help us until we take that step. Repent really means to reverse direction. If we have been gobbling down second and third helpings of rich, fatty foods, repentance means turning away from the table. It means turning around and leaving the kitchen and the refrigerator. It means turning away from the easy chair and going outside to exercise.

Sometimes we do not want to admit that the way we eat or what we eat is wrong. We delude ourselves into thinking it is not that bad. Yet deep down we know that it is and wonder why God is not helping us. He is not helping us because we are not allowing Him to.

Lord, help me to turn around from my bad habits and run toward healthy ones. Help me to really understand my need to change.

You enlarged my path under me;
So my feet did not slip.
—2 SAM. 22:37

When I was bulimic I said to myself more than a thousand times, Tomorrow I'm going to quit. Before I knew it I was bingeing again. Sometimes I could not get through a day, hardly a week, never a month. I dreamed of a lifetime of freedom from the terrible monster I had inside me.

If your bad eating habit is not as serious as mine, your hope of overcoming it is still in taking the first step. Ultimately my first step was the first mile I drove out of Little Rock on the road to Dallas and to the Minirth-Meier Clinic.

Addiction to food in whatever form it takes, bulimia, anorexia, compulsive overeating, eating for reasons other than hunger, is still addiction. As with any addiction, there is always that first step. For the smoker, it is saying no to that first cigarette of the day. For the alcoholic it is turning down that drink. But for the food addict there is a significant difference. The smoker can live healthily never inhaling another cigarette. The alcoholic can survive without taking another drink. But the food addict has to eat to live. The food addict cannot just swear off food. We must eat to live.

While we are eating to live, we must walk the careful line between nourishment and over- or undereating. We must choose our steps carefully.

Lord, help me to take that first step toward health. Help me have wisdom in the steps I take and my eating choices.

When wisdom enters your heart,
And knowledge is pleasant to your soul,
Discretion will preserve you;
Understanding will keep you.
—PROV. 2:10–11

Choices. Our lives are full of them. At first it might seem that what we put our food in would not matter, but sometimes it does. If we are watching television and we decide we want something to drink we have a choice. We can use the drink container, or we can use a large glass or a small glass. If we are not careful and take the container with us to our seat, it is easier to drink the whole thing while we are watching television. Those unnoticed calories can really add up. Instead, use the small glass, and if you are still hungry, drink some water.

When having ice cream for dessert, we can choose the large soup bowl to serve it in or the small fruit bowl. Since we naturally want to fill up either bowl (it looks better that way) we could be serving up twice as much ice cream in the large soup bowl.

Often we are doing something else while we are eating. We do not even realize how much we have eaten. So instead of a large slice, take a small one; instead of four dips, make it two; instead of eight ounces, make it four. In this way you will be cutting down on the amount you eat and still meet your need to have a little something while you read or watch television. In time you may decide to cut out that snack altogether.

Lord, help me to use wisdom in my eating habits, and help me to follow through.

I have chosen the way of truth;
Your judgments I have laid before me.
—PS. 119:30

Whole milk. Half and half. Pure cream, 2 percent milk, 1 percent milk, 1/2 percent milk, skim milk. Going to the grocery store is not simple anymore. An 8-ounce serving of whole milk has 160 calories, and a significant amount of fat. Eight ounces of nonfat milk has 90 calories, but only a trace of fat.

Wisdom is required for even the little choices we make for ourselves and our family. By choosing intelligently at one small area of the grocery store we can save hundreds of calories while still providing the important nutrients dairy products give us.

So often we go to the store with no set plan in mind. We seem to fill up the cart at random, as if we are on automatic pilot. We buy whole or 2 percent milk because we have always bought it, or because that is what we had in the refrigerator when we were growing up. Seldom do we stop to actually read the back of the carton to see what is inside. We might be surprised if we did. We should use wisdom in our choices and take advantage of the information.

If this seems like a unpleasant chore to you, think of it as a treasure hunt. Waiting for you there in that jungle called a supermarket is a treasure of good food for yourself and for your family.

Lord, help me to make wise choices in the food I buy for myself and my family. Help me to avoid buying food on impulse.

With her enticing speech
she caused him to yield,
With her flattering lips
she seduced him.
—PROV. 7:21

With the best of intentions, we went out to our favorite restaurant to have a "lite" lunch. My friend and I knew what we wanted and when the waitress came to our table, we both said, "The number five, please."

"Will that be all?" she asked. "How about an appetizer? French fries, onion rings, nachos, fried cheese?" We looked at each other and hurriedly said, "No!"

"Are you sure?" she asked again. "They're really quite good." Our "no" turned into a "well, why not?" We soon had both french fries and onion rings.

We'll eat just a few, we said to ourselves, besides, we are having a low-calorie entree. The order came and they smelled *so* good. One bite led to two, then four. Before we knew it we had eaten every crumb. Our salads came, but we weren't hungry.

So much for our "lite" lunch. We started out with the best of intentions and ended up with a belly full of fried food. Next time, we will try to stick to our guns.

Let's let our "no" mean just that.

Lord, give us an extra measure of determination to stick with what we have decided. Help us not to be swayed from our purpose.

The simple believes every word.
—PROV. 14:15

Across the television screen a colorful, enticing picture flashes. With three scoops of luscious ice cream nestled between two banana halves, covered with chocolate, strawberry and pineapple sauce, with whipped cream and nuts on the top, you wish you could reach into that picture tube and yank out that banana split. You can almost taste it. The woman in the ad savors it with a contented smile. The announcer extols the deliciousness of the banana split and adds that it is now half-price, the perfect reason for running out and buying one.

Unfortunately you have just finished a full meal. So what, you think to yourself, I deserve to celebrate. What better way to celebrate than a sale! Besides, it is a great value. The ad made it look like everyone and his brother was down at the restaurant eating banana splits, so off you go to join them.

Wait a minute. What just happened? A minute ago you were perfectly happy and content with your meal, and now all you can think about is leaving your house and driving to a restaurant miles away just to have a banana split. Whether you know it or not, somebody else is tugging your strings and pulling you out of yourself, so they can fill you up with their messages. You are being manipulated. Think about what you are doing and why. Did you need that banana split before you saw the ad on television? Take back the control.

Lord, I need more of You in my life instead of more food.

> *But Daniel purposed in his heart that he*
> *would not defile himself with the portion*
> *of the king's delicacies, nor with the*
> *wine which he drank.*   —DAN. 1:8

Nancy Reagan was asked by a little girl what she should say to someone offering her drugs. Mrs. Reagan replied, "Just say no." Her answer captured the imagination of the country and before long there were "Just Say No" clubs all over the United States. Billboards and bumper stickers sprang up with the slogan.

I think the reason this answer caught on so much was because of its simplicity and its truth. The major step in fighting any bad habit, and destructive behavior, is to "just say no" to it. This may be simple and true, but it can also be excruciatingly difficult. Saying no implies that you do not want what is offered. Where food is concerned that is not always the case. We must be truthful about the answer we give. We must truly *believe* that those extra helpings or those oversized desserts or those in-between-meal munchies are not good for us. We must mean it in our hearts when we say no to them, or our answer will not mean very much.

Like Daniel, we must have the purpose set in our hearts. We must understand what we are saying and why. From that truth in our hearts we can find the strength to say no and mean it.

Lord, help me to have the will to say no when I'm tempted. Help me refuse to continue in those eating patterns which are not good for me and replace those bad habits with healthy ones.

> *And when Asa heard these words and the
> prophecy of Oded the prophet, he took
> courage and removed the abominable
> idols from all the land.*
> —2 CHRON. 15:8

When Asa became king of Israel the people had built altars and were worshiping foreign idols. But Asa determined to do God's will in spite of the people who were not too thrilled with their new king. Before Asa started he needed the courage he could only get from God.

Courage. It was out there waiting for Asa to take it, and it is out there waiting for you. God is waiting for you to accept the courage He can give you.

Recently I met a twenty-seven-year-old woman. She had a beautiful smile and exuded confidence. I could tell, however, that she was nervous. Before long she blurted out that she had been bulimic since she was eleven. She told me she had read my book, *The Monster Within,* and it had given her hope for the first time of being cured. She said, "You'll never know how long it took me to get the courage to talk to you."

Because she took the courage to speak to me, I was able to give comfort and encouragement to her.

Are you needing to take courage from the Lord for the way you are eating? He is ready and willing to give that courage to you. All you have to do is ask.

Father God, today give me the courage to tear down the altar I have given over to food.

> *He also brought streams out of the rock,*
> *And caused waters to run down like rivers.*
> —PS. 78:16

Water, water, everywhere, nor any a drop to drink." That line from Coleridge's "The Ancient Mariner" came to my mind the other day as I stood in the diet and nutrition section of my local bookstore. I counted more than fifty books dealing with dieting. Every title seemed to suggest that it was the answer to happiness and health. How? Most methods boil down to proper eating habits.

Who could argue with that? Everyone knows that eating properly will improve one's health. But these books seem to overlook the fact that people who are addicted to food could care less about a balanced diet.

I thought, Books, books, everywhere, and not a word of help. All the diet books in the world will not take off permanently one pound from those who are addicted to food. They have an inner turmoil that they refuse to acknowledge or may be totally unaware of.

If you are overeating and do not know why, you need to talk to a professional who can help you answer the *why*. Buying a diet book may help you feel better for a while, but it will do nothing to answer the why. All the new recipes in the world will not do you a bit of good if they never get off the page.

Father, help me to understand if and when I need help. Give me the courage to seek out help in whatever form.

Better is a little with the fear of the LORD,
Than great treasure with trouble.
—PROV. 15:16

I have met some pretty amazing people. They have quit their destructive habits cold turkey. They emptied the last bottle of scotch down the sink and never drank another drop. They threw their last cigarette pack into the fireplace and smoked no more. They laid their cards down on the table and never bet again. Others have given up sweets and did not eat another piece of German chocolate cake.

I must admit that these people are rare souls. Habits are hard to break. Compulsive habits are seemingly impossible to break. Most of us give up a little at a time. We constantly regress.

For most of us a little of anything is not enough. The more we can consume, own, or use, the better. Solomon contradicted our "wisdom." He said that a little is better than a lot, if the fear of the Lord is within us. We have seen in our own lives how plenty sometimes comes with plenty of trouble. In this land of plenty, plenty of us have weight problems. We have not learned Solomon's lesson of little is better. In this age of consumerism, we consume much more food than we really need. We consume food when we need something else.

———————————

Father, give us wisdom to know when little is better. Help us to take courage and example from those rare souls who have made a decision to stop their bad habits. Help me to stop mine.

*You have made profit from your neighbors
by extortion, and have forgotten Me.*
—EZEK. 22:12

Lose weight while you sleep!" The promise screams out from the page. All you have to do is order their magic pills for $29.95 and take one at bedtime. Of course, that money is only for the first batch, good for a month's worth of pound-shedding sleep.

My dad has a saying: "That which promises too much usually picks your pocket." The only thing those pills are going to burn is your money. There are no magic pills.

At one time in my life I thought I had found magic pills. They were called laxatives. They caused my body to reject the food I ate before it could be absorbed. They also brought me to the brink of death.

There is only one way to lose weight. Eat less and increase your activity. It is not magic. The answer to losing weight and conditioning your body for healthy living is mundane.

The next time you see an ad promising to "burn fat while you sleep," remember, the only thing you will reduce is your bank account. The people who run those ads are counting on your misery to stay in business. They have no concern for you and your need. The only thing they are interested in is your money.

Do not give in to their false promises. Turn to God for His true promise for grace, salvation and love.

Thank You, God, for always being true to me and for loving me eternally.

The sleep of a laboring man is sweet,
Whether he eats little or much;
But the abundance of the rich
will not permit him to sleep.
—ECCL. 5:12

How many times have you gone to bed only to get up an hour or two later to stumble into the kitchen in the dark to find that little roll of pills? There was a party and you ate too much pizza, or the in-laws came over and you had one too many helpings of enchiladas. Now it is time to sleep but your stomach is in an uproar trying to digest the massive amount of food you have fed it. You ask yourself, Why?, and unable to come up with a good enough answer, you promise never to do it again—at least, not for a while anyway.

It is nights like that when we become our own worst enemies. We overeat and overdrink to satisfy some need that has nothing to do with hunger or thirst, and end up miserable, burping and belching all night. With all of that rich food and fatty dessert we are really asking our bodies to do a lot. It answers back with its own language of heartburn. When are we going to stop and listen to it?

God has made our bodies special. They are intricate and work in an amazing way. We have a tendency to take our bodies for granted. We ask our bodies to process too much of the wrong kind of food. It is no wonder it exacts its price from us.

Father, give me the will to eat regular, well-balanced meals. Help me to not take the body You have given me for granted.

Then those of Israelite lineage separated themselves from all foreigners; and they stood and confessed their sins and the iniquities of their fathers.

—NEH. 9:2

We live in a time when fathers and mothers have ambitions that take them away from their children for days, weeks, or even months. There are many justifications for their absence.

"I'm in the military and the defense of this country is more important than being home right now."

"I'm trying to build a better life for my kids. I want them to have all the things I never had when I was growing up."

"The work of the Church is more important than anything else. God said I have to give up everything to follow Him."

What are these statements really saying to their children? "You aren't very important to me." "My work is more important to me than you are." "Things are more important than you." "What I do for myself is much more important than what I can do for you."

Few parents intentionally send these messages to their kids. Intentional or not, tender-hearted children hear them. Lonely, these children take out their despair in food, drink, sex, drugs.

What are you using to cope? Has that coping mechanism turned destructive for you? Understand where it came from and why. Stop coping and start living.

Father, forgive me for hurting those closest to me. Help me to forgive those who have hurt me.

When I was a child, I spoke as a child,
I understood as a child, I thought as
a child. —1 COR. 13:11

Church can be a fascinating place to watch people. I have observed interesting behavior in the church pews. Some parents allow their children unlimited freedom. They climb over and under the pews, talk, and play during worship.

At other times I have seen parents slap their children for the slightest whisper.

Parents often go to extremes, and many find it difficult to strike a balance between not enough leeway and too much lenience. Those whose hands lay heavy on their children often ask "When will you grow up?" The message they give to their children is, "You're not acceptable to me as you are. I want you to act like an adult." That is an impossible when you are a child.

When this is repeated often enough, children begin to believe that they are unworthy and incapable of pleasing their parents. Children can take this concept of unworthiness to unhealthy extremes themselves. One extreme is an eating disorder.

Is your life being defined by an extreme? Are you using food in an unhealthy way? Ask God to help you put your life back in proper balance. If you are a parent, are you showing extreme behavior to your children? Ask God to help you put their lives back in proper balance.

———————

Lord, help me to never expect too much of a child. Help me to understand that children speak, understand, and think as children.

Be still, and know that I am God;
I will be exalted among the nations,
I will be exalted in the earth!
—PS. 46:10

Quick! Rush! Now! We are so busy rushing to and fro that we find it difficult to take the time to be still. We have jobs, cooking, cleaning, soccer, PTA, church clubs, social clubs, business clubs, and a host of other distractions.

Many families seldom eat together after the children start school. Preparing regular, well-balanced meals that nourish our families is difficult. So why not pick up a dozen doughnuts for a quick breakfast? And there is always pizza for that evening when cooking dinner is just more than we can do. Besides, the kids love going to McDonald's, right? Who has time to eat anyway?

Sometimes we eat, snack, nibble, and drink our way through the little breaks in our day, never realizing we have not really had anything nutritious and consumed thousands of empty calories. As we get busier and busier, we may put on more and more weight, while life seems less than satisfying.

We need to slow down, even to stop. We need to be still and acknowledge God. He rarely fits into our busy, overextended schedules. We need to find a quiet time to meditate on His Word, His power, His grace. We need to fill ourselves up with His presence. If we can take time to do that, we will not need to fill ourselves up with so much junk.

Lord, help me to stop long enough to be still.

Out of the depths I have cried to You, O LORD;
Lord, hear my voice!
Let Your ears be attentive
To the voice of my supplications.

—PS. 130:1–2

From the depths of despair we sometimes shake a clenched fist at heaven and cry, "Why are You doing this to me, God?" We long for Him to answer.

I know a woman who struggles with depression. She sought counseling and confronted the pain of emotional and verbal abuse from her parents. She remembered as a small curious child she had poked a finger into her mother's apple pie. The mother went into a rage, tied her daughter's hands to the crib, and left her there.

If God really loves me, she asked herself, why did He allow my mother to hurt me? Her anger at God eventually caused her to reject Him.

This woman came to the wrong conclusion. It was not God who abused her; it was her mother. It was not God who caused her depression; God is love. He must have shed many tears for this woman. He was always with her even when no one else was.

Today let us unclench our fists and raise our hands to our true Daddy. Let's ask Him to use our past pain for His glory. I believe He allows our pain to happen so we can choose to be better, not bitter.

Father God, today I open my arms to Your comfort, and to Your strength. Today I ask that You use me for Your glory.

> *Give us this day our daily bread.*
> —MATT 6:11

Our Father in heaven. When we say, "Our Father," we are saying, "Daddy, I need You."

Hallowed be Your name. His name is holy.

Your kingdom come. Your will be done on earth as it is in heaven. Jesus did not ask for His own request to be granted or His own will to be done, but His Father's.

Give us this day our daily bread. Notice there is no request for extra food. Jesus asked God to provide food that will simply sustain our bodies.

And forgive us our debts. Forgive me, Father, when I do not eat right, when I eat more than my body needs, or when I do not deal with my life in a healthy way.

As we forgive our debtors. God, it is not easy, but I forgive those who have hurt me, who anger me, and who say things that break my spirit and my heart.

And do not lead us into temptation, but deliver us from the evil one. Jesus knew our nature is one of weakness. He knew the world would tempt us. He prayed that His Father will help us to do right and to live for only Him.

For Yours is the kingdom and the power and the glory forever. Amen. Jesus was saying, "Everything is Yours, God. You are the Creator. You are the Author of our lives, and the Power and the Glory of the whole world."

God is near. God is listening.

Lord, we give our needs to You. Fulfill our needs with Your love.

For by grace you have been saved.
—EPH. 2:8

Today come to the door of grace. Your Father God freely gives it. You cannot buy it. You cannot earn it. Grace is a gift of God.

Paul wrote, "For by grace you have been saved through faith, and that not of yourselves; it is the gift of God." No matter how good we are, we will never be what we need to be. But that is OK in God's eyes. He gives us a beautifully wrapped package with a bright bow called *grace*. Inside is forgiveness and love. Oh, how He yearns for us to open up that package and be delighted. Instead, how often do we reject His free gift?

"God couldn't possibly like me. Look at me. I'm fat."

"How could God save me? I'm out of control. I'm not what He wants me to be."

"I'm such a bad person. I never do anything right. God surely can't call me His child."

"I don't deserve such a beautiful gift."

Today, God's door of grace is wide open. He loves you despite your sins. If you are too skinny, too fat, too tall, too short, too whatever, He loves you anyway. You have been saved by His grace. It is a gift. Take it. Cherish it. Receive it freely.

Father, thank You for Your mercy and grace and love.

> *That the God of our Lord Jesus Christ, the Father*
> *of glory, may give to you the spirit of wisdom*
> *and revelation in the knowledge of Him.*
> —EPH. 1:17

Today let us lift up prayers asking God for a spirit of wisdom.

Wisdom to know right from wrong.

Wisdom to do what is right even though it is easier to do what is wrong.

Wisdom to take charge of our lives.

Wisdom to seek help if life is not working anymore.

Wisdom to eat what is good for us and not what will hurt us.

Wisdom to love ourselves so we can love others.

Wisdom to know we cannot do it on our own, but with God's strength and spirit, we can.

Wisdom to search our heart for answers to how we can be more holy and pure in heart.

Wisdom to select food that will nourish our bodies so we can better serve God.

Wisdom to speak words that will touch lives.

Wisdom to be at peace.

Proverbs 3:13 says, "Happy is the man who finds wisdom, / And the man who gains understanding." May we seek wisdom and ask God to help us find it.

Father, give me a spirit of wisdom.

*At twilight you shall eat meat, and in the
morning you shall be filled with bread. And
you shall know that I am the LORD your God.*
—EX. 16:12

As the children of Israel traveled out of Egypt, God provided manna in the morning and meat at night. They were to gather just enough for that day's needs; they were not to hoard. But some of the Israelites disobeyed the rules and took too much. The leftovers bred worms and smelled really bad.

How many times do we stock up our freezers and refrigerators with high-calorie goodies, using the excuse, "Well, company may drop in and I'll need this food just in case"? The company never comes, and we conveniently eat the food to cover up our loneliness.

Or: "I'll buy candy and potato chips for the kids." Then we end up putting them up on a high shelf where the kids cannot see or reach them, or we just happen to eat them as a snack when the kids are away at school.

We set ourselves up for failure when we buy junk food for somebody else. What we are really doing is rationalizing our need to have that food on hand, in case the day does not go as we planned or we feel bad or discouraged about something.

Today let's stop lying to ourselves about what we bring home from the store.

---

*Lord, help me to be honest with myself about the food I bring home
and eat. Help me not to be a secret eater.*

*A false balance is an abomination
to the LORD,
But a just weight is His delight.*
—PROV. 11:1

Carol is short and gains weight easily. She finally reached a weight where she felt miserable and invested in a diet program, the kind where you buy their food and get weekly counseling and behavior modification classes.

Her counselor did a computerized analysis of how much weight she should lose and told her, "Fifty pounds would be best, Carol."

"Wait a minute," Carol objected. "I haven't been that thin in twenty-five years! That's too much—thirty-five pounds is right."

I met Carol when she had lost ten pounds. She felt great. Three months later, she had lost twenty-five pounds. She looked great. She has ten pounds to go to reach her goal.

There is a lot of pressure in the world to look like the pencil-thin models. The truth is most of us do not have the body structure to be pencil-thin. Carol got on the diet to gain back a measure of health, not to exchange one unhealthy condition for another.

Carol accepts herself and her figure, and she feels good about the choice she made. How about you? Is the pressure on you causing failure? Today, determine what is best and healthy for you.

God, help us to decide wisely what weight we will be comfortable with.

The LORD has been mindful of us.
—PS. 115:12

I didn't have an opinion until I was thirty years old." Carol laughs at the absurdity of her statement, but it was a fact. She was always afraid to express her feelings on any subject so she kept her mouth shut. When she was a child her father let her know that his opinion was the only one that mattered. She grew up believing she had nothing important to say.

One night at a party, Carol blurted out an opinion on what everyone else was talking about. Wonder of wonders, other people agreed with her! She was utterly amazed. She felt sure someone was going to react as her dad always had, but they did not. They actually respected what she had to say. "It felt so good to be respected," Carol told me.

That experience caused Carol to probe inside herself to understand what she was afraid of. She learned she had a fear of being rejected for her thoughts and feelings. She had to accept the fact that her father's assessment of her opinions as being "stupid" was wrong.

Isn't it wonderful to know that we have a heavenly Father who wants to hear what is in our hearts—our opinions, our feelings, our struggles and victories! He desires us to be honest and open with Him. He is a God of patience and understanding. No matter what we say or if we sin, He loves us. He wants to be our Father.

Today, God, may we be honest, expressing our needs and our hearts.

> *You shall love your neighbor as yourself.*
> —LEV. 19:18

The next time I see Carol I know she will be at her goal weight. She is resolved to keep it off. Carol's new motto for her life is, "Be good to yourself." For Carol that means speaking up for herself and being heard. It also means she does not have to deprive herself. Just the other night she went to a party with tables of food everywhere. She did not panic. She felt at peace because she was not terrified of eating too much or nothing at all. Instead of eating platefuls of stuffed mushrooms, little quiches, bacon-wrapped liver, or potato skins, she was good to herself and only selected two things to eat. She savored those two. "There's no guilt involved when I'm good to myself," she said.

Carol has not been caught up in the all-or-nothing trap. She goes ahead and eats what she wants but in a limited way. She is living with a rule that instructs her, "Don't deprive yourself." She has a cookie—one cookie. She does not say to herself, You can never have another cookie as long as you live. She does not let food control her. She controls her food; what she eats and how much. Just because she has one cookie does not mean she is doomed to eat the whole bag.

Carol's motto is an excellent rule we could all use when it comes to our dealing with food.

Lord, help me to use these two guidelines in my life. Help me to know that food is a gift from You, and that I do not have to deprive myself to eat in a healthy way.

And you shall know the truth, and the truth shall make you free.
—JOHN 8:32

Honesty means freedom. I really believe this is true. I remember that when I was a child my emotions were so sensitive. My conscience was easily pricked if I did something wrong. If I told a lie, I would hurt so bad I just could not hold it in and I would have to go and make it right. When I did tell the truth, there would be such a release of the heaviness I had been carrying, and peace would come. I felt as if I could go on with my life.

As we get older our conscience does not seem to be as sensitive, however. We start a habit of telling ourselves those little white lies.

"Everybody else is eating ice cream so I should too."

"You have to eat buttered popcorn and chocolate covered raisins when you go to the movies."

So off we sail on the wind of these little white lies and end up floundering on the shores of obesity, out-of-shape and depressed. Those excuses might sound good, but they are not based in truth.

We do not have to eat just because everyone else is eating.

We can watch a movie without the food.

The first step to freedom is being honest.

Honesty is saying, "Am I really hungry? What do I really need?"

———————

God, for today, help me not to do something just because I have always done it. Help me to not follow the crowd.

Who touched Me?
—LUKE 8:45

There was a woman who suffered from a serious malady for twelve years. She had spent all of her money on doctors and no one could heal her. She had heard about Jesus' healing powers, and she thought, If I could just touch Him, I'd be healed. She was scared, but she felt it was her last chance. She watched as He passed her in the crowd, and she was able to reach out and touch the hem of His garment. She was healed.

Jesus did not see the woman, but He felt the healing power going out through His body. He stopped, and looking around, asked, "Who touched Me?" The woman was terrified. Trembling, she fell down before Him and confessed.

Jesus looked at her tenderly and said, "Daughter, be of good cheer; your faith has made you well. Go in peace" (Luke 8:48).

After twelve years of struggling with my eating disorder, I longed to be healed. I longed to touch the hem of Jesus. I prayed long, agonizing prayers during those twelve years. When I finally sought professional help, I was healed. During all my struggles I wanted to give up, yet I did not. Now that I am well, I sometimes hear Jesus gently say, "Who touched Me?" I answer without fear, "I did, Lord."

And I go in peace.

Lord, thank You for touching my life, changing my life and giving me hope.

And having been set free from sin,
you became slaves of righteousness.
—ROM. 6:18

It is amazing how when I am honest, the next person feels free to be honest too. When I was released from the Minirth-Meier Clinic, I went to stay at a friend's beach house in Oregon. For three weeks, I prayed to God to tell me what to do with my life. My career was waiting for me back home but deep inside it just did not feel right to go back.

My time at the clinic changed me forever. I found out why so many people hurt and struggle and have addictions. I felt moved to do something. After those weeks in prayer, I decided to go public with my story.

As soon as the stories ran, my phone began to ring. Now, seven years later, it has not stopped. Because I was honest, others could be too. I heard painful stories that had never before been told to anyone. My honesty gave those people a sense of safety and brought us all one step closer to freedom.

One bulimic person who told me that her daughter was killed on an amusement ride, and she could not let go of the pain of knowing that she did not get on the ride with her daughter. I heard stories of terrible abuse, of trauma, of lonely abandonment—stories kept hidden away from themselves and others.

Honesty does mean freedom. Today, find a safe person with whom you can be honest. It will be a triumphant step toward freedom and wholeness.

Father, thank You for giving me the courage to be honest.

> *If you knew the gift of God, and who it*
> *is who says to you, "Give Me a drink,"*
> *you would have asked Him and He would*
> *have given you living water.*
> —JOHN 4:10

Jesus did not come down hard on the woman He met at the well. When He asked her to go get her husband, she answered by saying that she had no husband. Jesus said to her, "That's right. You have had five husbands, and the man you now have is not your husband" (see John 4:17–18). If she had lied, Jesus would have known. He did not condemn her for what she said.

Jesus brought up the one area in her life where she was experiencing glaring sin. What would His question have been to us if we had been that woman at the well? What if, instead of asking for water from us, He had asked us for some food? We might have answered, "There is no food in my house." He might say, "There is no food in your house now, but there was this morning and you ate it all." How would we have responded?

Jesus is at the well with us every day. He knows our weaknesses and our struggles. He knows our every need. The woman at the well did not need five husbands; she needed Jesus. We do not need food to fill us up; we need Jesus to give us His food and His water so that we will never thirst or hunger again. What a wondrous feeling it is to know Jesus is at the well, knowing all about us. He is there, longing to give us the fountain of everlasting life.

God, You are all-knowing. Help me to expose my half-truths to You.

*I have food to eat of which you do
not know.* —JOHN 4:32

Food can become such a trap in our lives. Adolf Hitler, in the days before he came to power, would get a bushel of bread, take it into the poor neighborhoods, and give it freely to hungry people. The food was a trap so people would believe in him. We know what happened as a result.

When Jesus was led by the Spirit of God into the wilderness to be tempted by the devil, he had fasted for forty days and nights. The Bible says, "Jesus was hungry." Satan knew this, and tempted Jesus with food.

Satan said, "If You are the Son of God, command that these stones become bread" (Matt. 4:3).

Jesus could certainly have done that. He was hungry and He had the power to do so. But there was more to it. Jesus knew Satan was using food to set a trap, so He responded, "It is written, 'Man shall not live by bread alone, but by every word that proceeds from the mouth of God'" (Matt. 4:4).

Today, let us look to Jesus for our example. Jesus knew when Satan was using something good to set a trap for Him. We need to strive to be like Jesus and see those traps. Seek to be able to put food in its proper place and in its proper perspective. Jesus did not let food get in the way of God's will. Let's not spring Satan's trap when we set our table.

Father, help me as I struggle to look to Your Son and His example.

> *My food is to do the will of Him who*
> *sent Me, and to finish His work.*
> —JOHN 4:34

When I resigned my television career to help people struggling with eating disorders, I thought support for my endeavor would abound. I was wrong. In fact, few people truly understood why I wanted to educate the public and provide answers. Although I knew in my heart what I needed to be doing, when I shared this with others, they would say with exasperation, "When are you going to go back to your real job?"

What these friends did not understand was my "food" is to do the will of God. My objective is to do His will. His will turned out to be writing a book called *The Monster Within,* and later another, *The Courage To Go On.* His will for me was to speak to people searching for answers and to listen to broken hearts and encourage them to seek professional help.

One person who criticized me for quitting my career and helping others believed my only motive was my own therapeutic reasons. That person was wrong. My motive is I know how it feels to be so lonely you want to curl up and die. I know how it feels to have only food and a toilet as your best friends. I know the desperation of being near death; yet I also know the feeling of being truly alive.

What is God's will for you? He has a purpose for you. Receive His food and you will be truly filled up.

Father, help me to discern Your will for my life.

Blessed are those who hunger and thirst
for righteousness,
For they shall be filled. —MATT. 5:6

As I reflect on my experience with bulimia, I now realize that food was not my problem. After hospitalization, therapy, and time to reflect, I am able to realize what I hungered and thirsted for all along. I hungered for acceptance. I thirsted for the knowledge that I was not "damaged freight." I hungered to know and understand that man judges wrongly, by the outward appearance. I thirsted to know that God judges by the condition of our hearts. I hungered to know that my inner beauty was what really mattered. I thirsted to know that I truly could be called God's child.

It was no wonder that I "stuffed" myself with my bulimia. I was trying desperately to fill myself up, but with the wrong things. God knows what we need and why. He knows how to fill us up. Until I gave over the control to Him and stuck with my own choices, I was never full no matter how much I ate.

You know that you hunger and thirst. But do you know for what, or why? You may not have the answers, but God does. He not only knows why you thirst and hunger, but also He already has the answers to make you really full. Pray that He will send those answers to you, in whatever form or person they may take. Be alert to the answers. They may surprise you.

Father, provide me with the food and drink of righteousness.

> *For He looked down from the*
> *height of His sanctuary;*
> *From heaven the LORD viewed the earth,*
> *To hear the groaning of the prisoner,*
> *To loose those appointed to death.*
> —PS. 102:19–20

My dad has a very dear friend who was in World War II. He fought in Germany during the Battle of the Bulge and was captured. The Germans marched him and the other captured soldiers for days, to a prison camp near Berlin. By the time they arrived at the camp every man was starving.

The conditions at the camp were terrible. A single bowl of cabbage or turnip soup each day was the standard meal. Dysentery was rampant, and during the winter the only heat to be found was from the bodies of the other prisoners. In order to prevent frostbite on their feet, the men would lie so that the feet of one rested within the armpit of the other.

This friend told my dad that the hunger was indescribable. He said he could feel the hunger eating at his bones. When he dreamed at night, it was not of home but of food. Even today that specter of hunger is never far from his thoughts.

If physical hunger can be so consuming, how much more intense is the hunger of our souls? God's desire is to set us free from our prisons. He hears our groans. He desires to loose us from our addictions. How long will it be before we take Him at His word?

Lord, help me to feed my soul. May I feel Your presence in my bones and may I be nourished by Your comforting promises of freedom.

*In weariness and toil, in sleeplessness
often, in hunger and thirst, in fastings
often, in cold and nakedness.*
                    —2 COR. 11:27

These words were written by the apostle Paul. He was writing the Corinthian churches about what he had experienced in the name of Christ. He became a shepherd to the lost but often those he had come to help turned on him. He was driven out of their cities. He was thrown into their jails. Hunger and thirst were constant companions. Paul was willing to suffer those tribulations for the sake of Christ.

Are you willing to suffer a little hunger for your own sake, for the "cause" of your own health? The body is really a wonderful thing. It has the ability to adapt to changes in what we eat and how much. The first few days of a diet can be rough. But before long, the stomach shrinks and that constant hunger is curbed, not by eating food, but because less food lets you still feel full.

By eating such large meals all the time, we are setting ourselves up for hunger later on. We stretch that stomach out to the limit. The next time we eat, it wants the same amount of food to feel the same degree of fullness. By changing our eating habits, we can cut down on the hunger we feel. Smaller meals, eaten on a regular basis, can actually help shrink our stomach and give us added energy.

Paul's hunger stemmed from a basic need for food. Frequently, our hunger stems from habit.

Lord, help me to distinguish between my daily bread and all the junk food and sweets I want to eat.

> *So they gathered it every morning, every*
> *man according to his need.*
> —EX. 16:21

There it is, screaming at you in neon-colored letters, "All-You-Can-Eat!" It is a breakfast buffet, or a salad bar, or a pasta and seafood spread. All those beautiful colors and smells waft up to greet you as you walk in the door. And such a deal—only $4.95 for breakfast or $9.95 for dinner. They will even bring you a new plate so you can pretend the current heaping of food is really just the first.

Though you are not that hungry, it is too good to pass up. You order and then it's up to you. Surely with all those people going back and forth, no one will notice how many times you've gone back for more. Besides, the more you eat the better the value, right?

Of what value is it to eat until you cannot walk? If you order from the menu, you can enjoy a perfectly good meal for less money without having to loosen your belt a notch or two. When the sign reads "All-You-Can-Eat," you take it as permission to stuff yourself, a kind of justified gluttony. It seems you always eat more than you should, or really want.

Next time you go out to eat, don't punish yourself. Choose something besides the "All-You-Can-Eat" selection; or, revise it in your mind to mean, "All-You-Should-Eat."

Lord, help me to have self-control, no matter how much food is available. Help me to be wise in my choices. Help me to avoid situations that might tempt me to eat unwisely.

So Jonathan arose from the table in fierce anger, and ate no food for the second day of the month, for he was grieved for David, because his father had treated him shamefully.
—1 SAM. 20:34

We have all probably been in situations in our lives when we could not or would not eat. We sometimes lose our appetites when experiencing extreme anger, sorrow, or fear. Guilt can be so consuming that we stop consuming food. I have talked with many anorexics and bulimics. In almost all of them a deep-seated anger exists, for a variety of reasons.

The anger may be because of a divorce, or death, or a sense of abandonment. Many times the anger is in response to abuse they suffered as children. It could be simply because Mom or Dad seems to be more interested in jobs, hobbies, or social activities.

"Mom's got thirty kids she looks after at school. They're more important to her than I am!"

By either eating too much or not eating enough, children attempt to assert some control over their own lives and the lives of their seemingly disinterested parents. Sometimes the anger is so deep that the people who are its object do not even know the anger is there.

Are you struggling with deep anger? You need to dig deep and ask why, and against whom. Food is not a very realistic way of letting people know you are upset with them. If you want to make sure they know you are angry, a better way would be to tell them yourself.

Lord, help me to recognize the source of my anger. Help me to confront it and the people involved.

> *Be anxious for nothing, but in everything*
> *by prayer and supplication, with thanksgiving,*
> *let your requests be made known to God.*
> —PHIL. 4:6

We have all been there. Two days ago you decided to cut down on your eating to take off those extra pounds. Now water and celery are your constant companions. It is going to work this time. Slim figure, here I come!

Then the phone rang. "A dinner party?" you asked, heart sinking to your knees. "Sure, we'd love to come."

Oh, no, you thought to yourself as you hung up the phone, how am I going to handle this?

The day of the party arrived. You had just water and celery all day, plus a few other little things to take the edge off your hunger. Of course you do not want to offend your hostess, and you have all those calories saved up, so you eat some of this and some of that, and just a little more please, of that over there.

By the time you are done you have irrevocably ruined your diet. Or have you? You blew it for today, but there is always tomorrow. And what have you learned? Maybe next time you will eat more sensibly during the day, or try taking smaller portions, or not try everything.

Of course you could have explained to your hostess over the phone that you were cutting back. She might have prepared something with you in mind. Try it next time. You might be surprised.

Lord, help others understand about my diet. Help me take pride in trying to do what is good for me.

Have you found honey?
Eat only as much as you need,
Lest you be filled with it and vomit.
—PROV. 25:16

In the courts of the Roman Empire, those in power would hold huge feasts, which lasted for days. The finest food and the best wines would be served. The Romans ate and drank, taking great pleasure, and when they had had enough, they went into another room and induced vomiting to clear their stomaches. Then off to the food tables they went to start all over again.

Many years have passed since the last days of the Roman Empire upon this earth but the practice they were famous for is still going on today. It is called bulimia, and it is not just cultural practice; bulimia is an addiction.

Solomon, who wrote that there is nothing new under the sun, also wrote the warning above. Today, if you encounter honey, or chocolate, or candy, or whatever your weakness is, be careful. "Eat only as much as you need!" Otherwise, you could find yourself miserable. Out of physical need or the fear of getting fat or fatter, you may be tempted to induce vomiting like the Romans.

What a waste—acid in your mouth, food up your nose, vocal chords strained, watery eyes, nausea. Sometimes, eating only as much as you need may mean not eating at all.

Lord, I know that my addiction is a sign of sickness, either physical or emotional. Help me to know if I am going out of control. Help me, Lord.

> *So the elders of his house arose and
> went to him, to raise him up from the
> ground. But he would not, nor did he
> eat food with them.* —2 SAM. 12:17

David had just been visited by Nathan, the prophet,
who told him a story about a rich man and a poor man.
The rich man had many sheep, while the poor man
had one only which he loved dearly. The rich man, instead of using one of his many sheep, took the one
from the poor man to have at a feast for a visitor. After
David expressed his indignation at the rich man in the
story, Nathan told him, "You are the man" (2 Sam.
12:7). Nathan was speaking about David taking Uriah's
wife in adultery and of having Uriah killed in battle.

Upon hearing this, David refused to eat for seven
days. The guilt of what he had done drove out any desire for food.

Some people who have lost spouses or children have
starved themselves to death in grief. Starving becomes
a way of coping and avoiding. We must acknowledge
and confess the sin in our life. We need to let out the
pent-up grief we feel. If we cannot do it on our own, we
must seek out those who can help us.

Not eating because of grief can be natural but only
for a short time. Eating often means accepting reality
and getting on with our lives. If you are using food as a
means of coping with grief or anger, you are not coping; you are avoiding.

----

*Lord, give me the strength to take a look at my relationship with food
and go on with my life in the healthy way You want me to.*

*And you shall eat and not be
satisfied.* —LEV. 26:26

In this Scripture, Moses understood that you can have an abundance to eat and still not be satisfied.

Often when we are in doubt about what is best for us, or are torn between several options, we develop stress. Under stress, we can have a tendency to overeat and overdrink. The problem with this is the guilt and discomfort of weight gain only increases our stress.

In the opposite direction, the stress in our lives can lead to deciding to stop eating altogether. We feel more in control of uncontrollable circumstances if we maintain rigid control over our eating.

Both methods are highly ineffective. What we need to do is to seek to learn God's will in handling our problems. We can read it in His Word. We can pray for wisdom and discernment. We can pray for peace of mind while we consider our possibilities. We can seek the counsel of others.

Instead of relying on food to cope with the stress of life's situations, try these other options. A sympathetic friend is much more filling than a slice of pie. A hug from a family member leaves a better feeling than a large order of fries. The helpful counsel of a professional will do more to ease your mind than a quart of ice cream. The sense of control you feel when you actively seek answers to your problems leaves a better feeling than starving yourself all day.

Father, give me the food to be wise, to be honest and to trust in You.

> *Whoever has no rule over his own spirit*
> *Is like a city broken down without walls.*
> —PROV. 25:28

I have a friend who loves doughnuts. It seems to her that there is a doughnut store on every corner, in every mall. They call out to her while she is driving, promising sweet, warm delights just inside their doors. Often the invitation is more than she can resist. It would not be all that bad if she could stick to just one doughnut. Unfortunately, she has taken the saying "cheaper by the dozen" to heart.

One occasional doughnut will not have a long-term effect on anyone's weight. A dozen, eaten frequently, definitely will.

Another woman I know buys large boxes of candy bars. She tells herself she is saving money. In truth she wants a ready supply available whenever the urge for one hits her. She might not go to the store to buy just one. Buying by the box, she rationalizes that she can have all she wants and save money too.

Instead of saving money, they are both gaining weight.

Do you ever rationalize about the things you buy? Is your motive really to save money when you buy bulk quantities? And what do you buy that way—chips, candy bars, doughnuts? Next time try buying just one. It is a great way to save money and save yourself from excess weight.

———————

Lord, help me not to deceive myself about the food I buy.

Speak to the children of Israel, saying:
"You shall not eat any fat, of ox or sheep
or goat."
                                    —LEV. 7:23

Did you know that the federal government is interested in your health? Every food you buy must be labeled and meet certain governmental standards. Part of the information that must be on the package label is the fat content.

Have you ever wondered why God prohibited the eating of animal fat? The children of Israel were hardly as interested in their cholesterol level as we are today. They had never heard of hardening of the arteries or triple bypass heart surgery. The only reason they knew fat was bad to eat was that God did not want them to eat it.

Many of the food restrictions listed in the Bible have sound medical reasons that we can appreciate today.

God was interested in keeping His people healthy then, and He is just as concerned with your health today. It is part of His will that we treat our bodies well and eat food that is good for us. When we deliberately choose to harm our bodies we are not in His will.

Why should God care what we eat? After all, we are all going to die anyway. Why the big deal about don't eat this or eat only that? Because God made our bodies, He knows what works best. Isn't it about time we accepted His decisions?

Lord, I trust You for my strength and wisdom. Give me the wisdom to make the best choices and the strength to carry through with the decisions.

> *But instead, joy and gladness,*
> *Slaying oxen and killing sheep,*
> *Eating meat and drinking wine:*
> *"Let us eat and drink,*
> *   for tomorrow we die!"*
> —ISA. 22:13

God sent Isaiah to Jerusalem to warn the people of their impending doom. Instead of mourning, weeping, and begging God to change His mind, they decided to have a "going out of business" party, saying, "Let us eat and drink, for tomorrow we die."

There are many people today who have the same frame of mind. Instead of changing their destructive habits, they cling to them doggedly.

The smoker will say to himself, "You've got to die from something! Why not cigarettes?"

The overeater rationalizes, "What's wrong with being fat? I'll never die of starvation."

What is wrong with this line of thinking? Have you ever heard a smoker cough and wheeze in an attempt to get a breath? Have you ever watched an overweight person gasp for breath while attempting to walk up a flight of stairs?

We cannot live our lives as if death were going to solve all our problems. Instead, let us resolve to live here and now, today, to the best of our ability. Let's give up those dangerous habits that keep us from living today to the fullest.

Father, today is a new beginning. Help me to take care of myself so I can better serve You.

Death is swallowed up in victory.
—1 COR. 15:54

Jesus said to those who followed Him that we must die to ourselves. It sounds strange, doesn't it? How do we die to ourselves? For me, dying to myself meant first determining why I was self-destructive, so I could love myself, grasp life, and become whole. After I really knew who I was, then I could die to myself.

When I was self-consumed with my body, food and dieting, I was into only *me*. I thought only about me—what I wanted, what could fulfill me. I needed help desperately. God opened the door for me to get the right kind of help. Then I started to live. I started to love me. When I learned to love me, I learned I could love others as well.

The first time I shared my story with others I died to myself. I felt God needed me to tell it, and after I did, I have been overwhelmed by the needs of those around me. By helping a lost person, by touching an unloved person, by seeking out those who need someone to talk to, I think of others instead of just me. I have found that through dying to myself, I really do live.

There are times when a need arises and I think, I don't want to do this, God. But I do it anyway. After I give of myself, I feel so good. Dying to yourself means being a servant instead of being the "monster."

Be a servant today. Be alive!

God, help me to die to me. It's so hard, God. I live in a "me" world, but God, help me to love in Your world. Help me to live for You by giving to others.

*For if we live, we live to the Lord; and
if we die, we die to the Lord. Therefore,
whether we live or die, we are the Lord's.*
—ROM. 14:8

As we reach for the goal of dying to self, let us also take care of ourselves. Sometimes we translate dying to ourselves to mean we shouldn't take care of ourselves. That isn't what God intends.

After I went public with my story and was so overwhelmed with the needs of hurting and desperate people, I felt an intense drive to do everything for everyone. It reached the point where I could not sleep. All I thought about was helping others.

"Slow down, Cynthia," my therapist firmly told me. "You're not everyone's savior. First you must take care of you. Think 'balance.' If you don't, you won't be up to helping anyone before long."

He was right, of course. It took me a while to learn how to balance my life. The people I help have to save themselves. I cannot do it for them. I have to let go of that person and give him to God. Dying to myself does not mean getting so drained I make myself sick.

Jesus Himself took the time to rest, pray, slow down.

Maybe you feel as if you cannot give anymore. If you do, it may mean you are giving too much. Take a step back and take time for you. It is OK to take care of yourself too.

*God, we get frazzled sometimes and think we have to save everyone.
We have to remember that You are the Savior. Use us, God, but help
us to understand our role.*

And he prayed that he might die, and said,
"It is enough! Now, LORD, take my life."
—1 KINGS 19:4

Are you tired of being obsessed with calories? Are you weary of always feeling bad about how you look? Maybe you are in therapy and it is so hard to face your pain, you wonder if you are going to make it.

I remember times when I did not want to get out of bed because I felt so bad about me. There were many days I asked God to take my life.

I believe the story about Elijah in 1 Kings makes it clear that he was depressed. He had fled from the wicked queen, Jezebel. He was burned out, scared, dog-tired. All his friends had been brutally murdered, and he was next. He was tired of the good guys taking a beating. Elijah cried out to God in a weary voice, pleading with God to take his life.

The story goes on to say that Elijah slept, and when he woke up an angel said to him, "Arise and eat." Before him was a baked cake and a jar of water. He ate and drank and laid down again. He did this for several days, just eating, drinking and resting. Then one day he got up and was ready to continue doing God's work.

Even prophets of God get tired and depressed. Rest and good food were what Elijah needed. God knew this and made sure he got what he needed.

What about you? Are you tired or depressed? Give it to the Lord. Talk about it. Rest and replenish your body. God understands and He will be there for you.

Lord, please replenish me and fill my emptiness.

> *Then the man said, "The woman whom You gave*
> *to be with me, she gave me of the tree, and*
> *I ate."*
> —GEN. 3:12

Recently I spoke at a church service and afterwards a beautiful young mother approached me with tears in her eyes. Her name is Janet. We sat down together in a quiet place and she told me her story. She was ten pounds overweight and her husband hated it.

"He tells me if I'd just lose my ten pounds he wouldn't have such a problem with lust."

"Passing the buck" is not new. Adam tried it in Eden.

While talking with her it became clear that Janet's husband had problems stemming from his childhood. Her husband's dad had told him, "You'll never amount to anything." To prove his father wrong, he became a successful businessman and married a beautiful wife. When Janet put on the extra ten pounds she ceased being beautiful to him. He has a problem with lust for other women and refuses to take responsibility.

Janet loves her husband. She does not love herself. If she did, she would have the strength to say to her husband, "My ten pounds is not the cause of your problems! You need to get help!" If she loved herself she would be able to love him better.

Is someone displacing their problems on you? Are you blaming your problems on someone else? God does not hold us responsible for the sins of others.

Father, help me to not live for others. Help me to live for You.

Let the lying lips be put to silence,
Which speak insolent things proudly
and contemptuously against the
righteous. —PS. 31:18

Sometimes speaking with the people I meet is like opening up a Pandora's box. One thing after another comes pouring out, often heartbreaking events they have never shared with anyone else. It was that way with Janet. She told me her husband prayed she would become bulimic or anorexic to lose her extra weight. She then revealed issues she was not dealing with.

Janet's father abandoned her and her mom. Her mom married another man who sexually abused Janet's sisters. Their mother knew but did nothing. His abuse took other forms as well. At mealtimes he would force Janet to fill her plate to overflowing with food. As she started to eat, he would say to her, "You're such a pig! You're going to look just like one!"

Janet grew up being abused and married someone who abused her too. She has never stopped long enough to recognize the pattern in her life.

I think about all the other Janets, the ones who do not come up to talk to me, or who do not ever get the chance. Are you a Janet, walking around with a Pandora's box full of unresolved conflicts and hurts in your life? If you are, it is time to open the box and expose that painful past to the fresh air of healing. Janet took a risk and talked to me. Find someone with whom you can open up. Please, don't wait too long.

Father, help the Janets of this world find a safe place to open up.

> *To everything there is a season,*
> *A time for every purpose under*
> *heaven. . . .*
> *A time to gain,*
> *And a time to lose.*
> —ECCL. 3:1, 6

You are looking in the mirror and those pants just do not fit the way they used to. The band around the waist pinches, and the fabric around the thighs just keeps getting stretched a little more each month. Sucking in your stomach does not work as well as it did. You do not even want to look in the back. It is decision time.

God reminds us there is a time for everything, even gaining and losing. You have gained it; now it is time to lose it. But you are finding it so hard to do by yourself. That is OK. There are ways you can do it with the help of others. Many programs are available to give you the personal support you need. Of course, these might cost money that you do not have. Perhaps you can find a friend who will agree to work with you. It means you will have to open yourself up to that person and reveal a little bit of yourself.

Each of us reaches a point where we know it is time we did something about our weight. There are very few of us who will be able to do it on our own. Most of us will need others to help us. If you are smart, you will go to God for it. The last time I checked, He didn't charge.

Lord, help me to understand that now is the time for me to take control over my weight. I need Your help and support.

> *Therefore, my beloved, as you have always obeyed,
> not as in my presence only, but now much more in
> my absence, work out your own salvation with fear
> and trembling; for it is God who works in you both
> to will and to do for His good pleasure.*
>
> —PHIL. 2:12–13

Every person who makes radical changes in their lives must take the first few steps. The first step is to decide to change when you are tired of the way things are. You have to make up your mind to change.

The second step to change is to *do* something about the way things are. God works through both thought and action. He "works in you both to *will* and to *do* for His good pleasure." Through His word He helps us to be able to see and understand the need for change. His Holy Spirit lives inside us to help bring conviction to our hearts and minds.

Next, God gives us the ability to take the action we have decided on. He does not help us understand the need for change only to abandon us without the help and support we need to accomplish the change. God is a transforming God. It is "His good pleasure" that we constantly change for the better!

We do not struggle alone. We labor together with God. He is ready and willing to help as we "work out our own salvation." It is up to us to decide and to act if we are going to change. Yet we can be sure that God promises to be there with us.

God, work in me as I make the decisions that will get my life under control.

> *When I remember You on my bed,*
> *I meditate on You in the night watches.*
> *Because You have been my help,*
> *Therefore in the shadow of Your wings*
> *I will rejoice.*
> —PS. 63:6–7

Only the lonely know the way I feel tonight," Roy Orbison sang. Country songs have a way of expressing deep truths in a simple way. Some people I know are "social butterflies." They love parties, gatherings, anywhere there are people. They excel at chit-chat.

There are others I know for whom socializing is a nightmare to be avoided at all costs. People frighten them. New situations present a complex set of dangers to be negotiated only with the greatest care.

I have felt both ways. There have been times in my life when I loved being with people. But as my bulimia reached its later stages, I began to withdraw.

I was sick and lonely. Snickers bars, chocolate cake, pecan pies—those were my friends then. These "friends" were killing me, but no one seemed to understand. "Only the lonely know the way I feel," I thought. That is why I did not share my "monster" with anyone.

How many of us have felt weighted down by despair at some time in our life? "Only the lonely" may number a lot more than we think.

Are you hesitating to talk to someone because you don't think they will understand? You may be surprised. Give them a chance. Making friends sometimes involves great risk. The reward can be great.

God, help me to seek people to share my life with.

And do not lead us into temptation.
—MATT. 6:13

On one occasion when I flew home to Oklahoma City for a speaking engagement, Dad picked me up at the airport. As we were driving to his home, he told me he was going to buy me the most delicious morsel I had ever put in my mouth. We pulled up to the restaurant, got out, and Dad proceeded to order fried peaches.

"Wait a minute," I protested. "Fried peaches?"

The order arrived, and it did not take me long to get over my initial hesitation. Each slice was deep-fried in a crispy batter, and they came with a sauce made of sour cream, brown sugar, and cinnamon. They were about the best thing I had ever tasted.

Now every time I fly home to see my parents I stop off at that restaurant. In this way I created my habit of fried peaches. I am lucky that restaurant is far from where I live now. What is your habit? A friend of mine has a doughnut habit. Unhappily for her, there is a doughnut store around every corner.

It is staring you in the face! What do you do? Take another way home. Use another store. Eat before you go shopping. Don't put your mind on automatic pilot. Be aware of your habit and be smart about it. Yes, it is all right for me to have fried peaches when I go home, and it is OK for my friend to have a doughnut, now and then.

Lord, help me to enjoy the delicious morsels You have put on this earth, but to be smart in my enjoyment of them.

> *But if you have bitter envy and self-seeking in your hearts, do not boast and lie against the truth.*
> —JAMES 3:14

When tragedy strikes our lives, sometimes we scream at the top of our lungs, "No, this can't be!" or "Tell me I'm dreaming!" The denial of some people is so acute they cannot even weep at the funeral of a loved one.

It is that way with an eating disorder. We will deny our eating disorder to ourselves and to others for as long as we can, sometimes to our last breath. I have counseled anorexics who weigh seventy-five pounds or less, and who will look up at me with the wide eyes of the starving and insist they do not have a problem with food.

Denying serious problems is a natural reaction. Doctors tell us that people faced with a terminal illness go through a process that includes denial. We think that if we deny the truth, it will simply go away. Not all denial is bad for us, however. Denial can give us the cushion we need to get over the initial shock.

Facing the truth can be an excruciating experience, yet it is vitally necessary if we are going to get on with our lives. I have known of several people who denied their problem to the bitter end.

What are you denying about yourself?

Lord, help me to face the reality of my disorder, and let it out to those who are able to help me.

Do not remember the sins of my youth,
  nor my transgressions;
According to Your mercy remember me.
  —PS. 25:7

An addiction creates such great losses in your life. The loss of love. The loss of friendships. The loss of opportunities. After my hospitalization I was well on the road to wholeness. Yet there were times when I felt overwhelmed with sadness thinking about all those years wasted because I was obsessed with my body. I felt as if I lost my young adulthood. I felt I lost the prime time of my youth. I grieved over the loss of relationships that never were. I grieved because my fears overshadowed my dreams.

As I grieved over missed opportunities and friends, I realized I also had to forgive, mostly for the wasted years. I had to grieve and forgive myself so I could go on.

If you are caught up in the frenzy of food and dieting, you can stop too. Take the time to think about what you're giving up, what you're losing. Take a risk and get help.

Today you have the opportunity to quit losing and start winning. Don't let it pass.

Show me Your ways, O LORD;
Teach me Your paths.
—PS. 25:4

As I walk this road called life, I am constantly reminded that God and I are not in synch. His timing is not my timing. While I've had to grieve over the loss of my youth to bulimia, I stand amazed at how our God is one of healing. He isn't a God who stays in the past; He's a God of healing and He renews each day.

As time passed after my therapy, as wounds healed and as my life changed in a productive, wondrous way, I began to feel so alive. It was as if God had wiped the slate clean. He had taken away the grief, the past pain, and said, "Here, Cynthia, the slate is clean. Start over." Today I rejoice because, as time has gone by, I've recognized the past hurt but I took responsibility to change and I can start over.

God is a "start over" God. He doesn't remind us of how bad we were. He wants us to know how good we can be. He wants us to trust Him.

As you change and grow, know today that He wipes the slate clean each day and gives us the loving opportunity to start over.

Father, thank You for the chance to start over each day. Thank You for loving us and concentrating on our todays, not on the past.

*Wait for the LORD, and He will
save you.* —PROV. 20:22

Peter tells us, "But beloved, do not forget this one thing, that one day with the Lord is as a thousand years and a thousand years as one day" (2 Peter 3:8). It sure seemed that way to me at times during my bulimia.

You may be in the midst of the battle and crying out to God, "Help me!" But you hear no answer. I understand.

When I was sixteen there wasn't even a name for the binge-purge cycle. I was too immature to know this was not normal behavior. When I was twenty-three, I was caught shoplifting peanuts by an undercover cop. I realized something was wrong, but I couldn't find anyone to understand. At twenty-five I was into my career and I thought surely I could beat this thing by myself. I didn't rely too much on God. By the time I was twenty-eight I was desperate, but I denied how bad it was. I went on with life until my body and my mind broke down. At that point, I surrendered and gave up the idea of doing it myself. I said, "Only God can help me."

Through it all I feel God was saying, "When you're ready to give up control, then I'll know you're ready."

Waiting on God's timing is difficult to do. Yet somehow we've got to believe that there is a purpose in feeling stuck in the waiting room. God could be with us in that waiting room, waiting for the moment when we're ready to get up and open the door.

God, waiting on You is so hard when I want the answer now. Help me to trust You when You say "wait."

> *And we know that all things work together*
> *for good to those who love God, to those*
> *who are the called according to His purpose.*
> —ROM. 8:28

God is planning for our lives even when we don't realize it. I look at my twelve years with bulimia, and during that time I was a successful TV news reporter. I believe He was allowing me to learn to communicate so He could use that gift. The timing of my downfall was at a point in my life when I gave up the control. As a result I had to totally rely on God to give me strength. I was so far down, the only way to get out was to go up.

In the psychiatric ward He opened my blind eyes to see why people hurt and behaved destructively. God was planning for me to serve Him. He didn't coerce me or force me, yet He gave me every opportunity to learn from my experiences. Because of all the struggles I've been through, I'm more compassionate, more understanding. I have learned the answers to some of the questions so many people ask. To be honest, I wouldn't want to go back through the same experiences, but I praise God for taking what was bad in my life and using it for something good.

He will do the same for you. He doesn't play favorites. He promises that if we love Him all things work together for good.

Believe the promise.

Father, help me to look to You to be the Author of my life.

*But Jesus said, 'Let the little children
come to Me, and do not forbid them; for
of such is the kingdom of heaven.*
—MATT. 19:14

My niece Danielle and I are buddies. When she was three, I rented a house on the beach, and Danielle and her five-year-old brother, Uriah, came to spend the night with me. We had a great time playing on the beach. Uriah finally fell asleep.

"Danielle," I asked, looking out at the waves, "who made the ocean?"

With the assurance only a three year old can muster, she answered, "Uriah."

"Well, who made the blue sky?" I asked, smiling to myself.

"Uriah," she answered.

"What about the moon and the stars, Danielle?"

Her answer didn't change. "Uriah," she told me.

At three years old Danielle looked up to Uriah. He was her big brother. She not only thought he hung the moon, she thought he made it!

God wants us to have the faith of children. He wants us to believe in Him like Danielle believed in Uriah. He wants us to believe He's bigger than anything we face.

How big is your God? As big as the ocean? As bright as the stars? Does He fill up your sky? Have you put God in a box, and can't understand why He won't help you. Let Him out. Let Him fill up your world.

Father, help me trust You to care for me.

> *If anyone comes to Me and does not hate*
> *his father and mother, wife and children,*
> *brothers and sisters, yes, and his own life*
> *also, he cannot be My disciple.*
> —LUKE 14:26

From birth we are taught to love and respect our parents, brothers, and sisters. We then are taught to extend that love and respect to our grandparents, uncles, aunts, and cousins. One big happy family.

But what happens when that love is turned into horror? What happens when we're sexually abused by an uncle, or our mother yells at us and calls us trash? We're trained to protect our family name. We never talk about what happens behind closed doors.

Dad is drunk? Keep it quiet! Mom beats you? Wear long sleeves and tell lies about falling down stairs. Uncle John likes to fondle your sister? Shove the terror behind the locked door and throw away the key.

Old habits are hard to break. But what happens when the horror of those secrets continues to intrude on the present? Keeping the secret damages the family more in the long run. You've got to let someone know. Find someone to talk to.

It's wonderful to have pride in our family. There is no pride in abuse. If you're afraid of the "hurt" that would be done to your family if you tell the secrets, just think about how much hurt has already been done. If you don't tell, neither you nor your family will get any better.

Lord, give me the courage to see that the light of truth is greater than the darkness of denial.

> *But they all with one accord began to make excuses.* —LUKE 14:18

It's so easy to deny reality and make excuses for our overweight condition. We say, "I'm a natural size sixteen." "I'm big boned." "All my family has large frames." "I'm perfectly happy with my size; why should others care?" "Fat people have more fun." "It's just my metabolism."

For the most part, these are lies and we use them to deny our real condition.

Big bones do not produce fat.

Big frames can easily carry a normal weight.

Others care because they know that overly fat people are usually unhappy.

How much fun can it be to have to wedge your body into a theater or airline seat? Is it really more fun to sit on the sidelines and watch other people participate in sports? It isn't more fun to huff and puff trying to tie your shoes, or having to bear the brunt of fat jokes.

It is true that some people have a genetic predisposition to gaining weight, but that isn't an excuse to become obese. These people must take special care in how they eat, just like people with family histories of heart disease or diabetes have to be careful in what and how they eat. Denial won't save their lives.

Dear Father, help me to rid my mind of the excuses I use to deny my weight problem. Help me to get on the path to recovery and better health.

> *For forty years I was grieved with that generation.*
> —PS. 95:10

God was ticked off with the Israelites. All they'd done since He rescued them from slavery was whine and complain. Then they had the audacity to make and worship the golden image of a calf. They practically slapped God in the face. He reacted pretty much as we might expect. "He swore in His wrath, 'They shall not enter my rest.'" God got really mad.

Were you ever allowed to be mad when you were a kid? Are you allowed to be angry now? Or do the people around you tell you to "calm down"?

In my house, if we got mad, Dad would cool us off by throwing a cup of water in our face. "Nice children don't shout." So we'd pout. "Nice children don't pout either." And then there was the ever popular "Children are to be seen and not heard." If we were mistreated by a teacher, a coach, or a mean kid on the playground, we were told to "take it like a man!" We weren't allowed to express our anger, so we stuffed it deep inside. By the time we hit puberty, we were dealing with our anger through food.

Paul said, "Be angry and do not sin." Jesus said, "If your brother sins tell him his fault between you and him alone." In other words, it's OK to be mad. You don't have to stuff it anymore. You don't have to starve it anymore. It's time to get out your anger in a healthy way and get on with your life.

Father, forgive me when I stuff my anger. Help me to express it and get on with the day.

We know that we have passed from death to life, because we love the brethren. He who does not love his brother abides in death.

—1 JOHN 3:14

What do you mean, I'm in denial? Who are you to judge me? Who made you my keeper?

God made me your keeper. It's part of His plan that we care for one another. Part of that caring sometimes comes through painful confrontation.

When I was bulimic, no one knew but one friend. No one took the time to get to know me well enough to peel through the layers of my protection and confront me with the truth. I would have vehemently denied it.

We're taught to be self-sufficient from the time we're born. "Be the captain of your own ship and the maker of your own destiny," we're told.

But sometimes we're doing such a poor job with our lives that we need someone to interfere. We need someone to stop long enough to see we're having trouble.

Has someone tried to confront you with the problems in your life? What was your response? Do you think he or she will try again after how you responded the first time?

Have you seen friends in trouble? Have you tried to help? If they didn't respond as you wanted, will you try again?

We need to be concerned and care for one another. We're all in this together.

Father, help me to be open to a friend's constructive criticism and to learn from it.

> Coming to Him as to a living stone, rejected
> indeed by men, but chosen by God and precious,
> you also, as living stones, are being
> built up a spiritual house. . . .
> —1 PETER 2:4–5

Jenny was outwardly beautiful. Inside, however, there were self-hatred and many questions. Her dad had abused her. Her mother never protected her. As a young adult, Jenny searched for love with abusive men. She was once engaged, but her fiancé dumped her. She vowed she would never be hurt again. She turned to food; now she's obese.

Jenny has a good job and many people love her, but she doesn't like herself. She wants to be accepted the way she is—obese. Recently she saw a hat with words on it that said, "Save the whales, harpoon a fat chick." She cringed—the message was so typical. "If you're fat," she said, "you're not acceptable. Whales are more important than people."

She readily admits, "I'm hiding under my fat, daring people to love me. If they later reject me, I can always believe they left because I'm fat."

The world rejects Jenny because of how she looks. Jenny rejects Jenny because of how she looks. God will never reject Jenny because of how she looks. He knows all about rejection. He was perfect. Yet He was despised, spit upon, and nailed to a cross.

If you feel rejected by the world, remember you have a Lord who understands.

I have become the ridicule of all my
people,
And their taunting song all the day.
—LAM. 3:14

The brain is like a tape player. It records everything. The playback of messages is too often negative, even from family. "If you were thin the boys would knock down the door." "You realize that baked potato would be better for you if you wouldn't have the butter and sour cream." "You have such a pretty face. You would be beautiful if you could lose some weight."

And then there are the flashbacks of what strangers say. Children stare and say, "Mommy, look at that fat lady." Two teenagers whisper to each other, "I'll never get fat like that lady."

Jenny feels as if they are holding back all their love until she loses the weight. So she keeps it on, forcing them to love her the way she is.

Jenny blames her weight on their unacceptance. But she does not accept herself, either. Jenny is allowing those negative messages to control her.

It is wonderful to know that God is a God of positive messages. He tells us over and over again how much He loves us. He not only tells us He loves us, but also He showed us by sending His Son to die for us. What greater proof do we need?

Father, help me to listen to Your words and not to the words of the world. Help me to know that You love me just the way I am and that You only want the best for me.

> *Behold, I say to you, lift up your eyes*
> *and look at the fields . . .*
> —JOHN 4:35

After I learned why I was bulimic, it dawned on me that if I kept my eating disorder a secret for twelve years, there probably were others just like me.

When I finally got help, very little was known about my disorder. Bulimia had not yet become a household word. After I made my decision to go public, the local newspaper ran an excellent account on the front page of my battle.

I was not prepared for the deluge of contact from others suffering from eating disorders. I heard from bulimics who were married to doctors, and whose husbands did not know they were bulimic. Dietitians, secretaries, and housewives all called me to share accounts of their addiction. I was overwhelmed with the stories and their desperate need for answers. Because of all the calls, I set a time and invited all those who called to come and hear my story. Around one hundred people came. Parents came who had bulimic daughters. A lawyer brought his wife. Single women came.

As I told about how bad my life was, what it took to get help, and the pain of therapy, I looked out in the audience and saw tears running down faces. My narrative gave hope and answers. It let them know they were not alone and that there was a name for what they did.

Father, help me to name my struggle and to see it for what it is. Help me to have hope.

. . . for they are already white for harvest.
—JOHN 4:35

God used what I had been through to help others. When I look back to my news reporting days and my communication skills, I see how God was preparing a ministry for me. Now I lecture full-time, sharing my story in a firsthand way, giving answers and hope.

The first time I rented that lecture hall and invited people to come hear my story, I had no idea that my life would change as it has. I only knew that if I could give hope to someone struggling as I had, it would give purpose to my struggle.

Today, I want to encourage you, if you have struggled and overcome, to seek one person who is struggling and reach out. You may be that one person who will help save a life. You may be the one person who can break through the shell of denial and help lead that person to the truth of her addiction.

The field is white. There are so many out there hurting; they need someone to take an interest in them, someone to say, "Hang on! There is hope. Let me tell you what I've been through." I believe Jesus can use your past pain to touch a lost life. God can and will use you if you allow Him.

_____

Father, today, use me to touch a hurting soul. Thank You for being there for me when I was down. Help me to be there for someone else. May I touch someone today as You have touched me.

> *So Jesus answered and said, "Were there not*
> *ten cleansed? But where are the nine?"*
> —LUKE 17:17

When you open your heart to the world, look out. I have learned when you deal with hurting, unwell people, a lot of things can happen. My most painful experience has been the transference of anger.

Many of the people I encountered in my ministry sought help at the Minirth-Meier Clinic. I thought they would be like me after they worked through their issues, rejoicing and thankful for a new chance at life and wholeness. Instead, they were angry people, angry at me because I had urged them into a collision course with their painful past.

Now I realize how Jesus must have felt after He healed the ten lepers, and only one thanked Him.

But as I struggled with my hurt feelings, I felt a tug on my heart. The voice said, "Who are you doing this for? For the gratitude of other people, or for Me?" I promised myself, It does not matter if I never hear a thank you from anyone; I will tell my story of hope in the name of the Lord.

Perhaps you feel alone in your ministry, or maybe even close friends or family never say thank you for all your efforts. Know that Jesus is saying thank you to you. When we give love and it is not returned, Jesus knows and is waiting with His thanks.

Jesus, thank You for saving me. Thank You for loving me when no one else does. Lord, please help me to know You love me as I do Your will.

For to this end we both labor and suffer reproach,
because we trust in the living God, who is the
Savior of all men, especially of those who believe.
—1 TIM. 4:10

In therapy I learned that I was trying to be the savior of my family. I took on the role of savior early in my life because there were so many conflicts going on. My dad was consumed with work. Mom suffered from health problems and depression. My brother was rebellious and always in trouble. As a child I felt a deep need to save the family and to make everything better. I became the perfect child who did no wrong.

I also became bulimic and attempted a form of slow suicide because I was mad at my family for making me feel as if I needed to save them. As I worked through my anger, I had to let go of trying to be the savior. Somebody else already had the job. Trying to take on the role was preventing me from living for God.

I had to learn the truth that Jesus is their Savior. I had to stop dying for everyone else and start living for me. My sacrifice was not needed or required. He died on the cross for my mom and my dad, for my brother, and for all the hurting people who come to me for help.

The burden of saving the world has been lifted from my shoulders, where I imagined it was, and put squarely where it belongs, with Jesus.

Are you dying for someone you love? Stop. Give the job to Jesus, because He has already done it.

Jesus, help me to serve You, and as I serve other people, help me to know that I do it for You and not for me.

But indeed, O man, who are you to reply against God? Will the thing formed say to him who formed it, "Why have you made me like this?"

—ROM. 9:20

We all like to have someone else to point the finger at, don't we? We want to be able to say, "It's their fault." "They" can be our parents, our spouse, our children or our fellow church members. Blaming someone else takes the pressure off us.

Some of us even blame God for the way we are. We say to ourselves, This is just the way God made me. If there is something wrong, then it's His fault! While it is true that all of us are made in the image of God, we have made a few modifications to His original design.

We were created by God for His glory. Each of us is *unique*. We often forget we are *special* too. Our voices, fingerprints, and footprints all are different. God even knows the different number of hairs on our heads.

God made us, but He does not control us like robots. We choose to be depressed or obsessed with food.

We can use our bodies for God's glory, or we can abuse those same bodies through the choices we make. Instead of blaming God for our wrong choices, we should praise Him for the bodies He has given us, and petition Him for the help we need to get our bodies back into healthy condition.

God bore the punishment of our sins when His Son's earthly body suffered on the cross. Let us start taking the responsibility for our own bodies.

Lord, thank You that You made me with the power of choice. Help me to make the right choices.

For bodily exercise profits a little, but godliness is profitable for all things, having promise of the life that now is and of that which is to come.
—1 TIM. 4:8

During the past several years, store fronts in malls across this country have undergone a transformation. Out with the doughnut shop, the dry cleaner, and the stationery store, and in with the fitness center. Scores of women and men appear there regularly, wearing leotards, tights, shorts, and gym shoes, determined to shape up their bodies.

Flatten that stomach! Firm those thighs! Obliterate those saddlebags! Not only are tremendous amounts of energy expended toward this goal, but also money and time. For some, the pursuit of fitness almost becomes a religion. In fact, many work harder at working out than at working out their salvation!

Exercise is profitable. The Bible says so. It profits us here and now. Exercise helps us to keep our bodies in working order. But if we concentrate on that to the exclusion of our spiritual health, we are missing out. The apostle Paul did not say not to exercise and keep yourself in shape; he said do not neglect your soul for the sake of your body. You only have the body on a short-term lease anyway.

Father, help me to be disciplined in exercising this body You have given me. Help me to understand I need to keep it in shape so I can work for You. But, Father, help me to remember that I need to exercise my spirit as well. Help me to get my soul in shape so I can better serve You, my family, and those around me.

> *So she caught him and kissed him . . .*
> *"I have peace offerings with me;*
> *Today I have paid my vows.*
> *So I came out to meet you . . .*
> *Come, let us take our fill of love until morning."*
> —PROV. 7:13–18

The harlot knew just how to seduce. She promised a good time without guilt. She had already brought the peace offerings she needed to make to the Lord for those sins. She thought she could do what she wanted as long as she paid for it.

But in verse twenty-five Solomon warned, "Do not let your heart turn aside to her ways."

It is easy to get caught in this kind of trap. Many of us go ahead and eat rich food thinking tomorrow I'll diet.

Dieting is our penance for overeating. We also do the opposite—starve ourselves so we can have the reward of indulging. The extreme of this starve-to-eat game is the binge-then-purge nightmare of bulimia.

Are you on that roller coaster of starving and indulging? Do you eat rich, sugary foods and justify it by starving yourself the rest of the day? Do you diet for days just to indulge at some special event? Your body deserves better. Your body needs nutritious, regular meals consisting of a moderate amount of food. Remember, you are along for whatever ride your body is on; you will feel the effects of a stable, healthy road, or a wild, uncontrolled journey.

Father, I need balance in my life. Help me to understand my needs.

*For He satisfies the longing soul,
And fills the hungry soul with
goodness.* —PS. 107:9

We are made in the image of our eternal, all-knowing God. He is the source of life, light, and all that sustains us. Embedded within our hearts is the need to be filled with His love, power, and goodness.

All of us have that nostalgic desire to go back to our roots, to walk through the rooms of our youth, to visit schools we have attended. We enjoy reliving the past.

We go back, only to find the ceiling is not as high as we remember; the room is not as big; the path is not as long. Only the trees have grown. Sometimes we discover that what we are looking for is not there anymore.

For most of us, there comes a time when we desire to go back to our spiritual roots. We seek God. He created us for greatness. God wants us to be His children. He wants our paths to be straight. He wants us to enjoy the cool waters, the green pastures, the quiet streams. He promises safe passage back to where cups overflow and there is goodness and mercy.

Living with God means the deepest longings of our souls will be met. The greatest hunger of our hearts will be filled. As we search for our roots, let us determine to go back to the very source of our being. Only there, with our Father, can we be truly satisfied.

Father, guide me back to You. Guide me back to Your love. Help me to turn to You to fill myself up.

> *A satisfied soul loathes the honeycomb,*
> *But to a hungry soul every bitter*
> *thing is sweet.* —PROV. 27:7

Solomon was right on target. Not only was the honeycomb filled with delicious honey, but also the honeycomb itself was good to suck on.

We do not suck on honeycomb today, but from the time we are born we have our share of things put into our mouths. Some mothers start their babies off with pacifiers. The child cries, and in goes the pacifier. The child learns that when she cries, something popped into her mouth will make her feel better.

The pacifier or the bottle soon get replaced with a piece of gum or candy. Often, parents use these to avoid the real reason the child is complaining in the first place. The child learns that having something in her mouth stalls dealing with a problem. So many of us start off in life sucking or chewing our "honeycomb." Once that pattern is set, it is hard to change. As we get older and have more control over what we eat, the pacifier or piece of candy becomes anything sweet.

We need to grow up. We need to recognize that childhood pattern and take the adult responsibility of changing it. If our problems are beyond us, we need to find someone who can help us.

———————

Lord, give me the understanding I need to change bad habits. Help me to turn to you and to others instead of something sweet when I have a problem.

And when those came who were hired about the eleventh hour, they each received a denarius.

—MATT. 20:9

Jesus told a story about a wealthy landowner who went out early in the morning to hire workers for his vineyard. He kept returning later in the day for more workers. Those he hired in the morning who worked all day received the same wage as those he hired late in the day. Naturally, there were some complaints about fairness. The ones who had worked a full day resented those who had only worked a few hours.

But Jesus reminded his listeners and us that those who had worked all day agreed to work for the wage they were paid. He also reminded us that it was the landowner's money—he can do whatever he wants with it.

Instead of dwelling on what seems to be an unfair situation, we need to rejoice at the mercy of God. When we turn to God, even late in life, the reward is the same as if we had always followed Him. The promise can perhaps be stated, "It's never too late."

How many of us use the excuse, "It's too late to change." So we do not even try.

It is never too late to start taking care of yourself. It is never too late to give up a bad habit. And it is never too late to stop living for yourself and start living for God. The rewards will still be there.

Lord, help me to know the power to change is still there, and to instill in me the will to improve my life.

I, therefore, the prisoner of the Lord, beseech you to have a walk worthy of the calling with which you were called, with all lowliness and gentleness, with longsuffering.
—EPH. 4:1–2

There are times when I just do not want to change. I do not want to do better and I do not appreciate people trying to make me change. I have reasons for the way I am. Do you ever feel this way? When I do, I want those around me to accept my reasons and to leave me alone. I want them to be longsuffering with me, even if they do not understand why I feel the way I do, and even if my actions hurt them.

What about when the shoe is on the other foot, and it is my turn to put up with a sullen spouse or a friend who really does not want to talk? I want those around me to go the second mile with me, but I have trouble going the second mile for them. Too many times, I want to shake them and try to make them better. It is hard for me to remember that, just like me, they may need to be left alone.

Each of us has a time in our lives when we need the people around us to give us a break. That requires patience and longsuffering. It does not mean you care about that person any less; you are just giving them the time they need to work it out by themselves. Some tasks are better done alone.

Lord, give me the wisdom to know when to seek the help of others and when I need to work through my problems alone with You. Help me to be as patient with others as I ask them to be with me.

*But the fruit of the Spirit is . . .
kindness.*   —GAL. 5:22

A song I know declares, "Show a little bit of love and kindness." The more I live in this world, the more I realize we do not need a *little* kindness; we need a lot. Sin and its ravages are everywhere. There are places in this world where children grow up never knowing peace. War and death are all they know.

The United States may not be at war with another nation, but there is a war being fought in the streets with drugs and violent crime. Our homes are no longer a safe haven from the world; abuse and domestic violence intrude even into that sanctuary.

Where does kindness fit into this picture? There is a lot in the world that we are powerless to change. But what we *can* do is be committed to treating others with kindness. We can make the decision to treat those around us as we want to be treated. God has given His love to us. We can spread it around a little.

And while we are spreading it around, let us not forget to save a little for ourselves. It is very difficult to love those around us if we do not first love ourselves.

Be good to yourself. Learning to love yourself frees you to extend that love to others. The source of that love is God. If God, knowing you better than you know yourself, still loves you, how can you not love yourself? Trust Him. He has not made any mistakes.

Father, open my heart to be kind to those who come into my life.

> *Come to Me, all you who labor and are*
> *heavy laden, and I will give you rest.*
> —MATT. 11:28

In the days of Christ, just about everyone was a laborer. The average man and woman of that time lived a life of hard work. There were slaves during that time whose lot was even harder. How much Jesus' words must have meant to them!

Our lives are not as rough today, but His words are still true. Today, we face mental and spiritual burdens, which in some ways are much harder to bear than mere physical labor. In our society, we are taught "if you want something done right, do it yourself." We struggle under the weight of trying to earn our own salvation.

Christ died to free us from that burden. We are not under a law, but under grace. We have the freedom to change and grow and make mistakes. Our God does not expect perfection from us.

That thought really helps me when I feel down on myself for something I have done, or did not do, or said, or did not say. In those times, it is a great comfort to know I am forgiven. It gives me the courage to pick myself up and do better. Whether it is in my relationship with God or with other people, in the way I treat others or the way I treat myself, it is good to know God understands. Rest replaces anxiety. I can rest on His promises. I can rest in His love. I can rest.

Father, thank You for allowing me to give You all my worries and burdens. Thank You for giving me rest.

*Therefore do not worry about tomorrow, for
tomorrow will worry about its own things.
Sufficient for the day is its own trouble.*
                                    —MATT. 6:34

The old saying, "Never borrow trouble from tomorrow," is a lot easier in principle than in practice. Yet it is the principle that Jesus wanted us to understand, no matter how hard it is to put into practice. Before He said these words, He assured us of God's concern for us and His ability to provide for our needs.

Jesus did not tell us never to plan, or never to strive toward a future goal. He did not want us to lie around, doing nothing for ourselves. The point Jesus made is God is in control, and worrying about a future that may never come is counterproductive.

There is great peace to be found in giving our future to God and approaching each day as a gift from Him, unencumbered by the mistakes of the past or the uncertainty of tomorrow.

Do you live in the past? Are you consumed with what will happen next? Then you are not living for today. Yesterday is gone and tomorrow is not a guarantee. All we have is today. It is a gift for which we should be grateful.

When I was bulimic, each day was a battle. Now that I am well, life is wonderful. Each day is something special. I still have hard days as does anyone, but my focus is no longer on my past.

Lord, help me to live for today, not in the past, or waiting for the future. Help me to live one day at a time. I gladly put my tomorrows in Your hands. I gladly give You my past. Thank You for my today.

> *I know how to be abased, and I know how*
> *to abound. Everywhere and in all things*
> *I have learned both to be full and to be*
> *hungry, both to abound and to suffer need.*
> —PHIL. 4:12

The apostle Paul led a balanced life. He had his priorities in order. He learned to be content in all circumstances. That is a tough lesson to learn.

I learned it with great difficulty. There have been times in my life when I have been down to my last dollar, my last loaf of bread, my last friend, even my last chance. I have learned to walk in faith, without the security of a job, or even a home. When I entered the hospital for my bulimia my insurance was going to run out in two weeks. My bank account was hovering around zero. God came to my rescue through my parents and my church.

When I left the hospital, I gave up my job, and God gave me caring friends who supported me as I started lecturing and wrote my first book.

When cancer struck my life I was without insurance, and again God provided the means for me to pay my bills. When I was sure that I would be single all my life, God provided me a wonderful mate who loves me.

I had more security with nothing to eat in the house than during my days of bulimia, when I had a house full of food. I have learned not to count on things to make me happy. I have learned to let God, not food, fill up my empty places.

Lord, help me to look to You for every need. Thank You for giving me what is best for me.

Therefore with joy you will draw water
From the wells of salvation.
—ISA. 12:3

Joy. According to Paul, it is part of the fruit of the Spirit. When we have joy in our hearts, our burdens seem lighter. Our trip seems shorter, and our difficulties become easier for us to manage. With joy in our hearts, our lips sing, and praise rises from our tongues. We are thankful to God for our blessings.

Being secure in our relationship with God brings joy. From the wells of salvation we draw joy and peace.

I have not always felt such joy in my life. Now that I have given myself to God and accepted His forgiveness, I am free to experience the joy of a right relationship with Him. With all my heart I wish that you may feel this joy as well.

Do you feel as if that joy is far away from you now? Are you struggling with your relationship with God? Please know that God is doing all He can to bring you into a relationship with Him. He desires you more than you desire Him. Trust Him. Search His Word. Search your own heart and your own life. Decide to place yourself completely in His hands.

It was necessary for me to reach the bottom before I completely put myself in God's hands and under His control. I held out a long time, almost too long. Please don't wait as long as I did. Joy awaits.

God, thank You for the joy that I can draw on from the well of Your salvation. May my life be filled with gladness as I seek to do Your will.

> *Love never fails.*
> —1 COR. 13:8

It is difficult to define or even to describe love. We use many words to describe many types of love: brotherly love, physical love, loving a pet or a favorite television show. All of the love we can talk about will fail us at one time or another. We get angry at our friends and out goes brotherly love. Marriages end. That pet we love dies, and that television show we love is cancelled.

God's love never fails. God has proved His love to us over and over again: "For God so loved the world that He gave His only begotten Son."

So often we choose another solution to our problems besides the love which never fails. And when we do, we are doomed to failure. I turned to food to fill up my broken heart. It failed. Others turn to alcohol or drugs, a multitude of relationships, social position, or abundance of wealth, but all these things will fail to satisfy the deep needs of our hearts.

Look at your life. What are you turning to to fill you up and to satisfy your needs? If you are turning to anything but the love of God, you are headed for disappointment.

God manifests His love in a variety of ways. He shows His love through His Spirit. He shows His love through the words in His book. He shows His love through the actions of others. I have seen His love in my life in all of these ways. Look for it in yours.

Father, help me to be aware of the many different ways that You show Your love for me.

And having food and clothing, with these
we shall be content. —1 TIM. 6:8

Contentment is contrary to Satan's wishes. He does not want us to be satisfied. Rather, he wants us to be always grasping and stretching, wanting for more, never happy, always in turmoil.

We have just bought a new house and Satan whispers to us, "But you didn't get the pool." Our child gets a B in school and Satan speaks to our child through us, "Why couldn't you get an A?"

How many times have we said to ourselves, If I only had this, then I'd be happy! Sometimes wishing is often more fulfilling than having. As soon as we get what we sought, off we go in search of something else.

While we wait for that thing that we think is going to make us happy, we are anxious. We pace the floor and cannot sleep. And often, during that time of waiting, we eat, just to fill up the time and to get our minds off the nagging emptiness. Sometimes we do not even know what we are waiting for—just anything, something different, something to change the way things are. When the waiting is too hard to bear, we turn to food, something to get our mind's attention.

We have to stop looking for happiness in things. As Dorothy said in "The Wizard of Oz," If she ever went looking for her heart's desire again, she would not go any farther than her own back yard.

Lord, help me to be content with having enough instead of yearning for an abundance. Help me to better understand that life's great gain is in being content in You.

> *You shall not eat any detestable thing.*
> —DEUT. 14:3

In the Old Testament, God's laws governing food were strict, and His punishment was sure. Certain animals could be eaten, and others were forbidden.

Do you ever wonder what God might ban today if He planned our menus? Traditional foods, and new substances in our diet, have been found to pose serious health risks. We used to think that a big breakfast of whole milk, bacon, and eggs would get us through the morning, or that a lot of red meat was good for our bones and hair.

If God were prescribing food laws for us today, He might be more concerned with *how much* than with *what* we eat. Eggs are an important source of protein, yet we should avoid too many of them. Milk is essential for strong bones and teeth, but we should limit its butterfat content. Even bacon is all right, every once in a while.

Today, God's grace guides us instead of His law. God expects us to use our best judgment in choosing what and how much we eat. With choices comes responsibility. Sweet treats are a wonderful part of life but a steady diet of sweets is an irresponsible choice.

God made the Israelites responsible for the foods they ate. He holds you responsible today. If eating too much or too little food is a problem for you, you need to take responsibility for your behavior. Seek His help if your behavior with food is destructive.

Father, thank You for loving me even when I'm not responsible.

*When you have eaten and are full, then you
shall bless the LORD your God for the good
land which He has given you.*

—DEUT. 8:10

In this warning from Moses to the children of Israel, he
reminded them that, after they were full, they needed
to remember the source of their fulfillment. God,
through Moses, promised them a land flowing with
"olive oil and honey." He promised them beautiful
houses, clear waters, crops, herds, silver, and gold
(Deut. 8:8–13).

He also included a disclaimer. They were to remember that their hands had not brought about their prosperity. The Lord had done it.

Whether we drive a fancy sports car or nurse along
a dilapidated junker, we need to acknowledge that God
gives us these things.

With a full stomach, it is very easy to forget to thank
God for the food. It is easy to delude ourselves into
thinking that it is our money, that we've earned it. We
say to ourselves, I've worked hard to get it, and I'll do
with it what I want!

We need to remember to thank God, not just with
our voice, but by the way we use what He has given
us. Our thanks are expressed by eating wisely, by using our money wisely, and by giving to those in need.
He wants our verbal thanks, and He also wants to see
our thankfulness in action. He knows we speak best
through our actions instead of our words.

*Lord, help me to remember to thank You for the things You give me.
Help me to use these gifts wisely.*

Another man dies in bitterness of his soul,
Never having eaten with pleasure.
—JOB 21:25

When I was growing up, my dad used to tell me stories about the hard times of the depression. He described many meals consisting of only red beans and cornbread, or cornmeal mush and biscuits. He often went to school with a lunch of only two cold biscuits.

Dad was never embarrassed, he said, because everybody else lived that way too. Except for one child. His parents had a little extra money, enough to buy the boy a new lunch box. He had a sandwich made of store-bought white bread and bologna. Often he had a piece of cake for dessert. While my dad and his brothers and sisters washed down their hard biscuits, this boy ate with pleasure. Needless to say, the others ate in bitterness and envy.

I have often wondered how that boy could eat in pleasure when all around him were envious looks from those who had less.

God expects us to share whatever we can with those who have less than us—our food, or time, or money, or just understanding. When we help others, it helps us to be able to live with pleasure.

Today, let's remember to thank God for what we have, for there are so many in this world who have less. We can thank God by not wasting what He has given us.

_____

Father, thank You for the pleasure of eating. Help me to approach my food with a feeling of thankfulness and not of dread. Help me to be wise with what I have.

*Then Elijah said unto Ahab, "Go up, eat
and drink; for there is the sound of
abundance of rain."* —1 KINGS 18:41

How often do we wish that God would zap our problems away as miraculously as He did in Elijah's time! Elijah prayed that it would not rain, and it did not rain for three years. King Ahab and all those he ruled were punished for the evil they did.

When the punishment had ended, "Elijah prayed again; the rain came and the earth yielded its fruit." One prayer and the rain stopped; another prayer caused it to start up again—a miracle.

In our own battle with food, we may wish that a miracle would make our weight go away. We do not want to have to work at it. We do not want to have to change what we are doing.

God does not want us to suffer. He wants us to learn. We did not put on the weight overnight, and it is not going to come off overnight. It takes time to unlearn bad habits. Do not despair if it seems as if your goal weight is impossibly far away. The journey itself may yield more rewards than reaching the end.

The quick fix may seem like the ideal answer, but it took three and a half years for the rains to fall again. During that time the people turned back to God.

Don't concentrate merely on the end of your diet, but on what God has in store for you along the way.

God, it is exciting to know that You have plans for my life. Help me to trust You as I give my life to You.

The poor shall eat and be satisfied.
—PS. 22:26

The author of that passage never sat by the two women I ran into the other day. A friend and I were at a cafeteria, and we happened to sit down near two elderly women. Both of them were extremely overweight. They were also very hard of hearing, which made overhearing their conversation unavoidable.

Each of them had selected enough food to feed three people. As they shouted to each other my friend and I learned they lived in a small house, on income from social security. After they ate everything on their trays, one lady yelled at the other, "Well, are you satisfied?!" "I could use another helping of that blackberry cobbler," the other shouted back.

"Me too," the first lady agreed at the top of her lungs. So off they went for another dessert.

Later, their conversation turned to money. "Well," the first lady bellowed, "we could also leave the air conditioner off 'til our checks come."

These two women were poor, barely mobile, and were ready to suffer the heat of the summer to conserve money. Yet they appeared to place a high priority on gorging themselves on food. It seemed that, no matter how much they ate, they were never satisfied.

What price do you pay for food? God expects our lives to have balance, including the way we eat.

Lord, help me not to allow food to rule my life.

Give me children, or else I die.
—GEN. 30:1

Children. How do you describe them? It saddens me that, as we grow up, so many of us love the simple, precious qualities of a child.

Find a child today, and watch him. Children are curious. They ask all kinds of crazy questions. They are so hungry to know and to learn. What an example they are to us. If they feel like giggling, they do. If they feel like crying, they make sure the whole world can hear them. Children are honest. They have the disturbing capacity, to adults anyway, to say exactly what is on their minds. It does not take much to fill a child with joy.

I saw a little boy at church running and running in a circle, round and round. When he got tired, he fell to the ground laughing. It felt so good to him just to run and fall. As we grow up, we adults lose the simple joy of running and falling and laughing. We get so bogged down with life and its struggles.

Children are a gift from God. Take time out of your busy life to learn from them. Through children, God is trying to remind us of what is important. Let the child in you giggle and find joy in the simple things.

Father, sometimes it feels as if I have lost the little child I used to be. Sometimes it seems that I cannot find that place anymore where all my joy and wonder is stored. Help me to find myself again, Father. Help me to take time out from being an adult to enjoy being a child again, for a little while.

> *They send forth their little ones like
> a flock,
> And their children dance.*
> —JOB 21:11

Last summer I visited my niece, Danielle, and my nephew, Uriah at my parents' house in Oklahoma City. I had planned to take them to a water slide park, but on that day Oklahoma was having severe thunderstorms. We were all disappointed until Danielle came up with a great idea. "Let's go outside and play in the rain!"

So thirty-four-year-old Aunt Cyndi, eight-year-old Danielle and nine-year-old Uriah went outside and played in the pouring rain. It was a deluge. We had a ball.

Danielle found a spot at the side of the house where a drainage pipe had broken and the rain was gushing down like a water fall.

"Look, Aunt Cyndi," she cried out, "my own private shower!" Under it she went, moving her arms as if she was putting on soap and washing her hair, singing all the while at the top of her lungs.

My mother took a picture of us. We look like drenched rats, but we look so happy.

Uriah and Danielle bring such simple joy to my life. Every time I am with them they teach me to take time and enjoy God's free gifts. Maybe, if we all took time to dance in the rain, we would not be so bogged down with low self-esteem and stuffing our feelings.

Thank You, God for the example that children offer us. May we grasp them, observe them, and learn from them.

How forceful are right words!
—JOB 6:25

An important lesson I have learned from children is honesty. I know a woman who lost a lot of weight on a diet, then she gained it all back. I was out shopping with her, and suddenly her little boy said, "Mommy, you sure are fat again. You need to go back on your diet."

His mother was hurt by his truthful words. "Well, thanks for that little reminder, Jimmy!" she retorted. We start out teaching our children they should always tell the truth. Then we spend the rest of the time explaining why that is not always the best idea. To children, things are simple. This little boy wanted his mother to lose her weight. He was honest.

There was a time in my life when I was deathly afraid of flying. I asked my niece one day, after she got off a plane to visit me, "Do you like to fly, Danielle?"

"I love it," she told me, "especially taking off." "Boy, that's great. I shake every time I take off in a plane."

Danielle frowned for a minute, then she told me, "Then you're in the wrong business, Aunt Cyndi." I began to laugh hysterically. Her simple statement made me reexamine why I was afraid. It was as if she was saying, "Face your fear. God will be with you."

Maybe today we, like children, should look inside ourselves, be honest with ourselves, and do something about it.

———————

Father, thank You for children and all that they teach me about being honest.

> *Out of the mouth of babes and infants*
> *You have ordained strength.*
>
> —PS. 8:2

Danielle, if you could fly up to a rainbow, what would you do once you got there?"

"I'd slide down it, Aunt Cyndi."

"What if you got to the rainbow and there wasn't any color on it. What would you do?"

"Oh, Aunt Cyndi, that's easy! I'd go buy a bunch of paints and then I'd go back to the rainbow and paint it."

Out of the mouth of a babe comes such easy, uncomplicated answers. Why can't we be like that? As adults we know logically that we cannot go to the rainbow and slide down it. But we can dream. We know we can not go paint a rainbow if one lost all its colors, but we can pretend. We can use our imagination.

Adults get so caught up on the complicated answers. It makes our lives seem so hard to deal with sometimes. I have to lose weight. I have to weigh my food, and myself. We get so caught up in our complex lives we do not take time to stop and dream. It is fun to stop and think. What if I could paint a rainbow?

We can paint rainbows. We can paint love where there is hate. We can paint cheerful thoughts where there is negativity. We can go to a park, slide down a slide, and make believe it's a rainbow.

God gives us so many opportunities. Look for an uncolored rainbow today.

Father, help me to never quit dreaming.

Sorrow and sighing shall flee away.
—ISA. 35:10

What do you do for fun, Cynthia?" my therapist, Mike, asked me once.

"Fun? What's fun?" I replied. My eating disorder consumed me. It took my time and squelched my ability to love and give. I did not have time for fun. As a result, I felt dead inside.

Mike asked, "Well, can you swim? OK, then, I want you to go with a friend you enjoy to a really neat water park."

"A water park? Oh, come on! I'm twenty-eight years old! I don't want to go to a water park where you go down slides and scream."

"It's mandatory," Mike informed me sternly. "You have to go."

I went, and guess what? I laughed and screamed as my body swirled and swayed down those huge slides. I had a blast. I relaxed on a float in a man-made ocean.

When was the last time you had fun? When did you really allow yourself to let go, to relax, and to just enjoy yourself? If you cannot remember, it has been too long. Why has it been so long? Go ahead.

Father, the pressures of this world are so great sometimes. Money problems, weight problems, blowing our diets, family hassles, work frustrations—they all rob us of our ability to have fun. Lord, there is a time for everything under Your heaven. Thank You for allowing us time for fun.

> *He who trusts in his own heart*
> *is a fool.* —PROV. 28:26

Do you agree with the statement, "God helps those who help themselves"? A girlfriend and I were talking about the struggles people face, and my friend said, "You know, Cynthia, in the Bible it says, 'God helps those who help themselves.'"

I had to tell my friend, "That statement is not in the Bible. And besides, it sounds good, but it's so far from the truth. God wants us to rely on Him: His wisdom, His strength, His power, His love."

I believe that God helps those who *can't* help themselves. God knew what was best for the children of Israel, but every time He made a rule, they broke it. They trusted in themselves, and it just did not work.

The apostle Paul experienced horrible suffering. God certainly did not say, "As soon as you start helping yourself, then I'll help you." Rather, God helped him specifically when Paul could not help himself.

People who struggle with food sometimes say to themselves, If I were thin, God would love me and help me, or, God won't help me because I just can't get started on my diet. Such thinking is wrong. God picks us up when we are down. God loves us even when we cannot love ourselves.

Our lives are happier when God and the person work as partners. But when we cannot be there with Him, He is still here with us. He loves us anyway.

God, help us when we can't help ourselves.

Blessed is the man who trusts in the
   LORD,
And whose hope is the LORD.
For he shall be like a tree planted
   by the waters,
Which spreads out its roots by the
   river,
And will not fear when heat comes;
But her leaf will be green.
   —JER. 17:7–8

A commercial shows several people exercising. They do not look like they need to, but they are busy at it anyway. The screen goes blank except for these words, "Just do it." That makes me really mad.

The attitude is, "Do it now. If you cannot, you are not disciplined. You are not worth much."

After I see that commercial, I want to say, "Wait a minute! You are demanding perfection. You are saying if I don't 'just do it,' then I should feel like a failure."

I am so glad God does not demand that I "just do it." He wants me to be whole and healthy, but He gives me the free choice to do it. And even if I don't, that does not mean I am less valuable to Him. If I go ahead and "just do it," there is no guarantee I will not fail.

People who struggle with their self-esteem and pressure from the world to be thin do not derive motivation from television commercials that make them feel more inadequate. We need to know we are accepted as we are and understand *why* we feel badly about ourselves. I am so thankful God is a God of patience.

Father, I thank You for always being patient when I fail.

> *No longer do I call you servants . . .*
> *but I have called you friends.*
> —JOHN 15:15

God calls us so many reassuring names in the Bible. Before Jesus was betrayed in the Garden of Gethsemane, He talked to the disciples about many things. In John's version of the story, Jesus called them, "my friends." Not only are we the children of God, but He calls us *friends*. It makes me realize that God wants to have a close, personal relationship with us. He is the key of all keys. He is the creator of the universe. He can do anything. Yet all the while, He calls us His friends.

Some people say, "Jesus is my best friend." It makes me so happy to hear that. It means they feel a kinship with Jesus. It means they have a personal relationship with Him. What is even better to know is that Jesus considers me His friend. It is not a one-sided relationship. God desires a oneness with me!

During the times that I've felt despair and devastation, even though I had no one to talk to, I always turned to Jesus. He knows my sorrows. He is my friend and He understands. I have a picture that says, "When you get to the place where God is all you have, you know He's all you need." Jesus is our true friend. He will never leave me.

Thank You, Jesus, for being such a friend.

And all things, whatsoever you ask
in prayer, believing, you will receive.
—MATT. 21:22

As I grew healthier emotionally, my relationship with God grew too. No longer was He the Father who could not possibly have time for me; instead, He was the Daddy who would stop anything He was doing for me. As I grew to realize the depth of His love (I am still realizing it), and that He longs to have a personal relationship with me, I have come to the conclusion that He does not want me to hide anything from Him. He wants me to trust Him.

I said before that honesty means freedom. I especially feel this way when I share with Him all my thoughts, feelings, and desires.

If I have a dream, I tell Him.

If I am hurting, I tell Him.

If I am angry at Him, I tell Him.

If I am happy, I tell Him.

If I need answers, I ask Him.

Sometimes I do not even feel like praying. I am overwhelmed with life, and I just do not feel like talking. He knows that. I am honest with Him, and I tell Him, "God, I'm empty and I don't have words to express the feelings I need to let out. Thank you for loving me anyway."

_____

Thank You, Father, for listening to me and understanding me.

Watch, stand fast in the faith,
be brave, be strong.
            —1 COR. 16:13

A friend I look up to is always telling me, "Cynthia, as long as I'm trying, I'm not a failure." Gary is legally blind. He grew up with parents who were totally blind. He was put in a school for the blind as a little boy, and there he was told he would not amount to much in this world. He refused to believe that. He fought for the right to attend public school and won. There kids ridiculed him, and teachers continued to tell him, "You're not going to make it." Gary refused to be a failure. He refused to give up. Now he is a professional lecturer with a powerful message that encourages teenagers to dream and not to give up.

Gary's motto is true. He believes, "Yes, I'll make mistakes and blow it sometimes. I'll be rejected along the way, but as long as I don't give up, as long as I'm at least trying, I'm not a failure."

If you feel as if you have failed or blown it, do not give up. Examine why you blew it, and start over. Pick yourself up and try again. You are not a failure; you are trying.

On any weight program, there will be days when you go off the plan. That does not mean you have failed. With a "keep it up" attitude, you would be surprised what is possible.

Father, help me to keep trying even when I feel like giving up.

Mercy and truth have met together.
—PS. 85:10

Setbacks can be temporary. Candie overate. She went off her diet, and as a result, she beat herself up verbally. Why did you do that? she asked herself. "You've blown it. You were so good, and now look what you have done! The more she beat herself up, the more she ate. Finally she stopped and asked herself, Why do I feel such a need to overeat?

Candie looked at her life, and she saw that there were many pressures. She had just separated from her husband. While she hoped for a reconciliation, he was against it. A new job was creating pressures at work, and food was an island of escape. She thought about and wrote down her feelings, telling herself, OK, I had a setback, but look at all the success I've had. She had lost thirty-five pounds and had kept it off for five years. Instead of dwelling on the negative, she decided to start fresh and learn from her experience.

Setbacks can be temporary. Have you suffered from a setback recently? Has it sapped your resolve to go on? Go back and think about why you relapsed. Admit you did and decide to make it temporary. Remind yourself of the reasons why you started in the first place. Remember all the success you have had, and how wonderful you have felt. Recommit yourself to your diet plan and stop blaming yourself.

Father, help me to get back on my diet. Help me to make this setback a temporary one, and to learn something from it.

Cleanse me from my sin.
—PS. 51:2

I was told that I would be released in two weeks. I had told myself I was never going back to bingeing and purging, but after hearing this, I had a relapse. I did not know it, but I was scared. A friend had gotten out of the hospital, and had gone back to his drug addiction. I was angry at him, and scared for myself. In order to numb those confusing emotions, I binged.

My therapist helped me understand that, instead of dealing with the fear and anger, I had numbed it with food. "Cynthia," he said, "when you fail, you have the choice of understanding why you fell back. Once you understand, you can be ready for the next time you feel like numbing yourself with food. Regression means growth, Cynthia."

He was trying to tell me there would be times I would want to regress, and as long as I examined the reasons, I could grow in my understanding. Eventually I would learn I did not need to run to food.

Change is a process. Learning is a process too. Understanding the reasons behind the need to eat can help us learn to deal with our failure.

It is not easy to look our failure in the face. But if we do not, it remains a failure. When failure becomes a learning experience, we are taught to fight the urge to fail in the future. God calls it maturing. I call it the only way to live.

———————

Father, help me to forgive myself when I fail and keep picking me up when I do.

For each one shall bear his own load.
—GAL. 6:5

Talking about weight loss is a beginning. Visualizing weight loss is even better. Realizing I can change my weight, with God's help, is the key to success.

Candie, who lost thirty-five pounds and kept it off, has learned that she must be responsible for change. When she decided to lose weight, she believed that she and God were a team. Together they could do it. Candie looks at her life as a journey. She says it takes strength, courage, and wisdom from God.

Responsibility first, she told herself. I need to lose weight. Then she imagined what she would look like. She liked what she saw. With God's help, she took on the responsibility day by day, step by step, to accomplish what she set out to do.

You will never be able to lose your weight, or overcome your eating disorder, until you take responsibility for it. That may mean getting professional help. It does not mean turning over the responsibility for getting well to someone else. It *is* important to get help, but the responsibility will stile lie with you.

The strength, courage, and wisdom to accomplish change comes from the Lord. Together, you and He can do anything!

The longest journey starts with one small step. You and God will be taking that step together. Isn't it time to get started?

Father, taking the first step can be so hard. Take my hand and walk with me.

> *Be of good courage,*
> *And He shall strengthen your heart.*
> —PS. 31:24

Jesus never promised our lives would be perfect once we accept Him. He did, however, promise us there would be trials and tribulations. As explained in the book, *Love Hunger,* those who struggle with overeating are really looking for love and comfort that they were denied, usually in childhood. They feel compelled to seek comfort from food, and they are driven to it by the severity of their emotions.

It seems to be easier to feed our pain than to deal with it. But if we do not confront our pain, our disappointments, our losses, our brokenness, we end up numb and frustrated and filled with self-hatred.

Today, let us stop and recognize what situations trigger in us: the drive to hide from them, and to eat. We need to be ready with an alternative to stuffing our feelings. We can try expressing our hurt. Admit we are angry. Admit that it seems a whole lot easier to avoid the problem, but that is not the best solution. Admit that any problem we are running from simply follows right behind us, and will eventually catch up with us, whether we are ready to face it or not.

Facing our problems can be frightening, but God does not expect us to do it alone. He has provided caring people who can help us, and He is always with us.

God, help me to stop running from my problems to food. Help me to face my problems and come up with solutions for my life.

No one, having put his hand to the plow,
and looking back, is fit for the kingdom
of God.   —LUKE 9:62

Potential: to be capable of being or becoming.

We all have potential, although some people feel that they cannot change. How often do you hear someone say, "He'll never change," or, "She's too old to change." These words simply are not the truth. We all can choose to change and all of us have the God-given potential to change.

Potential, however, does not come without commitment. Potential without commitment results in nothing. If we want to reach our potential, first we must understand that we need to commit ourselves to taking the steps necessary to accomplish that goal. We reach our objective through firm, productive, balanced steps, and sometimes a step back, or two.

Some people can lose five pounds a week. Others lose only one pound. Doctors say that two pounds a week is the most reasonable and healthiest way. Some weeks you may not be able to lose any weight at all, but that does not mean you should give up, or give in. We have the potential to change, and with commitment, it will happen.

Father, You know my potential better than I do. You know what steps I need to take to get there. Be with me, Father, as I take those steps to reach the potential You have given me.

> *O LORD, why do You cast off my soul?*
> *Why do You hide Your face from me?*
> —PS. 88:14

When I met Mac, he was seventy-two years old. He had a constant, joyful gleam in his eyes. Mac had not always been like that, however. When he was sixty-two he had a heart attack. It forced him to retire early, and he was miserable. He wanted to give up on life.

Mac felt sorry for himself. Then, when he was reading the newspaper, he saw an advertisement asking for volunteers to deliver meals to shut-ins, elderly and handicapped individuals who could not get out but needed nutritious food. Mac said to himself, I can do that. He volunteered.

Every day he got in his car and drove around his city, knocking on doors, and delivering food. The people behind those doors touched Mac. He saw their loneliness, and he could relate to them. They gave him joy.

I produced a story on Mac when I was a news reporter. He said to me during our interview, "Cynthia, never say you can't do it. Say instead, 'I'm going to give it a try.'"

When I get caught up in the "I can't do it" syndrome, I stop and think of Mac. He could have remained bitter and lonely in his retirement. He could have said, "I can't," when he saw the ad, and just turned the page to something else. But he did not and his life was changed for the better.

Never say you can't. Instead, say you'll try.

Jesus, help me to keep trying and never give up.

Trust in the LORD, and do good.
—PS. 37:3

On any journey to lose weight or overcome an eating disorder, we reach *the plateau*. We get stuck at a certain weight loss, and we can not seem to go any farther. Or, we are in therapy, and we are stalled, not wanting to let go of the past and get on with today. When we reach that dreaded plateau, sometimes our reaction is to get discouraged and impatient with ourselves. We feel tempted to just give up. At times like this, we need to know that the Shepherd understands, and He will help us over our stalemate and through the valleys.

Hitting the plateau means we need to stop, sit back, and realize we are human. To go from A to Z means we have to work past B all the way through Y. It is a slow process, and we need to constantly remind ourselves that the plateau will not last forever.

God, when we succeed, the taste of success is so good. When we don't feel successful, we feel like a total failure. Help me, God, when I reach the plateaus in my life. Help me to get over those plateaus. Be with me as You promised, and help me when I feel discouraged.

> *Teach us to number our days,*
> *That we may gain a heart of wisdom.*
> —PS. 90:12

Feelings come and go. Yet sometimes we feel as if the pain in our lives will last forever.

There was a time in my life when I was rejected by someone I loved. I remember how much my heart hurt, and I cried so hard I did not think the tears would ever stop. I was sure the pain would never go away. But it did, with time.

When I went through "emotional surgery" in therapy, I felt as if I had lost forever pieces to the puzzle that was my life. Yet with time, they were found. The pieces were put back together, and I became a whole person.

I have learned that no matter how I feel today, it will not last forever. I allow myself to feel, and I assure myself that with time, life will go on.

When I get on an airplane and the weather is stormy, I absolutely dread the bumps and turbulence I will experience. But I have learned that above the stormy, dark clouds the sun waits for me. I'll tell myself, Hang on, Cynthia, we'll be through these dark clouds soon. Then I will look and there will be the sun and blue skies.

My feelings are like that. Today I feel bad but tomorrow I won't. I know that after the storm passes, there will be a brighter day waiting for me.

Father God, thank You for the stormy days because they enrich the sunny days even more.

The LORD will be your everlasting light.
—ISA. 60:20

Life will not always be consistent. Variety and flexibility are good and healthy; change is inevitable. There are no guarantees we will always be healthy. There is no written assurance that happiness and joy will be our constant companions.

A lady with five precious children and a husband she adored told me, "You know, I love my home and my family and I hope to be with them always, but life can change all of what I want. A fire could destroy my home. My children could die. My husband could leave me. If I put all my trust and faith in people, I'm sure to be disappointed. My faith has to be in Jesus. He is the only consistent person in my life, and I know as long as I trust in Him, I'll be OK."

I felt very uncomfortable when she told me this. I would be devastated without my husband, David. But the more I thought about what she said, I realized she was so right. If we put our trust in the things and people around us, sooner or later we will be disappointed. The fact that we love these people and things is no guarantee that we will continue to have them.

Yet the unpredictability of life need not be a frightening thought. God is our constant. We can trust Him to keep us, no matter what happens in our lives. We need not fear the future, for God is there, waiting for us.

Father, I put my life and those I love in Your hands. Help us as we face the uncertainties of life.

A friend loves at all times.
—PROV. 17:17

If you have friends in your life who encourage you, thank God for that. If you feel all alone and do not know where to turn, find a friend. Join a support group or a church, and seek out friendship. Life is harder when we have to go through it on our own. It is said that a burden is lighter when shared by two.

If the burden is weight loss, it will be easier to carry with the help and support of caring friends.

There are times in our lives when we naturally turn to God for comfort, and at other times we want someone here to listen and talk to. We want a hug or a smile or someone to tell us that everything is going to be all right. God knows this.

God seems to put people in our lives at the most appropriate times. When I was in the Minirth-Meier Clinic for three months, my friend, Nancy, sent me a funny card every day. Every single day I would get a card that made me laugh and made me feel loved. She invested time and money to say to me, each and every day, "I believe in you, Cynthia. Don't give up."

There is a saying, "To have a friend, you must be a friend." It is a beautiful two-way relationship that provides for so many of our needs.

If you do not have friends, pray that God will bring one into your life, and be ready to be a friend back.

Father, thank You for giving me good friends.

*Present your bodies a living
sacrifice, holy, acceptable to
God, which is your reasonable
service.*
—ROM. 12:1

Before Martha lost her weight, she was determined to set a goal and eat right. She reached her goal weight but something was missing. My body needs a change, she said to herself, so she started going to an exercise class. Martha found that exercise enhanced her weight loss program, and it helped improve her moods.

Depression would often set in during her therapy sessions. She found that adding exercise to her routine helped her work through those dark thoughts. Physical activity became a tool that helped her realize well-being and success with weight loss.

Martha told me that when she felt least like exercising was the time she knew she needed to get up and go anyway. After she exercised, she found her whole outlook had changed. She did not allow her feelings to dictate whether or not she took care of herself. She made a decision and worked her way through the depression. She took control of her life and emotions.

Do you wait until you feel like it to diet? Is exercise on your schedule only when you are in the mood?

So many people have told me that once they started exercising, it changed their whole outlook on life. How about giving it a try?

Father, I give You my body to serve You in a healthy, whole way.

> The backslider in heart will be filled
> with his own ways,
> But a good man will be satisfied
> from above. —PROV. 14:14

Laura views her out-of-control eating habits as an addiction. She sought help, and now she is doing great. She says her addiction was painful, self-destructive, and scary.

Through therapy, Laura learned that when she was obsessed with food, it meant she needed something more, something else—comfort, a hug, reassurance, forgiveness. Now every time she wants to eat and she is not really hungry, she stops, and thinks. She puts herself on hold long enough to ask, What do I really need? When she figures it out, she seeks to fulfill her need in the proper place. Her self-confidence returns because she is in control of her life, not food.

Now when she fulfills a need, it is satisfied. When she stuffed her needs with food, they never really went away. She says she has a great feeling of accomplishment. She feels strong.

Isn't it wonderful when we take back control of our lives? The feeling of accomplishment we experience gives us the strength to overcome till next time we are tempted to backslide. Laura has learned the satisfaction that comes from going forward. She has learned to turn her negative past into a positive future.

Father, help us to take pain and make it into something positive.

*Thus the children of Israel were sub-
dued at that time; and the children of
Judah prevailed, because they relied on
the LORD God of their fathers.*
—2 CHRON. 13:18

After my hospitalization, I had dreams where I would eat three chocolate cakes, four pizzas, and twenty candy bars. I woke up in a panic and thought, Did I really do it? Then I realized it was just a dream, and the panic would subside. But the dream ignited my fear of going back to my bulimia. I promised I would never do that, yet the fear of it was always there.

Fear can paralyze us. Panic is even worse. There are times when it seems as if our world is unraveling, and we do not know what to do. We feel totally out of control. Who can we rely on? Who is our calm amidst the storm of panic? God is our rock and our refuge. Jesus is our ever-present help.

When our reliance is on God and His Son more than on ourselves, then we really can go on. Sometimes in our panic it is all we can do just to hold on to Jesus as we ride out whatever storm we are experiencing.

What do you grab during your times of desolation? Do you reach for the comfort of a piece of candy, or does your appetite leave you completely, and you refuse to eat?

Nothing you hold on to but Jesus will be of any real value. He is your only rock. Hold on.

*God, help me know that nothing is too hard for You. Help me to hold
on to You when it seems like there is nothing else to hold on to. Today,
I give You my fears, and I promise to rely on You.*

> *Thus also faith by itself, if it does*
> *not have works, is dead.*
> —JAMES 2:17

Faith without works is dead. God calls us to an active faith, alive with possibilities.

Faith is believing in something we cannot see but believe one day we will see.

Faith is not knowing all the answers to all the questions we have, but knowing our heavenly Father is holding those answers for us.

Faith is believing God wipes away our tears even though we do not see Him.

Faith is knowing God gives us the ability to face ourselves and our problems, and to overcome.

Faith is trusting God to know us better than we know ourselves. Faith is giving control of our lives over to Him.

Faith in ourselves and in God is so necessary to accomplish goals. It is what gives us the strength to continue to work, and to build upon our relationship to God.

Today, have faith in yourself. You can reach your goals.

Today, have faith in God. He wants you to reach your goals.

Nothing is impossible with God. Faith is our victory!

Father, increase my faith in You. Thank You for the faith I already have in You. Thank You for giving me the ability to have faith in myself. Thank You for Your love and faith in me.

If the ax is dull,
And one does not sharpen the edge,
Then he must use more strength;
But wisdom brings success.
                        —ECCL. 10:10

Life is so hectic at times; we do not even have time to sharpen our axes. We run from here to there with no time in between to breathe.

Is your day like this? You pushed the snooze button one too many times, and now you are running twenty minutes behind schedule. You rush into the car with half a piece of toast and a cup of coffee. By ten o'clock you are famished; you grab a candy bar. Lunch hits and fast food is the only thing you have time for. After your full day, you arrive home tired and unmotivated to fix a nutritious meal. You snack, then you pop in a TV dinner. A pretty sad picture, isn't it? Try it again.

You wake up in the morning twenty minutes early to spend time with God in prayer. With your spirits invigorated and your priorities in order, you take the time to eat healthy grain cereal and a piece of fruit. The night before, you packed a nutritious lunch to take to work. You rest during your break, and better still, you go for a walk too. Listening to Bible tapes or religious music on the way home from work helps you put work behind you. You prepare a healthy dinner, including lots of fresh vegetables and fruits, which you bought beforehand.

Much better, wasn't it? All it takes is a little planning. It is one of the benefits of an ordered life.

Father, help me to set priorities so I can feel healthier.

Hear my cry, O God;
Attend to my prayer.
From the end of the earth I will cry
to You,
When my heart is overwhelmed;
Lead me to the rock that is higher
than I.
—PS. 61:1–2

My phone rang this morning. It was Lauren, a girl struggling with bulimia. She looks so beautiful on the outside, yet behind her soft smile is pain and locked-up abuse and fear. Since we met, she has called me several times for help and encouragement. She finally found a competent therapist and he got Lauren to deal with the fact that she was verbally abused as a child. All her life Lauren was told: "Lauren, you never do anything right." "Lauren, we'll tell you what to do. You're too much of an idiot to make any decisions about the real world."

This morning she asked me, "I just need to know: does it get better? Therapy is so hard. I just need to know there is a light at the end of the tunnel."

"Lauren," I reassured her, "it will get better, but sometimes it gets worse before it gets better. Just hang on. When the truth is revealed it hurts, but God will get you through it. He's brought you this far, hasn't He?"

"Yes, I just needed to hear it," she said.

"Lauren, I'll pray for you today, OK? You're going to make it."

Before she hung up, she answered, "OK."

Father, thank You for loving me and understanding me.

Restore us, O God of hosts;
Cause Your face to shine,
And we shall be saved!
—PS. 80:7

Usually when Lauren calls, her voice sounds beaten and depressed. But I remember one call when she told me, "Cynthia, I feel happy. I feel for the first time in so long that there is hope, and because every time I call you I'm down, I wanted to tell you it's going to be OK."

"Lauren, that's great," I said. "It feels good to feel good, huh? So what's been going on?"

"After years of going to therapists who gave me no hope, I think I've finally found someone who is making me look at what's underneath my out-of-control eating. I'm getting answers to all my whys. I just feel as if I am going to get well."

"Lauren, I want you to remember this call. This is a monumental day for you. You feel good about life. You feel hopeful. Now lock it in your mind, because the next time you call and you feel like it's never going to be all right, I'll remind you of today. Then you'll know you did feel good."

Three months later, she called back, and needed to know it was going to be OK. She even had a tough time admitting she had felt the hope before. God blesses us so abundantly with a job, friends, and material needs, yet when we are disappointed or down, hurt or lost, we quickly forget His blessings.

Father, thank You for bringing me this far. Help me to remember that the tough times will not last forever.

*So they all ate and were filled, and they took
up seven large baskets full of the fragments that
were left.* —MATT. 15:37

When your heart is breaking, do you give your pain
to God? Or do you think, with all the world's problems,
God could not possibly care about you?

The twelve men who walked and talked and slept in
the same camp with Jesus could relate to how you feel.
Jesus fed five thousand men with only five loaves and
two fish. He healed the sick, and He walked on the
water. A few days later, Jesus spoke before another
large crowd of four thousand, and he told the disciples
He wanted to feed that gathering too. What was their
response?

"Where could we get enough bread in the wilderness to fill such a great multitude?" (Matt. 15:33). It was
probably not the response Jesus was hoping for. If I
had been Jesus, I think I would have said, "Wake up,
you guys! Don't you remember the five thousand?"

Jesus did not react as I would have. Instead, He commanded everyone to sit down. He prayed and another
miracle happened. Everyone was fed, and there were
seven baskets of leftovers.

Yet I can be so much like the disciples, can't you?
God opens a door for me that blesses my life, but then
another door closes, and I feel as if my life is over.

Today, when a door slams in your face, remind yourself that God has opened so many others. Praise God
for the open doors.

Father, thank You for opening so many good doors for me.

*Now may the God of patience and comfort
grant you to be like-minded toward one
another, according to Christ Jesus.*
—ROM. 15:5

Jesus' reaction to His disciples' lack of faith touches me. He did not yell at them. He did not say, "You're never going to make it!" No, He just went ahead and did His job and thanked God.

It was not always like this. At times of frustration, Jesus wondered if we would ever believe. But, always, Jesus was patient and understanding.

The Bible says that God is a God of compassion. He is a God of patience. Jesus was like His Father in all things.

How often do we say to ourselves in those dark moments, How could God possibly love me after all I've done? How can He hear my prayers? I wish we could talk to those twelve men who lived with Jesus. I think they would tell us about His understanding and His longsuffering.

I do not always understand things the first time around, however. Sometimes it takes what seems like a lifetime before I get the point. During those times I need people to be patient with me. I need a God of patience to stay with me just a little longer until I figure it out. When I am struggling, I need to understand God's patience and have a little of my own. Sometimes, in despair, I am too quick to write myself off. Jesus has not. I should not either.

Father, help me to be patient with myself and others.

*So He said, "Come." And when Peter had
come down out of the boat, he walked on
the water to go to Jesus.*

—MATT. 14:29

No one had done it before. No one has done it since. Only Jesus walked on water. Peter wanted to be absolutely sure it was Jesus, not a ghost, approaching the boat. He cried out, "Lord, if it is You, command me to come to You on the water" (Matt. 14:28). Jesus told him to come, and Peter got out of the boat and walked toward Jesus.

But Peter lost his nerve and began to sink. "Save me!" he cried. Immediately Jesus stretched out His hand, caught Peter, and said, "O you of little faith, why did you doubt?" (Matt. 14:31).

Some may wonder, why did Peter lose his nerve? What strikes me is that Peter actually got out of the boat! He lost his nerve along the way, but he had enough faith to start walking. Peter did not just sit back and watch. He did something. He is such an example to me.

Sometimes getting on with life means getting out of the boat, but it is safe in that boat. The water looks pretty deep out there, and we are not at all sure we want to venture out. The problem is, we are looking at the wrong thing. Instead of looking at the water, we need to be looking at Jesus.

Take a step of faith. Get out of the boat.

Lord, it is scary to get out of the boat and walk by faith. Help me to keep my eyes on You.

*But let him ask in faith, with no
doubting, for he who doubts is like
a wave of the sea driven and tossed
by the wind.*   —JAMES 1:6

Michael lost fifty pounds. Then, afraid of gaining
weight again, he fought his desire to starve himself.

When I talked with Michael recently, he sounded so
confident at first, but he quickly admitted it was just an
act. "My life isn't working," he said. He told me about
his driving need to *be* somebody.

"Who said you weren't somebody?" I asked.

"My father. He always told me I was nothing, that I
wouldn't amount to much."

"You're trying hard to prove him wrong. But trying
to prove him wrong is killing you, isn't it?"

"So it seems," he said.

Michael wears a very successful mask. People think
he has it all together, yet he lives with constant fear,
terrified of his eating habits and of gaining weight. Michael is afraid that someday someone will discover the
truth behind the mask.

Michael does not understand what that truth is. He is
angry at his father for never believing in him, so with
an "I'll show you" attitude, Michael is dieting himself to
death. Michael needs to take off his mask and face his
truth.

Like Michael are you wearing a mask? Do you live in
fear that someone will see past it? Instead of praying
that no one does, pray that someone will.

Father, help me to take off my mask and reveal my true self.

> *Stand fast therefore in the liberty*
> *by which Christ has made us free.*
> —GAL. 5:1

A mother whose eighteen-year-old daughter has anorexia said, "I'm a good mother." "I've brought my daughter up the right way: no drinking, no smoking, no dancing, no mixed swimming, no shorts. . . ." She did not understand that her rigid rules were having a profound effect on her daughter whose problem is not food. She is angry—angry at all those rules that keep her from expressing who she really is.

Children need guidance, but they do not need a straitjacket of excessive rules. Children need freedom to think, and to express who they are. God gives us, His children, that freedom.

Christians are free in Christ. Do you feel bound by past rules and regulations? Today, know that Christ paid the price for that freedom. Accept and exercise it.

God gave us commandments to live by, of course, because He knows what is best for us. But one of those "rules" is, we are free to choose. Sometimes parents do not understand as well as God does, and they make rules that are not good for their children. After all, they are just people, and they make mistakes.

Look at the past rules in your life. Did they guide you or cripple you? Are they affecting you today? Accept those that guide and reject those that hinder. Christ died for your freedom. Don't let anyone take it away.

Father, thank You for not being a God who is rigid but who is flexible.

All things are possible to him who believes.
—MARK 9:23

A father brought his son to Jesus. He had no where else to go. The disciples had been unable to cast out the demon that lived inside his son. The father told Jesus of the horrid life his son lived with this demon.

Exasperated, Jesus said, "O faithless generation, how long shall I be with you?" (Mark 9:19). In other words, Jesus said, "Haven't you seen all I've done? What more can I do to make you believe?"

The boy's father said to Jesus, "If You can do anything, have compassion on us and help us." Jesus answered his "if" with one of His own. "If," He said, "you can believe, all things are possible to him who believes." The father exclaimed, "Lord, I believe; help my unbelief!"

Over and over again I meet people struggling with eating disorders who do not believe in a future without their illness.

Belief involves risk. Ruts are deep and safe, and we can hide in them. They are also cold and damp and hide the brightness of the sun.

Do you believe that you can get better? Do you believe that God will be there for you? Do you believe He can help you slay your demon? Do you believe that all things are possible, including your own return to health? Today, say to our Lord and Savior, "Lord, I believe; help my unbelief!"

Father, sometimes it's hard to believe You are working in my life. Help me because I long to believe and trust You.

> *For we, being many, are one bread and one*
> *body; for we all partake of that one bread.*
> —1 COR. 10:17

Communion is a time when brothers and sisters in Christ glorify Christ's life, death, and resurrection. God intended for all of His children to share in this meal, and to remember His sacrifice for our souls. When we meet in sweet communion, together we recognize that He is our Lord and Savior.

In 1 Corinthians the whole church partakes of communion. Paul called it "the Lord's supper," a time of unity.

How often do we eat alone? How often do we eat in secret? The more we eat in secret, the guiltier we feel. The early Christians gathered in each other's homes to eat together. How often do you get together with friends and eat? And how honest are you when you do? Do you put all the "right" things on your plate, only to go home afterwards and eat what you want?

How do you feel when someone invites you over for dinner? Are you glad, or do you dread another evening of having to hide what you eat? Eating should be an act that brings people closer together. If you always want to eat alone, to conceal what and how you eat, you are hiding from yourself and others.

Today, determine to eat with other people. Invite someone over. Eat with your family. Don't wait until everyone is in bed, when you can have what you really want.

Lord, help me to examine when I eat, and why I want to eat in secret. Help me to be open and to enjoy the communion of others.

*For nothing is secret that will not be
revealed, nor anything hidden that will
not be known and come to light.*
—LUKE 8:17

It is such a sad existence to eat alone, bingeing in secret, avoiding people because we ate too much the night before.

Years ago, I was interviewed by a newspaper reporter for an article on singles. The reporter asked me what my favorite thing to do was. I answered, "I love going to a restaurant by myself, eating a meal and reading a book."

My answer was true, but when I look back on it, I feel great sadness. What an empty, lonely answer. Underneath was fear of intimacy and rejection.

What is wrong with eating alone and reading a book? If it is done to avoid people, then it is time to reevaluate.

The other night I was out walking, and I passed a doughnut shop. Inside were three people, each alone reading. I was reminded of my old life, and the sadness came back. Yet after the sadness I felt joy. If that reporter were to ask me the same question now, I would say, "My favorite thing? To be with people. To be a friend. My favorite thing now is to give to others."

Why do you like to be alone? Is it a healthy aloneness that recharges you, or a reason to stay away from love and loving? Instead of seeking solitude, seek a partner.

———————————

Father, help me not to avoid people and friendship.

> *By strength of hand the LORD*
> *brought us out of . . . the house of*
> *bondage.*
> —EX. 13:14

Bondage is another word for slavery. Bondage comes in all forms, some of which we bring on ourselves. Today I was at the store to buy some frozen yogurt. It has been really hot, and I could not wait to have some luscious, cool yogurt. As I was deciding on what flavor to get, I heard a woman behind me talking to herself.

"This says the four-ounce container has sixty-two calories, the two ounce has thirty-one, and the five ounce has eighty-three, and the hot fudge has 260 calories. . . ."

I turned around, and I saw she was thin as a rail. Perhaps she is thin as a rail because she counts calories, but the woman really put a damper on my enthusiasm for my yogurt.

In the drive to be thin, so often we lose the joy. I bet that, whatever size of yogurt she finally decided on, she began figuring out how much of what kind of exercise she would have to do to burn it off. She took all the joy out of a little bit of delight.

Freedom is not license. It is not wise to indulge however and whenever we want. But in your quest for balance in your eating, do not forget the joy. Do not give up the freedom to enjoy the wonderful gifts we have around us. Somewhere between obesity and calorie-counting, there is a happy medium.

Lord, thank You for the wonderful gift of taste. May Your gift remain a gift, and not become a curse. Help me to use Your freedom wisely.

*Better is a dinner of herbs where
love is,
Than a fatted calf with hatred.*
—PROV. 15:17

Food is merely food to me now. I eat when I am hungry, and I do not feel an urge to overeat. It has been seven years since I binged and purged. It took three months in the Minirth-Meier Clinic and a year of further therapy to reach the point of wholeness.

I hurt for people who still struggle after going through an intense therapy program. Therapists say the reason is something else needs to be dealt with.

At lunch one day I sat with a girl who had first been obese, then anorexic, then bulimic. She had gotten professional help, but was still struggling. I ordered what I wanted, but she began to almost hyperventilate because she had not planned her meals that morning, and she was not sure what she should eat. It took her twenty minutes to decide.

"Lynette," I gently said, "you are not free if you must agonize over what to order. Something else is wrong."

She broke down and admitted, "I'm so scared." Her mother was dead. Her father was terminally ill.

"You've got to grieve, Lynette. You've got to deal with what really hurts. Your obsession with food is your shield from the reality of pain. Let go, Lynette."

Letting go takes time and it is tough. Letting go is another way of allowing God to help us. If we do not let go, we are doomed to failure.

Father, free me from the pain and guilt I carry. Free me to be honest.

> *A merry heart does good, like medicine.*
> —PROV. 17:22

Don't you just hate it when you put your foot in your mouth? You intend to say something meaningful, and the words come out all wrong. Sometimes people look at you like you are an absolute idiot, and you feel like it. If you are lucky, the person will laugh.

At church I was talking to a husband and wife. The woman struggles with her weight. As our conversation ended, I blurted out, "I have to get my book on eating disorders finished. I'll call you this week for some ideas."

My husband, David, who was standing nearby, started laughing. I did not understand why he thought my remark was so funny. David explained, in front of the couple. "Honey," he said, "what an insult. You're doing a book on eating disorders and you'll call Bonnie for ideas?" I felt stupid. Bonnie just laughed.

She said, "I bet I can help Cynthia. Just this week I had work done on my teeth, and I asked my dentist if he couldn't just sew my mouth up so I would stop eating." We all laughed some more.

Bonnie was secure enough in herself to laugh at my "foot in mouth" comment. She taught me something about not being so sensitive.

We need to let people off the hook when they make an embarrassing comment like I did. Remember to be gracious and laugh if someone does it to you. The next time the shoe could be in the other mouth.

Father, thank You for the gift of laughter.

*For this reason I bow my knees to the Father
of our Lord Jesus Christ, from whom the whole
family in heaven and earth is named.*
　　　　　　　　　　—EPH. 3:14–15

Mike, my therapist, gave me four years to find a husband. He told me one day, "In four years you'll allow yourself to get married." Four years later, almost to the day, I married David Robert McClure.

David and I met at a Christian retreat. We were happy people, in love with God and life. I chose to be myself with David. I was interested in him, but I decided that he, too, had to be genuinely interested in me. I was confident around him, and David, because of his maturity, appreciated my spunk and confidence. He fell in love with the person.

I had experienced a lot of lonely, painful relationships with men because I was not happy or whole. I have learned that secure, healthy people make secure, healthy relationships. Too often, unhappy people look to mates or friends to meet their every need. They seek to find the resolution of their problems in someone else. But your problems are not dissolved by a relationship; you just bring them along with you.

Instead of seeking another relationship to mend your broken heart, seek the reasons why your heart is broken. True love is not about taking from others, but about giving. How can you give when you are empty inside? First, fill yourself up with God's help.

Father, mend my broken heart and when it is healed use me.

In God is my salvation and my glory;
The rock of my strength,
And my refuge, is in God.

—PS. 62:7

David and I fell very deeply in love, but three months into our relationship, our love was tested. I was told I had breast cancer. At age thirty I had a modified radical mastectomy. It was a devastating blow to my ego, and possibly to my future.

When I found out I had cancer, the news made me relive all the feelings of the past. Again I felt the fear of abandonment, the fear of loving and losing that love, the fear of dying. I had been free from my bulimia for two years; I was in love for the first time in my life; and now I had breast cancer. I thought David would leave me.

The first thing I saw when I woke up after surgery was David's face. We cried and hugged and David gave me a present. It was a bottle of perfume. It was just what I needed. David was telling me, "You're still beautiful to me. You're still a woman to me."

God gave David to me at a time when I needed a man to love and accept me.

On those days when I do not feel very pretty or feminine, I remember that perfume. David loves me with the love of God.

I wish everyone could have a David. More than that, I wish everyone could accept God's unconditional love.

Father, Your love for me is more than I can fathom. Help me to feel more deeply Your unconditional love.

*My brethren, count it all joy when you
fall into various trials, knowing that
the testing of your faith produces
patience.*
—JAMES 1:2–3

Just because you overcome one problem does not
mean there will never be another. That is when your
faith in God comes in. When you lose weight or overcome an addiction, some people think that life will be
just fine from then on. When another trial comes, they
are blown away.

When my cancer hit me, my bulimia was gone. I was
an author, traveling full-time and lecturing. I was helping people, and I was in love. Then wham, breast cancer. I was faced with the same choice I had with
bulimia: to give in to fear or to fight for my life, to
numb myself or to deal with the pain. I chose to deal
with it. I chose to fight.

A recent study was done with women who were told
they had breast cancer. In most of the cases, those who
took the news with the attitude, "I'm going to die," did
die. But most of the women who said, "OK, I've got
cancer. Now what can I do to live?" lived longer, or
they beat the cancer altogether.

Today, you can choose to seek help or stay stuck.

Today, you can seek companionship or be lonely.

Today, you can be a friend or lose a friend.

Today, you can seek God's love or reject His love.
The choice is yours.

Father thank You for giving me choices.

> *Do not boast about tomorrow,*
> *For you do not know what a day*
> *may bring forth.*
> —PROV. 27:1

If everyone had to experience chemotherapy for just one day, I think people would love life and themselves a lot more than they do now.

Patients on chemotherapy start out experiencing a low-grade nausea all the time. Large chunks of hair fall out. They lose a lot of weight. The reality of death hovers like a shadow around every corner.

Because of my cancer, I look at life differently. I hug life a little harder than I did. When I open my eyes in the morning, the first words I say are, "Thank you, God, for another day."

There was a time when I was bulimic that I actually thought to myself, I wish I'd get cancer and die. Some of you may think it looks like a good way out of your pain. You may already have *cancer of the spirit*.

I was lucky. My cancer could be cut out surgically. Emotional cancer must be cut away, too, and it is no less painful. During the twelve years of my addiction I had cancer of the spirit. With the help of a loving therapist and a loving God, that cancer was cut away, leaving the healthy tissue of a vibrant spirit.

It is never too early to start to work on your cancer of the spirit. The doctors always tell you, "The sooner the better." Decide to do it before it is too late.

Father, be with me as I examine my spirit. Help me to remove the hidden, painful things that are eating me up.

Behold, you are fair, my love!
Behold, you are fair!
　　　　—SONG 1:15

When I started losing my hair during chemotherapy, I went out and bought a Dolly Parton wig. David did not like it at all. He said it was not me. He liked me bald. It did not matter to him that I had no eyelashes and bald spots all over my head. I felt so ugly, but David constantly told me, "Cynthia, you're beautiful to me." Truly love is blind, and I thank God for a blind man named David.

God's love is also blind. He does not notice those scars, or the wrinkles, or the pimples, or the flab. He sees the one He loves.

David would lovingly rub my bald spots, and assure me, "The bald spots mean the chemotherapy is working. Your hair will grow back." The very thing I wanted to hide was the one thing that David dwelt on. To him those bald spots meant healing and life, not ugliness.

We are always trying to hide our bald spots. We cover them up with masks and dark colors and fragile laughter. God knows where those bald spots are. His desire is not for us to hide them from Him, but to recognize them. He realizes that our hair will grow back, and those bald spots will not be there forever.

David's love gave me the courage to love myself, bald spots and all. He helped me look at those spots from another point of view. God desires to do the same for each of us.

Lord, thank You for loving me even when I don't love myself.

> *The tongue of the wise uses*
> *knowledge rightly,*
> *But the mouth of fools pours forth*
> *foolishness.* —PROV. 15:2

I was sitting in my hotel room the other night after lecturing, and a new movie was reviewed. The reporter obviously did not like the movie, and one of the reasons he gave was, the two female stars in the movie were so fat. He called them "whales." I could not believe it. The two women appeared normal, healthy-looking, not anorexic, and certainly not fat. They looked like the rest of us. Then I got mad. If they *had* been overweight, would that have diminished their acting ability?

The attitude of this reviewer is typical of the emphasis today on being thin. You have to be perfect, lose weight, not eat—leading to the tragedy of anorexia and bulimia. This reviewer had a preconceived idea of these women's correct weight. Who was he to decide that for them?

In today's world, the pressure to be thin is great. Normal-looking is not good enough. We are told we have to whittle our bodies down to no body fat at all. Tall, thin models are the standard the world says we have to live up to no matter how we get there.

I used to think that way. I do not anymore. I have rejected the world's definition of beauty and substituted God's. His is the only one who matters anyway.

O God! Help us today to not succumb to the world's foolishness.

*A fool despises his father's
instruction,
But he who receives reproof is
prudent.* —PROV. 15:5

Whenever I am in the grocery store checkout line, I cannot help reading those outrageous tabloid headlines. The other day "Girl Sues Parents for 1½ Million!" caught my eye. The reason this lawsuit was "noteworthy" was the girl was suing her parents because she was "fat and ugly."

The girl fell for the message that fat and ugly people are nobodies. And since she was fat and ugly, and therefore disadvantaged, she was due compensation for her "handicap" from her parents.

I have met so many people who, like this girl, do not want to take responsibility for their own lives. Instead of taking steps to change, they blame family, friends, people at work. They walk around with an enormous chip on their shoulders and a negative attitude about the world.

Taking responsibility means we need to take charge of our lives by dealing with our families and their dysfunctional qualities. It means we need to confront our pain and the issues in our past. Ultimately it is our responsibility to take control of our lives and change.

Eleanor Roosevelt said, "No one can make you feel inferior without your consent." In other words, just because someone says I'm fat or ugly doesn't mean I am.

Father, thank You for accepting me when others reject me.

> *Whoever has no rule over his own*
> *spirit*
> *Is like a city broken down, without*
> *walls.* —PROV. 25:28

While reading the paper the other day, I saw a letter to an advice columnist by a pharmacist. He wrote to complain that he was sick and tired of seeing people take short cuts on the way to helping themselves. An obese woman comes into the pharmacy where he works every month, for more prescribed diet pills. Concerned for this woman's health, he suggested she get off the dangerous pills and lose weight in a healthier way. She told him that her metabolism was so slow she needed the pills.

Month after month she came in, never reducing in size, always getting more and more pills. Then one day he happened to see her at a buffet. He saw her take five times the amount of food that he had. His letter stated that he believed she was lying to herself. Her problem was with overeating.

I wonder if she was thinking, as she went through that line heaping food on her plate, Tomorrow I can use my diet pills. She was looking for a fast, easy short cut. But she was not losing any weight at all.

It takes time, discipline, determination, and love for yourself to do it the right way. Short cuts are not the answer. Going the long, straight way is usually the best on any path.

———

Father, sometimes the short cut looks so good to us. Give us the strength to take the right path.

*To him who is afflicted, kindness
should be shown by his friend,
Even though he forsakes the fear of
the Almighty.* —JOB 6:14

My husband and I were talking to a beautiful, talented, vivacious friend of ours. She told us about a music video she was going to produce. I asked her what she planned to wear for the video. She answered, "Something slenderizing."

My husband, David, kiddingly said to her, "Well, since you're doing the video on the beach, why not wear a bikini?"

"Oh no," she shot back, "I don't think people want to see a 'whale' in a music video."

David and I hurt for our friend. Though she has beauty and other amazing qualities, she is insecure with how she looks. She had had some hurtful relationships, and her self-confidence was low. We decided to let her know how we felt about her. We sent her a card and in it we wrote:

> You are beautiful inside and outside and we thank God for who you are and all that you are.

> Whether you wear a bikini or an evening gown in your video, we will see *you*—a beautiful, talented girl who is full of life and God's love.

Do you undermine yourself? Today, listen to how you react to others about yourself. If your response is negative, think about why.

Father, I'm so glad You look to our hearts instead of our bodies.

> *I lie awake,*
> *And am like a sparrow alone on the*
> *housetop.*
>   —PS. 102:7

Dorothy's parents divorced when she was a baby. Growing up, Dorothy lived in boarding schools. She was lonely.

Other children made fun because her skin was not the same color. Her mom was black and her dad white. Kids taunted her, "Dorothy has dirty skin! Dorothy has dirty skin!"

One day Dorothy approached her grandmother, her mother's mother, and asked her, "Why am I a different color from everyone else?"

"You're not different," her grandmother said. "You're the same. Color doesn't mean you're different."

As Dorothy grew up, she decided she was OK. Every morning she would look in the mirror and tell herself, "Dorothy, you are special. You are somebody." She is one of the most confident women I know. She made the choice not to believe what others thought of her. She knows who she is.

Just because someone's unkind words hurt us does not mean they are right. Just because our culture bases the worth of a woman on how she looks, or a man on how much money he makes, does not mean that is all that matters.

Today, may we be like Dorothy and tell our reflection in the mirror, "I am special."

Father, thank You for giving me life and making me unique and special.

*The fathers have eaten sour grapes,
And the children's teeth are set on
edge.* —JER. 31:29

I spoke about childhood messages at a retreat, and a woman in her fifties came up to me after my lecture. She was crying, and said that something I had said brought a forgotten memory to her mind. She was nineteen years old, going to college but still living with her parents. One morning as she sat down to eat breakfast, her dad came up, reading the newspaper. In it were pictures of all the Miss America contestants. He showed her the pictures and asked, "Don't you wish you looked like a Miss America?"

She was devastated. She had never thought of herself as particularly pretty, but she had never thought of herself as ugly, either, until that day. The memory still stung after more than thirty years.

She struggles with low self-esteem. Even now, when she thinks she looks good, it does not last for long, because she knows she will never look like a Miss America. Cruel words spoken so long ago continue to haunt her today. The little girl inside of her was hurt because Daddy did not think she was beautiful. Every little girl wants her daddy to think she's the prettiest little girl in the world.

If your "child within" remembers painful messages that still hurt, close your eyes very tight and, in your mind, hug that child. Tell her you think she is the prettiest girl in the world.

Father, help me to love myself like You do.

> *But you are a chosen generation, a royal*
> *priesthood, a holy nation, His own special*
> *people, that you may proclaim the praises*
> *of Him who called you out of darkness into*
> *His marvelous light.*
>
> —1 PETER 2:9

Struggling with our bodies instead of really living life can seem like one dark tunnel. Instead of enjoying life to its fullest, we get depressed with what we think we look like. All we see is darkness instead of light.

Take heart. Jesus called us out of the darkness into His marvelous light. He chose us. We are part of His royal priesthood. We are His own special people. Because He loves us and died for us, we can praise His name. Notice He did not say, "I'll choose you when you're perfect," or, "I'll choose you when you lose your weight." He did not say He would choose us *when;* we are *already* chosen.

God has more important things for us to do with our time and our minds than worrying about how fat we are. He has meaningful work and a purpose for us regardless of what we look like. May we savor the reality that He has called us out of darkness into marvelous light.

Father, thank You for choosing me. I love You because You first loved me. Father, You know me so well. Thank You for giving me a purpose for my life—Your purpose. Help me to stop dwelling so much on my body and to learn to focus more on You.

Behold! The Lamb of God who takes
away the sin of the world!
—JOHN 1:29

Sometimes the past haunts me. I feel so bad about abusing my body and for not loving God the way I should have. I grieve over the loss of twelve years of my life to bulimia and to the obsession with dieting. During my outpatient therapy, I talked about this with my therapist, Mike. We talked about my pain, and then he made me close my eyes.

"Now put yourself in a room," he told me, "and then put Jesus in the room with you. What would He be saying to you?"

I saw myself in that room, grieving. "Jesus," I said to Him, "how could I have done all that I did to you?"

Gently, Jesus answered me, "Cynthia, I've already died to save you and cleanse you of all your sins. The past is gone, and you have today to start over.

"I've always been with you, Cynthia," He reminded me. "I've never left you and I'll be with you always."

When I opened my eyes I felt a sense of healing. Now when I get overwhelmed with grief, I picture Jesus saying to me, "This past is gone, and you have today to start over."

Jesus forgives. Jesus heals. Today we can start over.

Jesus, thank You for your healing power and for loving me enough to go to the Cross.

> *I am He who lives, and was dead,*
> *and behold, I am alive for ever-*
> *more.*
> —REV. 1:18

If you are at the bottom of the pit . . .

If you are doubting whether God is alive . . .

If you fear God does not love you . . .

If you have been rejected, abandoned, beaten . . .

If you think life is over because of your sins . . .

Look to the Cross.

Look to the Cross, today. It is there, on a lonely hill in time, waiting for you. It is where our Saviour, our Messiah, died for us. He knows all about sin even though He never committed even one. He took all our sins and put them on His shoulders. He went to hell and back for you and for me.

The next time questions come that have no answers, come to the Cross.

When you feel so alone you think you are the only one left in the world, come to the cross.

It's so hard to grasp. Jesus came to Earth to heal people and spread the good news of salvation. He loved people and during the thirty-three years of His life, He knew He would die for me. To save my soul. To save the world. So as I struggle I will sit below the cross and weep for joy. Jesus died for you and me.

Jesus, thank You for going to the Cross for me.

He who disdains instruction despises his
own soul,
But he who heeds reproof gets
understanding. —PROV. 15:32

What is your reaction when you are criticized? Do you get mad? Do you believe every word and then overeat? Do you shrug off the criticism, and return it with an ugly gesture? Do you take it and learn from it?

Criticism is not much fun but I do have choices for how I deal with it. I used to believe every word of criticism; it would reinforce how bad a person I thought I was. I never stopped to think that maybe the person who criticized was wrong. I bought the whole line, and then I felt so bad I would go out and stuff myself with food in an attempt to forget the pain I learned that I can deal with criticism in a healthier way.

Constructive criticism is good, and I can learn from it, but sometimes the best way to react is to take it with a grain of salt—to consider the source.

When I am criticized I can say, "You're right. I'm a failure." Or I can say, "Let me think about what you've said and I'll get back with you." This enables me to put it on a shelf and examine it. Then I can come back and say, "you're right," or "you're wrong." Or I can simply say, "I'm sorry you feel that way. However, I have to disagree with you. Let me tell you why."

We do not have to succumb to hurting ourselves when we are criticized. Criticism is inevitable. When it does come, let us deal with it and learn from it.

Father, help me to listen to criticism and grow from it.

> *Seek the LORD and His strength;*
> *Seek His face evermore.*
> —PS. 105:4

We often feel so alone when we are struggling, hurting, and abused. We think, Who could possibly understand how we feel? When we feel this way, we forget that Jesus has been where we have been.

He felt everything we have felt.

His heart was broken.

His body was beaten.

He was rejected by those who claimed to have lived their lives looking for His coming.

His family turned against Him and did not understand who He was.

He cried alone.

He longed to have a friend stay up and pray with Him only to find no one had the time.

He was unpopular.

There is nothing we have been through that Jesus does not understand. We are not alone in our pain. Today, seek His strength. Seek His face. Today, seek the Lord.

Lord, I need You so much. Sometimes I feel so alone, as if no one else can understand what I'm feeling. Help me to remember that You understand how I feel, and that I can open up my pain to You.

There is therefore now no condemnation
to those who are in Christ Jesus, who do
not walk according to the flesh, but
according to the Spirit.   —ROM. 8:1

So many letters come to my office that say, "I'm a Christian but I'm such a bad person. How could God love me?"

"I've accepted Christ but I'm falling away because I feel I can't be a Christian and be fat at the same time."

Take heart. Paul said to the Romans, "For the law of the Spirit of life in Christ Jesus has made me free from the law of sin and death" (Rom. 8:2).

We are set free from sin and death when we believe Jesus died for us. This does not mean we will never fail or sin again. It means no matter where we have been or what we do, Jesus Christ forgives and does not condemn us. If Christ sets us free from condemnation, we must too. As long as we continually condemn ourselves, we lose sight of God's love and forgiveness.

We will fall but Christ will pick us up.

We will fail but Christ will give us victory.

Today, stop condemning yourself and forgive yourself. In Christ, the only condemnation is what you bring with you.

Father, thank You for forgiving me and setting me free from my past.

> *But seek first the kingdom of God and His*
> *righteousness, and all these things*
> *shall be added to you.*   —MATT. 6:33

Today, let us seek what God wants in our lives, not what we want. He promises that if we seek Him, saying, "God, I'm yours; what do you want me to do?" then He will bless us.

We sing in a hymn, "Have thine own way, Lord," but what we really mean sometimes is, "but I want my way first."

To seek His kingdom we must take His lead and let Him guide us. We must obey Him when He tells us the way we should go, no matter where that might be. We need to trust that no matter where we are, He will be with us.

If we start the day deciding to seek first His kingdom, God will take care of the rest of our needs. He does not promise to indulge our whims or give in to our destructive desires. He promises to take care of our needs.

What do you need? What do you desire? Are they the same things? If not, you cannot expect God to give them to you. Often what we want is not what is best. Do you ever wish that God would miraculously take away your problem with food? You are tired of it; you just do not want to deal with it anymore. You want God to just get rid of it for you. It does not work that way.

Father, forgive me when I say I'll do something for You and I don't do it. Be patient with me and help me to seek You.

*Call to Me, and I will answer you, and show
you great and mighty things, which you do
not know.*
                                        —JER. 33:3

Mandy is nineteen years old. She was anorexic, but now she eats all the time. She told me once, "I had a relationship with God but once the dieting started the diet was my God. The real God was left by the wayside. It's the same now, except food is king. Cynthia, I admire your ability to be so close to God."

Mandy had read my book, *The Monster Within*. When she expressed her admiration for my relationship with God, I had to explain to her that my belief in God was not always there. At one time food was my god, too. Like me, she had to find out why food was her king. She spoke a lot about food, but not of that which the food was numbing.

"I feel stupid when I pray," she told me. "I feel like no one is listening."

I can relate to how Mandy feels. Can you? God *is* listening. God does care about the Mandys of this world. God patiently waits for us to dethrone our obsessive diet plans and make Him King.

Father, I know it is wrong when I do not pray to You. Help me to know that You are listening, that You are not too busy to hear me. Father, I need to get rid of the things in my life that take Your place. Help me to tear down my idols of food and dieting.

> *I know your works, that you are neither*
> *cold nor hot. I could wish you were*
> *cold or hot. So then, because you are*
> *lukewarm, and neither cold nor hot, I*
> *will spew you out of My mouth.*
> —REV. 3:15–16

I told my therapist that I'd rather die than be fat." So goes a letter from Myrna. "As a child and all of my life, I've been told that I'm a 'big girl,' which I absolutely hate! I have always wished I was small and petite."

Myrna is seeking help, yet she says, "I want to be committed to getting thin, but I'm afraid of failing."

She lives with so many confused, mixed messages. She would rather die than be fat. She is not ready to give up food, her best friend and source of comfort.

If we are to get well and become whole, we cannot be lukewarm. We cannot go back and forth, vacillating between what we know we should do and what we want to do. We have to decide to face our pain, give up our control and our sin, and allow God to help us through our out-of-control behavior.

Instead of facing the reasons why she turns to food for solace, Myrna is angry and afraid. Yet the very comfort she seeks adds to her anger and fear.

Lukewarm can be such a comfortable temperature. We do not like things too hot or too cold. Sometimes being comfortable is not what we need.

Today, give up your back and forth ways and commit to healing, whatever it takes.

Father, help me to be strong in my faith in You.

> *Surely goodness and mercy shall*
> *follow me*
> *All the days of my life.*
> —PS. 23:6

I heard a minister propose another interpretation of the psalmist's words, "mercy shall follow me." He suggested the verse means God's mercy and kindness will *pursue* me all the days of my life.

God follows me! He wants to overtake me with His mercy and His goodness every minute, every day of my life. That means that no matter how bad we blow it, God has mercy on us.

Mercy means to have compassion for, or to bear with, no matter how much we fail or offend. We are in great need of the mercy of God. When I meet the Lord in heaven it is not justice I will want, but mercy.

Today, believe that God is pursuing you. He is seeking after you because He loves you. He longs to heal and comfort you. Even if you keep running away, He will still pursue you. Our God is an active God. He does not merely sit in some corner of the universe, waiting for us to have the good fortune to find Him. He is actively seeking us out. He knows and understands our nature. And He knows there will be times when He must come after us, as the shepherd pursued the lost sheep.

If you're running from God, stop. He'll catch up with you.

Thank You, God, for running after us, for never letting us go from Your love and care.

> *The fruit of the Spirit is love, joy, peace,*
> *longsuffering, kindness, goodness,*
> *faithfulness, gentleness, self-control.*
> —GAL. 5:22–23

Let the beauty of Jesus be seen in me" are words I can sing with great conviction. The song does not ask that the beauty of Jesus be seen in the clothes I wear, or the shape of my body, but in *me*. In me, where it really counts.

The Holy Spirit lives inside of us. Today may we allow the Spirit within us:

To show love where there is none.

To seek truth, instead of denying it.

To be kind instead of rude.

To be calm instead of in a rush.

To seek a need and fulfill it.

To be gentle instead of forceful.

Today, may we know that no matter what we look like on the outside, the Spirit lives on the inside. The love of Jesus can shine from the inside out to the world.

Do not worry so much about your outside but rather dwell on the beauty of Jesus that may be seen inside you.

Lord, I want to be more like You. I want Your beauty to shine from me. Too often I tarnish myself, so I do not shine as bright as I should. Help me to polish my life, Lord, so that Your spirit can show Your love to the world through me.

O come, let us worship and bow down;
Let us kneel before the LORD our Maker.
For He is our God,
And we are the people of His pasture,
And the sheep of His hand.
—PS. 95:6–7

Why is complaining so easy to do?

Why is it so much easier to focus on the negative instead of the positive?

Sometimes our prayers are just filled with complaints. While I believe God wants us to be honest with Him, it does the heart good to *praise* Him and to show our adoration.

Today, let us praise Him. Think of all that He has done, and say to our God,

"I praise you, God, for your salvation."

"I praise you, God, because you never let go of me."

"I praise you, God, because you fill up my empty spots."

"I praise you, God, for all your never-ending blessings."

"I praise you, God, for loving me, anyway."

"I praise you, God, because you always have time to hear my needs."

"I praise you, God, for you hang on to me even when I let go of you."

Father, I adore You. I love You and I am so proud to be Your child. I praise You, God.

> *Husbands, love your wives, just as Christ*
> *also loved the church and gave Himself*
> *for it.*
>   —EPH. 5:25

Because I have been writing and traveling and lecturing full-time, I have gotten out of shape the past few months, and it has gotten me down. I just feel better when I am exercising. But when you are out of shape, it takes time to get fit again.

Recently I underwent major surgery and my stomach muscles were cut open. As a result of the surgical trauma, I now have a funny-looking stomach pooch. I was looking at myself in the mirror the other day, and I started crying. I have one breast; I am out of shape; I have a scar across my stomach that looks funny because it bulges.

My husband, David, heard me crying, and I told him, "Look at me. How could you possibly love me?"

He gathered me up in his arms and said, "You're not ugly. I think you're beautiful!"

I am so glad love is blind. David, like God, loves my heart and my love for life and my love for God. David loves me so much it does not matter what I look like on the outside.

God does not see what I see when I look in the mirror. He sees the beautiful child He created, and He loves me no matter what. I thank God for that because it helps me to keep on trying.

How about you?

Father, thank You for families who love us no matter what we look like.

Anxiety in the heart of man causes
depression,
But a good word makes it glad.
—PROV. 12:25

When our self-esteem is low, we lose confidence. When we lose confidence, it is hard to stand up for what is right. Some people just do not feel as if it is their right to express what they are thinking.

During my bulimia, I had fruitless relationships with people who confirmed my feelings of worthlessness. I looked for people who would treat me that way. Through therapy, I learned that I was valuable.

After I left the hospital, Joel was the first man I dated. At first our relationship was good, but then I realized that Joel was not treating me with respect. I asked my therapist about it.

"If you want to break your pattern of dating," he told me, "you're going to have to stand up for your rights."

"If I stand up for myself," I protested, "I might be rejected."

"That's right. But at least you'll find out where you stand.'

Up to that point, Joel had been setting all the rules in our relationship. I prayed a lot about it, and then I went to talk to Joel.

Joel did not want to understand my rules or to compromise with me. We decided it was time to end our relationship. It hurt, but also it felt good to stand up for myself.

Father, help me to stand up for what I believe to be right.

> *For to this you were called, because Christ*
> *also suffered for us, leaving us an example,*
> *that you should follow His steps.*
> —1 PETER 2:21

Your whole life can change when you go through the intense surgery of emotions that takes place in therapy. I found that as I changed, my expectations of others became correspondingly high. Sometimes I wanted to scream to friends and family, "I've changed! Why can't you?"

I struggled with this frustration for eight months during my outpatient therapy, and then one day my therapist said something to me that struck like lightening.

"The only person you can change, Cynthia, is yourself."

In other words, I cannot change the past. I cannot change other people but I can understand my past and how it affects me. I can even explain my feelings to the people who need to hear them, but in the end the only one I can change is me.

If we think, Now that I've changed and understand, people in my life will change too, we set ourselves up for heartache and disappointment. Some of the people in our lives, as they see the change in us, will become even more entrenched in their own attitudes.

It is asking a lot to expect the world to change, too, when we take charge and change our lives. We hope those around us will desire to change as well. But we should not pin our hopes on that happening.

Father, help me not to worry about everyone else changing. For now, Father, help me change.

*Now we exhort you, brethren, warn those who
are unruly, comfort the faint-hearted, uphold
the weak, be patient with all.*
—1 THESS. 5:14

Last week I was on a call-in radio show to discuss my books. A few of the callers were very frustrated. A man called to talk about his bulimic daughter. He was angry because she ate so much.

"Her brother used to binge and purge all the time," he told me, "but he stopped. Why can't she?" The fact that he had both a son and a daughter who were bulimic told me the family had serious problems.

"Sir," I asked, "have you told your daughter what you just told me?"

"Of course I have."

"Sir, while I appreciate your call to me, I need to encourage you to seek professional help for your entire family. Your daughter needs compassion and under-standing."

Another caller said, "I know an eighteen-year-old guy who just got out of a thirty-day treatment center, and he's still sick. Why isn't he well?"

"It took him eighteen years to get to where he is today," I reminded him. "He's got to go back and un-derstand those years."

Families and friends sometimes want a quick fix. They want an easy answer so it will all go away. If you struggle with how long change is taking, be encour-aged. Take it one day at a time. God is patient.

Father, teach us to love even when we find it hard. Help us to realize healing takes time.

The LORD knows the thoughts of man.
—PS. 94:11

Rose Marie is obese. She cannot fit into a medium-sized car seat. She cannot take a trip on a plane because she needs three seats.

At one time Rose Marie was unemployed. One day an employer was able to see beyond her size and recognize her talent. Rose Marie is able to type ninety words a minute. She thanks God for her job, yet she still is not willing to do anything about her weight. She says she has prayed about it, and God has not healed her so He must want her to be her size.

Rose Marie is blaming God for her inability to lose weight. She is expecting Him to miraculously take the weight off for her without any effort on her part. God does not work that way. He wants us to know always that the journey is as important as the journey's end. There must be something here He wants us to learn.

Rose Marie's father is a prominent doctor who has disowned his daughter because her weight disgusts him. Maybe God wants Rose Marie to trust her heavenly Father more than her earthly father.

What does God have for you to learn on your journey? Do you really want to take the short cut and miss out on the discoveries along the way? The way is rough and hard sometimes, and we wonder if it really is worth it after all, but just hang in there and pay attention. Don't expect the gifts from God to start at the finish. The rewards may be waiting for you on the way.

Lord, help me to stop wanting a quick fix to my problems.

See that no one renders evil for evil to anyone, but always pursue what is good both for yourselves and for all.   —1 THESS. 5:15

It can be extremely difficult to express our needs verbally. When people are encouraged by their therapist or support group to confront their loved ones, they usually experience a sense of panic, fear, and dread. Some will even say to me, "I just can't do it."

I always recommend that they write everything down beforehand in a letter. The first draft should contain everything they are struggling with, or feel, or need. I encourage them to set the letter aside for a day, pray about it during that time, and then write it again. Next, I suggest they find someone they trust, ask them to read the letter, and ask them if they think the letter will help or destroy the relationship.

Writing a letter helps us to sort out our feelings whether we end up sending it or not. Attempting to get your feelings down on paper will help you to identify them. Often, we do not know why we are angry at someone until we have to put those feelings into words. Taking the time to write allows us to express what we need to say in the best way, divorced from the emotions of the moment. It also allows the person on the receiving end to read your thoughts in a safe way. Often, what we have to say is not pleasant.

Don't forget to give your thoughts to God. *He* will always respond to your letter.

Father God, thank You for always taking care of my needs.

> *A wise man will hear and increase*
> *learning.*
>   —PROV. 1:5

It is a sad fact, but often our families are the least likely to understand those of us struggling with our weight or with an eating disorder. After *The Monster Within* was published, a relative of mine talked to me about it. Ignoring the pain expressed in my book, and the joy that came out of it, the only response this person had was, "Don't you know you'd have gone to hell if you'd committed suicide?"

My suicidal behavior obviously shocked her, but of all the things in the book, I found it strange that that was all she commented on. I looked at her and said, "All I know is I was in so much despair I wanted to die. Only God knows my heart."

She could not understand my pain. It was not the first time relatives have not understood. Jesus' own mother and brother did not understand what He was doing. He reminded us that a prophet is never honored in his own country. The people who know you best often do not know you at all.

You may have relatives who have hurt you with their misunderstanding of what you have gone through, or what you are going through now. It may seem to you that no one understands. But remember, Jesus does. He has gone through the same pain. Don't give up. Look to Jesus.

Father, teach me patience with other people. Please soften the hearts of loved ones who don't understand.

"Why could we not cast him out?"
So He said to them, "This kind can
come out by nothing but prayer and
fasting."   —MARK 9:28–29

The disciples, who had cast out demons before, were confused because they were unable to cast a demon out of a boy. Jesus did it for them. The disciples wondered what they had done wrong. Jesus told them it was a kind of demon they had not encountered before who could only be cast out through prayer and fasting. It seems to me that Jesus said we need to be spiritually prepared for the times when we will come up against something that is really tough.

Jesus was always praying. He spent a lot of time alone with His Father, recharging His spiritual batteries. Are you spiritually prepared to face the demands of everyday life? What will you do if life throws you a curve? Jesus gave us the example of prayer and fasting as a way to get ready.

The fasting Jesus is talking about does not involve food—it is preparing your mind and body to be in tune with God. Until you are healthy and food is no longer a problem for you, fasting cannot possibly be what will draw you closer to God. It is your fasting that is drawing you farther away. Besides, God has always been interested in the condition of the heart. Bind yourself to Him in a way you can handle. He does not want it any other way.

Lord, draw me near to You. Help me as I grow spiritually to walk in Your ways.

> *As the deer pants for the water brooks,*
> *So pants my soul for You, O God.*
> *My soul thirsts for God, for the*
> *living God.*
> —PS. 42:1–2

We live in a complicated world. On the one hand, the secular realm says, "Do whatever feels good." On the other hand, I have heard ministers say, "Therapy is not from God. If you have problems in your life, just stop. You know what is right."

King David yearned for God in his days of distress. He longed for the presence of God to give him relief from his times of trouble.

At the end of this psalm, David wrote that his enemies taunted him, saying, "Where is your God now that you need Him?" David answered, "I will hope in God and I will praise Him anyway" (Ps. 42:11).

Even David, the man after God's own heart, struggled with prayer. At times he felt as if God was far from him. He anguished over the silence he felt came from God. Have you ever cried out to God, only to hear the echo of your own voice haunt you? You are not alone.

For every desperate psalm written by David, there is a multitude of others praising God for His ready answers. God did not change from one psalm to another; David's perception changed. God is everlasting. David learned to hope during those dark times when he could not feel God because he knew the light would eventually break through.

Today, if you are in darkness, retain hope.

Thank You, God, for giving me hope to overcome.

For He shall give His angels charge over you,
To keep you in all your ways.   —PS. 91:11

God orders His angels to protect us wherever we go. Think about it. Have there been times in your life when events happened that you could not logically explain? During my travels, I heard hideous stories of the abuse inflicted on people by relatives. I have often wondered how they made it this far.

My husband, David, has a friend who hitchhiked across the country. "Weren't you even scared?" David asked. "Did anyone ever try to hurt you?"

"Once a man stopped and acted so strange," he said. "Then the man drove away. I found out later that a man was arrested on that very road for killing hitchhikers. I guess I must have a guardian angel."

I look back on my years of destructive behavior, and I cannot believe I am still alive. Maybe God's angels were watching out for me. Then I ask myself, If He has angels watching over us, why do so many innocent people die, or struggle so? I do not have an answer for that, but I trust God does.

It is wonderful to realize how much God loves me, even when I do not understand how He could. Things happened that I see now as the hand of God in my life, whether through an angel or a friend.

I do not have all the answers, and I do not fully understand the angels, but I do know that God is watching out for me.

Father, thank You for watching over me and for Your constant love.

Do not lay up for yourselves treasures on earth,
where moth and rust destroy and where thieves break
in and steal; but lay up for yourselves treasures
in heaven.
—MATT. 6:19–20

Do you hide the best candy from everyone in the house, and eat it when no one else is home? Do you hoard food, and eat it as if there's no tomorrow?

I know a man who is thirty pounds overweight. When he eats he eats fast and packs in a lot of food. He grew up in Hitler's Germany. He and his family never had enough to eat. By the grace of God, they survived the war and came to America, to an abundance of food. He remembers vividly the joy of his first chocolate bar, and his very first hamburger. When he eats, he remembers always being hungry.

Sometimes I feel as if I need to eat chocolate, more chocolate than I really need. If I died tomorrow, there might not be chocolate in heaven, so I have to eat it now while I can. I laugh about this crazy reasoning, but the feeling is real.

For many of us, food is a treasure. It has always been meant by God to be a good, pleasurable thing. But our treasure in heaven is much greater.

If you have places in your house where you hide your food, go right now, and clean them out. Having food out in the open will make it seem less like a treasure.

Father, thank You for the treasures You have waiting for me in heaven. Help me to stop hoarding Your gifts on earth, and to start using them in the way You intended.

*Then God saw everything that He had
made, and indeed it was very good.*
—GEN. 1:31

As I sat on the beach recently on a hot summer day, I took time to just look at all the people. There were all kinds of shapes and sizes and, in their bathing suits, all the bumps, bulges, and pooches—or the lack of them—showed up clearly. It was very reassuring to me to look at all the different shapes, hardly any perfect.

I sat there and I thanked God for the diversity of His creation. Not one of us is just like anyone else. And one thought came to mind: God loves every single one of us. He loves the guy with a bulging stomach. He loves the woman with the fat thighs. He loves the fit lifeguard. He loves the girl with the flat chest and big hips. He even loves me.

Jesus loves the little children. Today, it is a good feeling to know Jesus loves all the shapes and sizes on the beach. Do you sometimes wonder if Jesus could love you in the shape you are in? He can, and He does.

Are you ashamed of your body? Do you avoid going to the beach, or putting on a swimsuit? Well, join the crowd at the beach! No one has a perfect body. Even that slinky one in the bikini probably has something about her body that she does not like. Don't let something unattainable keep you for joining in and having fun. God loves you and your shape. Everything He has created is good, and that means you too.

Father, thank You for the unique way You've created us.

> *Sing praises to God, sing praises!*
> *Sing praises to our King, sing praises!*
> *For God is the King of all the earth;*
> *Sing praises with understanding.*
> —PS. 47:6–7

My husband David loves to sing. One night I was discouraged and tired, and he said, "Honey, let's sing." We sat on our bed and sang praises to God. We sang about His wonderful love for us. We sang about the glory of His world. We sang prayers to Him. Singing with my beloved husband lifted me up. I did not feel discouraged or weary anymore.

God teaches us to be filled with the Spirit, speaking to one another in psalms, hymns, and spiritual songs, making melodies in our hearts. What a beautiful way to communicate to each other, to God, and to ourselves.

Few of us really hate to sing. If we do, it is probably because we do not think our voice is very good. But God could care less about how we sound. That is not the point. When we sing, we open our hearts to God with a personal expression of our inner selves. It is a way of showing who we are. Some of the most beautiful singing I have ever heard was created by people who could not sing a note.

Today, take time to sing. It is another free gift from God that lifts our spirits and puts our mind on praise rather than on the things of this world. Singing can be food for the soul. Fill up on song.

Father God, I praise You for the gift of song. Today, Father, I lift up my voice to You.

A soft answer turns away wrath,
But a harsh word stirs up anger.
—PROV. 15:1

On a stormy, winter night, the plane going home was delayed because of weather. I was tired. No one was sitting next to me, so I lay down on the empty seats. I was just drifting off to sleep when suddenly I was tapped sharply on my shoulder. "Get up, lady," I heard as I lifted my head. "That's my seat you're lying in. I've had a rough day and I want to sit down."

I could have responded in kind to this man's harshness. I felt like lashing out at him for his unbelievable rudeness. Instead I gently said, "Sir, I think I know just how you feel. I've had a rough day too." I sat up and controlled my anger.

After a few awkward minutes, the man obviously felt bad about what he had said. "Lady," he explained, "I'm sorry I was so blunt a minute ago, but I'm three hours late and I have to get to L.A. I'm just so frustrated."

"Yes," I agreed, "the weather has made it tough for a lot of people."

When we finally landed in Los Angeles, another man stopped me before we got off the plane, and said, "Miss, you sure handled yourself well with that ol' geezer at the airport. I was ready to punch his lights out."

I learned that day that my attitude can change someone else's, and I was reminded that you never know who might be watching you.

Father, help me to remember that a soft answer does stop wrath.

> *O My God, I cry in the daytime, but*
> *You do not hear.* —PS. 22:2

Prayer is direct communication with God. In 1 Thessalonians we are instructed to pray without ceasing. But sometimes we wonder if He is really listening. We pray about specific things, expecting an answer immediately. When it does not come right away, or is not exactly what we wanted, we wonder if He really heard us.

Is God deaf to our cries, or are we blind to His will? We do not get the answer we want so we assume He has not answered. In truth, He has answered us; we just cannot see it because we are looking for something else.

I think God answers prayers in three ways. Sometimes He says, "Yes." Sometimes He says a direct, "No." And at other times His answer is, "Wait."

When we are put in the "waiting room," we struggle. We get impatient and say, "God must not be home." We understand things according to when they happen. God is not bound by our time restraints.

It has been said, "All things come to those who wait." Of course, we do not know just how long that wait may be. We have to trust that God does hear our pleas and that He knows what is best for us, no matter how long the wait.

If you feel stuck, continue to pray. Gather your strength to wait from Him.

Father, help me to be patient as I wait on You.

The Lord your God is a merciful God.
—DEUT. 4:31

If God's mercy endureth forever, why is it so hard to give mercy to ourselves? If God can forgive us, why can't we forgive ourselves? After we have overeaten, how often do we beat ourselves and say, "I'm such a bad person! Why did I do that?"

In my therapy group I relived past sins, and I felt so bad. My friend, Stephen, said, "Cynthia, quit beating yourself. Guess what? Your pain proves you're really just a human after all."

Stephen's words helped me to be merciful with myself. I realized I had blown it like everyone else. I needed to go on.

The Bible is filled with stories and psalms about God's mercy. David sang, "His mercy endures forever" (1 Chron. 16:34). Today, be merciful to yourself. God is. He will never yank that mercy out from under you. It endures forever. Make it the foundation for your own mercy for yourself. Sometimes we need to put down the lash and give ourselves a break.

Merciful God, thank You for the love that only You can give. Thank You for Your mercy. As You show mercy to me, help me to show mercy to myself and to those around me.

> *A merry heart makes a cheerful*
> *countenance,*
> *But by sorrow of the heart the spirit*
> *is broken.* —PROV. 15:13

A young girl came to talk to me one day. She was very depressed. I could see that before she even opened her mouth. Her posture was stooped. Her face was sad. Her eyes were dull and listless. Her body mirrored the desperation inside. She had been sexually abused by her brother. She was angry and ashamed and did not know what to do.

"Have you been to a therapist?" I asked.

"Yes," she answered after a moment.

"Well, did he help you?"

"All he said basically was, 'If it's not broke, don't fit it.'"

The therapist told her to forget the past, and not look back. I recommended another therapist. She went and worked through her devastating betrayal by her brother. She even confronted him and her parents about the past, and now she is getting on with her life in a healthy way. It was broke, and she fixed it.

How many people are merely existing, walking around with broken spirits? This girl did not have to live alone in her depression.

God calls us to life. If you are not living but just existing, one step ahead of your past, it is time to figure out why.

———————

Father, help us to follow our hearts when we know we need help.

*Whether He is a sinner or not I do not
know. One thing I know: that though I
was blind, now I see.*   —JOHN 9:25

When I went public with my story, I was amazed at
how many people who came to me for advice were not
getting anywhere in their therapy.

"Has your therapist dealt with your past?" I asked.

"No, he (or she) just stares at me."

"You mean he doesn't probe beneath your symptoms?"

"No, he just says it's up to me to change."

They asked for referrals and I gave them names of
professionals I knew personally. I encouraged them to
seek other avenues of help.

Therapists may not see the answer to your eating
disorder; they may think they already have all the answers. Sometimes I feel like the blind man the Phari-
sees interrogated. They did not want to believe Christ
had healed him. I have wanted to say to some therapists, "Look, I don't know if this is the way you've
always done it, but I was sick and now I'm well."

People may not always approve of the route you
take to wellness. If you know it is the right road for
you, stay on it. Don't be sidetracked by the negative
comments of people who are not on the road with you.

*Father, give me strength and courage on my journey down the road
of wholeness.*

*A man will be commended
according to his wisdom,
But he who is of a perverse heart
will be despised.*—PROV. 12:8

Boundaries. Many of us who struggle with an eating disorder have trouble setting boundaries. They are either way too broad or way too narrow. We know we need balance in our lives but we do not know how to achieve it.

If we were abused as children, we can grow into adults who continue the theme of being abused. We attract people who hurt us and abuse us.

On the opposite side, sometimes we restrict ourselves far too much. We set harsh regulations for ourselves. We isolate ourselves from everyone. We starve and exercise ourselves to the very limit, thinking this is a way of maintaining control. Our narrow boundaries are so tight it is impossible to move, or to breathe.

Our lives need boundaries. We need to be able to put up a "No trespassing beyond this point" sign. We need to set a safe limit, to have balance and structure in our lives.

Where are your boundaries? Are you including things inside your boundary that are detrimental to you? Are you locking out good things because your boundaries are too limiting? You don't have to build your boundaries alone. Trust the Master Builder.

Father, help me to understand what my boundaries should be with other people and help me not to be afraid to use them.

He who says he abides in Him ought himself also to walk just as He walked.
     —1 JOHN 2:6

Mother Teresa has said that since Jesus cannot be on this earth in the flesh, we, His children, must be His eyes, arms, hands, ears, feet, and legs.

When our eyes see a need, do we fill it?

Do our arms reach out to hug and lift up the weak?

Do our hands reach out and touch, to soothe the broken heart?

Do our ears hear the needs of others behind the words?

Do our feet fly swiftly to help others?

Do our legs carry us to the far off places of the world where need exists?

In the Bible, the apostle John wrote that if you believe in Jesus, then you will walk as He did. How did Jesus walk, and talk, and interact with others?

Jesus always knew when to speak up, and what to say. He also knew when to keep silent. He hurt for the broken people of this world who constantly swirled around Him, desperate for hope. When He perceived a need, He filled it.

To walk as Jesus did means getting involved with others and putting your emotions on the line. It also means a life of purpose and communion with God.

Today, let us use our bodies to exemplify our Lord and Savior.

Father, use me as an instrument of Your love.

> *Do not be wise in your own eyes;*
> *Fear the L*ORD *and depart from evil.*
> *It will be health to your flesh,*
> *And strength to your bones.*
> —PROV. 3:7–8

We bend and stretch, and we twist our bodies into grotesque shapes—all in the name of shaping up. But while we are stretching our bodies, we may find our minds losing flexibility.

We can only eat certain foods. Stay away from those. These are the only ones we can have.

We are only allowed to wear certain clothes. Keep away from anything that might reveal too much of ourselves.

We should not seek out other people, lest we be tempted. We do not want to have to explain all our rules. Avoid anyone who might suggest something we just cannot do.

We have to stay on a schedule. There is no time to eat or to think of food. Food is the enemy, so we must fill up the time with things to do, more and more.

How much freedom are we willing to give up in order to achieve someone else's idea of perfection?

Today, be flexible. Allow yourself to change the rules. Sure, watch what you eat, but you do not have to set up rigid codes. Instead of wearing dark cover-ups, wear something bright. If friends ask you out, go. Don't exchange one prison for another.

Father, if I get too rigid, tug at my heart and help me to relax.

> *The lamp of the body is the eye. If*
> *therefore your eye is good, your whole*
> *body will be full of light.*
> —MATT. 6:22

Whenever I see Cora, I hurt for her. She has gained fifty pounds over the last three years, and her face is covered with acne. Her outward appearance is a sign of what is going on inside. Cora has locked-up sorrow. Her mother gave her away when she was a child. Her foster parents were good people but they expected perfection. Cora never felt like she measured up.

Cora longs to be married some day but her unhappiness and her neglect of her body hinders relationships. Cora does not care about herself, so it is hard to find other people who do. Everything about Cora screams out, Please, fix me! Underneath her severe acne is confusion and struggle.

Our bodies have a way of mirroring what is happening inside. When our body shows signs of distress, it may be a signal for us to take time to listen. It may be time to slow down, and to look beneath the surface into the real heart of the matter.

Today, take time to listen to your body. Our bodies and our minds work in conjunction with each other. Abuse or neglect on the outside is a sign that something is wrong inside, and we are trying desperately to fix it.

God, You have given me such a wonderful body. When something is wrong, it lets me know. Help me to stop and listen. Give me strength to do something about it.

> *Now may our Lord Jesus Christ Himself,
> and our God and Father, who has loved
> us and given us everlasting consolation
> and good hope by grace, comfort your
> hearts and establish you in every good
> word and work.* —2 THESS. 2:16–17

Cheryl woke up one morning and said to herself, I'm stuck. I don't control food; it controls me. She was sick and tired of the way she was. She did not like herself very much so she decided to find out why. Cheryl went to a counselor, and she opened up her past. She was sexually abused by her father. After the truth was revealed, her burden was lifted.

Free from her burden, Cheryl started a weight loss plan. Each day she set a goal for herself. As she lost her weight and uncovered the pain of her past, pride took the place of the hurt. For the first time in her life Cheryl felt pride in who she was and how far she had come. She started to wear new clothes that reflected her increased self-confidence.

Before her therapy Cheryl was not ready to lose weight because she did not feel proud of who she was. When she set a goal of losing thirty pounds, she was ready. The weight came off because the reason for the fat was no longer there.

Cheryl has some advice for anyone on a weight loss program: set little goals for yourself, and reward yourself for reaching those goals. (One word of warning, however: don't make food the reward.)

Father, thank You for helping me to stay on my road to change.

> *You almost persuade me to become a*
> *Christian.* —ACTS 26:28

King Agrippa almost became a Christian. The apostle Paul gave him a powerful testimony about what Christ had done in his life. It was almost enough. King Agrippa was almost ready. He was almost persuaded.

When it comes to changing the way we do things, we often are almost ready to act, but then we don't. It is tough to change things. We have to get around our traditions, our fears, our families, our own inertia.

Sometimes events in our lives cause us to take an inventory of our lives. We see things we need to change. But somehow we are never quite ready to do it. We can see we are in a rut, but we are afraid of what is outside our safe little rut. Why should we rock the boat?

There are many excellent reasons to get out of your rut. It could make you a better person. Perhaps your rut has resulted in your stagnation –emotionally, physically, or spiritually. You may find that it is not so bad outside the rut after all. You may even learn a thing or two. You will certainly enjoy life more if you are not closed in by those dark walls.

Almost only counts in horseshoes. It does not count in ruts. Climb out of yours. The sun is shining and it is a beautiful world out here. All you have to do is come out and experience it. *Almost* may mean *never*.

Lord, I want to get out of the rut and give my heart to You.

> *His rows of scales are his pride,*
> *Shut up tightly as with a seal.*
> —JOB 41:15

Job described an impenetrable sea creature that protected itself by closing its scales. Fish are not the only ones that can shut themselves off and shut the world out. We are pretty good at shutting out the world ourselves, and we do not even have scales.

When we have failed ourselves or others, often our reaction is to withdraw. The deeper our humiliation, the farther we shrink into ourselves. Some people even go so far as to remain continually in their house, never venturing out.

Have you ever pulled in the world after you? Have you shut the door and put up a "Do Not Disturb" sign for all to see? Is that what you really want? In Genesis, God plainly said, "It is not good that man should be alone" (Gen. 2:18). We are social creatures by nature. Isolation is not what is best for us.

All of us need time alone to sort things out and get our lives back into perspective. Sometimes it is nice not to have to interact with anyone else for a while. But it should be just for a little while.

So, get up and get out. Bless your family, your neighbors, your world, with *you*. Isolation is not the answer to life's pain—involvement is. When you are alone, all you have to think about is your pain. When you are involved, the pain is easier to bear.

Father, sometimes I just want to run away and hide. Help me to seek outward instead of inward.

> *Surely, as I have thought, so it shall*
>   *come to pass,*
> *And as I have purposed, so it shall*
>   *stand.* —ISA. 14:24

My father always recited a little poem to me whenever I was down:

> *'Twixt the optimist and pessimist*
> *The difference is droll:*
> *The optimist sees the doughnut*
> *But the pessimist sees the hole.*
>   *McLandburgh Wilson*

We focus on the wrong things too often. We do not look at the good about us; we focus on the bad. We may have a dozen right things going on in our lives, but we are devastated if we wake up in the morning with a pimple. We cannot try because all we will do is fail. We cannot lose weight. We will never be pretty enough, good enough, strong enough . . .

Enough for whom? For us? Who are we to judge what is enough? God is the only one who has ever had *enough*. And He does not ask perfection of us. In fact, He offers to fill up the gaps in us.

If our view of ourselves is always focused on perfection, we will always be disappointed. There is One we can focus on through the eyes of perfection, however, and never be disappointed. If you must look for perfection, look to Jesus.

God, it's such a relief to know I don't have to be perfect for You to love me.

> *The net takes him by the heel,*
> *And a snare lays hold of him.*
> *A noose is hidden for him on the*
> *ground,*
> *And a trap for him in the road.*
> —JOB 18:9–10

Little magic pills made of garlic and papaya are selling for one hundred dollars a bottle, an unbelievable deal considering you get twenty-four pills in each bottle. Advertised as the ultimate diet pills, they are purchased by the very rich or the very foolish.

The pill's creator says they are the best diet plan around. Druggists, nutritionists, and other health professionals say they represent the classic con job. Sales are going so well that they will soon be coming out with "Diet Water."

P. T. Barnum said, "There's a sucker born every minute." It would be humorous if it were not so sad. The people who buy these products may be wealthy and able to afford to throw money away chasing rainbows. But some of the people who plop down a hundred bucks a bottle will not really have the money to spend. They may give up buying food or shoes for the kids in search of the impossible dream these people sell.

There is no magic solution to your weight problem, no matter how badly you might wish for one. Garlic and papaya pills are not going to help you lose your weight, no matter how many movie stars swear to how wonderful they are.

Father, help me to watch out for the traps that lie along the road. Help me to use the common sense You gave me to avoid them.

*Owe no one anything except to love
one another for he who loves
another has fulfilled the law.*
—ROM. 13:8

Ahh, the magic words, "Charge it!"

Charge cards have not only put many of us into a financial crunch, but also they give us the illusion of escaping responsibility. One credit card company's television advertisements show people on vacation who change their plans and end up putting new clothes, food, transportation, everything, on their credit card. They did not like what they were doing, and they had the power to charge it and change it. A little piece of plastic made it all possible. Whenever I see that commercial I get an uneasy feeling. They have a marvelous time, the kind of fun only large amounts of cash can bring, but what happens when they get home? Sooner or later the bill comes, and it is time to pay the piper.

So many of us are like that when it comes to food. We recklessly charge into our food with abandon, thinking little of tomorrow and the price we will have to pay. But eventually the bill does come due in extra weight, upset stomachs, and a guilty conscience.

We need to be responsible to only spend and eat what we can afford to lose.

Father, sometimes I do not want to think about tomorrow. I say to myself, eat, drink, and be merry, for tomorrow we diet. I know that is not the way You want me to live. Help me to be responsible with the choices I make in my life.

> *Blessed is the nation whose God is*
> *the LORD.* —PS. 33:12

A national association reported in 1990 that sixty-five million Americans are dieters. We count calories, weigh portions, measure cupfuls and spoonfuls. We fuss over sugar, fats, cholesterol.

Researchers have found that children turned loose around a table laden with a wide selection of food soon tire of the sugary ones and soon select a fairly balanced diet. Somewhere we lose that tendency, perhaps when we turn to food for reasons other than satisfying physical hunger.

Maybe it is time to relearn what a healthy diet is. We need to return to food as simply food, not a way of numbing other things in our lives. Instead of naturally choosing those things that are good for us, we seek the sweet desserts to cover up what's really wrong.

Today, let us commit to putting food back into its proper place. Food is not a sedative or a crutch. It is what you need to keep your body running. The wrong amount or choices of food interferes with your body's proper purpose.

Lord, help me to see food as You see it—nourishment for my body and not god of my life.

O Lord, my strength and my fortress,
My refuge in the day of affliction.
                    —JER. 16:19

One type of abandonment leaves a trail of wounds and scars in the human heart that cannot be fathomed except by those who have experienced it: divorce.

Christians are taught that divorce is sinful, that men and women are married, "'til death do you part." At weddings the bride and groom vow before God to be faithful forever.

Contrary to the ideals of Christian upbringing, one out of two marriages in the United States ends in divorce. Guilt, feelings of abandonment, loneliness, rejection, and loss can be overwhelming.

The reality is that many of you, and myself, have been divorced. The task of rebuilding our lives is almost more than we can handle: We must reclaim our self-esteem, and maintain our belief in our own worth. Unfortunately, those around us do not always do or say things that help us to rebuild. Too often casual remarks destroy our already fragile spirits.

When we have lost a relationship, it can be very easy for us to turn to food for solace. We just cannot seem to feel good any other way. But food is not the answer. If your congregation offers no comfort and adds to your burden, find another church. If your family judges you, look to others for your comfort.

Above all, know that a merciful, loving God is always there, ready and willing to hear and to help.

Father, thank You for hearing my cries and never abandoning me.

> *Come to Me, all you who labor and are*
> *heavy laden, and I will give you rest.*
> —MATT. 11:28

When life is dealing us a seeming bad hand, when everything has gone wrong, when nothing seems to work and everything is breaking down, where do we turn? Where can we go but to the Lord?

There have been times in my life when I was down to my last dollar. My monster, bulimia, was consuming my income faster than I could make it. I could go to my parents for help, and they would. I could go to a friend for a short-term loan, just to get me by. Pretty soon there was nowhere else I could turn but to God. I had to admit that my life was out of control, and I needed God to take over.

Why is it that we have to be at the very bottom before we will look up and truly see God? Maybe it is just human stubbornness. We cling to the misguided hope that somehow we will pull ourselves out, even as we are sinking deeper and deeper into our pain.

What a joy it was for me to take His hand and be lifted up. What a thrill it was to be healed and forgiven just as I was learning to forgive myself. I am confident now, knowing through experience and through His promise that no monster is too big for Him to handle.

Dear Lord, I'm thankful that You are there always, calling me to You. I thank You for the comfort and strength You give me in all my struggles.

When my father and my mother
forsake me,
Then the LORD will take care of me.
—PS. 27:10

Very few of us get through life without feeling abandoned at times. Sooner or later we will be left alone, deserted by people we love. Do you ever remember being punished as a child, and instead of getting spanked, you were sent to your room? You could hear the sounds of the rest of the family in the other part of the house, talking or watching television. And there you were, all alone in your room.

Maybe you had older brothers and sisters who went off to camp during the summer. They were so excited about leaving. You were not old enough to go with them.

Did you experience the break-up of your family? Did you have to live with your mom, while your dad went off to live somewhere else? How many times did that father call, or visit, or write? Did he abandon you?

Some parents choose careers that take them away from their families. Whatever the reason, they are not there with you.

As children we cannot set the priorities of our parents. Feelings of abandonment may be at the heart of our eating disorder.

God is always there for the abandoned child. He has promised us that. Through His Son He has said, "I will never leave you nor forsake you" (Heb. 13:5).

Father, thank You for the security of knowing You will never leave me.

> *The other disciples therefore said to him,*
> *"We have seen the Lord." But he said to*
> *them, "Unless I see in His hands the print*
> *of the nails . . . I will not believe."*
> —JOHN 20:25

If only I could see His hands, then I would believe.

Conditions. Thomas had them, and so do we.

If only I could lose my weight, then I would be happy.

If only I were happy, then I could lose my weight.

If only my spouse were more understanding, then I could work on my self-esteem.

If only I could work a little harder, then I would be rich.

If only I had this dining room table and chairs, then I would be satisfied.

If only I could get away for a little while, then I would be nicer to my spouse and my kids.

A condition is also an excuse. If we put a condition on our actions, we have the perfect excuse for doing nothing. The condition was not met, so we are not obligated to act. But we are the ones who put the condition on the action in the first place.

If you must put a condition on action, make it a positive one. Tell yourself, If only God loved me . . . ; If only Jesus had died for me . . . ; If only the Spirit will help me. . . . You are bound to succeed, for He does love you; Jesus did die for you; and the Spirit will help you take the action you need to take.

Father, help me to grasp the love You truly have for me.

So God created man in His own image.
—GEN. 1:27

Did you know that no one can duplicate your finger-prints, or your hair strands, or your voice? You are unique. There is not another person like you in the world. No one can match your individual traits.

God creates individuals. He is not a cookie cutter God. He is a God who loves infinite variety. Why do you long to look like someone other than yourself? God did not make you that way.

In the Bible, God says that He created us in His own image. God made us to be like Him. We can feel sad-ness, anger, pain, happiness, joy. He likes singing and laughter. He grieves. God is like you and me.

In a world that is saturated with the message, "This is how you've got to look," it is assuring and refreshing that our God wants us to look exactly as He made us. If He had wanted all of us to look like movie stars, He could have. But He did not, so there must be a reason.

When you look in the mirror, stop wishing you looked like someone else and be glad you are you. That is just the way God made you. You can add to or subtract from what God originally gave you through improper eating habits, but with work you can get back to the original design. Trust your Creator. He did not mess up when He made you.

Father, thank You for making all of us different. Sometimes I want so badly to look like someone else. Help me to be happy with who You made me to be.

*And not only that, but we also glory in
tribulations, knowing that tribulation
produces perseverance.*

—ROM. 5:3

When Cheryl lost her weight she looked like a totally new woman. Her teenage children supported her all the way. They were thrilled with their new mom. Her husband, however, had a hard time accepting the new Cheryl. Threatened by her new beauty, he had an even harder time accepting the inner strength Cheryl was gaining from gaining control over her life. The stronger, more confident Cheryl intimidated him.

Her husband tried various ways to hinder her progress. But nothing would stop Cheryl from going forward with her life. She kept telling herself, I need to go on, in the face of his continued resistance. Sadly, he kept wanting the old Cheryl back. Unable to handle the changes in his wife, he left. They are now separated.

Cheryl learned the hard way that when you make a change in your life, it will affect your family. Everyone may not be ready to accept your change. Cheryl had to realize that she was responsible for putting her own life back together, confronting her past, and getting on with her life. She was not to blame for the inability of those around her to handle the change.

We are called by God to grow and change. He does not like stagnation. Unfortunately, some people really like the status quo.

Remember, the only person you can change is you.

Father, help me to focus on You when I feel like giving up.

*Beloved, do not avenge yourselves, but
rather give place to wrath; for it
is written, "Vengeance is Mine, I
will repay," says the Lord.*
                    —ROM. 12:19

She was a tall, beautiful girl of eighteen, with shoulder length blonde hair and perfect skin. Young men thought she was beautiful. They were afraid to ask her for a date, assuming the answer would be "no." After all she looked like a million bucks, was great in school, and her old man was a doctor with plenty of money.

This beautiful girl would have been surprised by what they thought of her. She saw every minute flaw in herself. She was brought up that way, groomed from childhood to mirror her father's success. Failure in any form was not an option.

Unable to withstand this pressure to accomplish the impossible, the girl turned to food. The backs of her fingers had calluses from jamming them past her teeth and down her throat to induce vomiting after bingeing.

Too often our parents attempt to relive their own lives through us. They want us to be all the things they were not. But you cannot live someone else's life without giving up who you are. Every time this girl vomited instead of confronting her father, she was killing herself.

You do not have to live anyone's life but your own. If you are being pressured to fit into someone else's mold, break free.

Father, be with me when I feel pressure to be what others want.

> *But my beloved had turned away*
> *and was gone.*
> *My heart went out to him when*
> *he spoke.*
> *I sought him, but I could not find him;*
> *I called him, but he gave me no*
> *answer.*
> —SONG 5:6

I know a woman who was left at the altar by her fiancé when she was very young. The jilted young bride found it impossible to develop an intimate relationship again for many years.

In order to protect herself from the pain of being rejected again, she began to put on weight. As her weight increased, her romantic interactions dwindled. She kept her weight on and her prospects off for forty years. When she was in her sixties she finally married a man in his eighties.

Her fat insulated her from revealing her true self and the possibility of being hurt again for years. She allowed the rejection she had felt so long ago to color everything she did later in life. Food became her lover.

Are you hiding behind your fat? Are you using it as an excuse not to develop intimacy?

God desires intimacy with us. Our relationship with our Lord is described as that of bride and groom. There is much the Lord wants us to know through the physical union called marriage. Don't miss out because of fear. Jesus risked death to become our mate.

———————

Father, help me not to be paralyzed because of my fear.

"I will never leave you nor forsake you."
So we may boldly say:
"The LORD is my helper;
I will not fear.
What can man do to me?"
— HEB. 13:5–6

In the past, there was not even a name for anorexia or bulimia. But now we can seek help. Frank Minirth, in his book, *Love Hunger*, lists twelve benefits that can be gained from joining a support group:

1. An antidote to the shame by providing unconditional love.
2. Fellowship which breaks isolation.
3. Ongoing encouragement.
4. A true substitute family.
5. Accountability.
6. A church in the broadest sense of the word.
7. Practical help and information.
8. Insight through the struggles of others.
9. Positive habits.
10. A reminder that food is not the issue.
11. A forum for the grief process.
12. A reminder that people should be put in place of food.

Lord, remind me when I want to hide that food is not the problem but how I see myself.

> *And do not be conformed to this world.*
> —ROM. 12:2

Remember Twiggy? Her boyish haircut and ultrathin mod look was the rage in the sixties. Like all rages, it soon burned itself out. But the feeling that we are all too fat was her enduring legacy. I think back to the glamour girls of the forties and fifties. You could have put two Twiggys into a Marilyn Monroe.

The only way many of us could look like Twiggy was to induce starvation, or develop a drug addiction. Faced with such an impossible idol, many of us just threw in the towel. "Forget it," we screamed. "I'll never look like that so why try!"

Fashion designers use people who look like that because their bodies are anonymous. There are no features to get in the way of their clothes. They use them as living mannequins. When a mannequin in a store is dressed, all you see is the clothing. That is the way it is supposed to be. Without its draping, it looks grotesque, oddly disturbing.

When people look at me, I want them to see me. I do not want to be so skinny that all they see is what I am wearing. That is not the look I am after. Don't be afraid to be who you are. Don't be afraid to show your shape. You don't have to look like Twiggy to be beautiful. She was never meant to stand out; you were only supposed to see the clothes.

Father, often what the world thinks is beautiful, or of value, is not. Help me to see beauty and worth through Your eyes.

*A certain man gave a great supper and invited
many, and sent his servants at supper time to say
to those who were invited, "Come, for all things are
now ready." But they all with one accord began
to make excuses.*
                                    —LUKE 14:16–18

It amazes me how the human mind can rationalize just
about anything. We really are inventive creatures.
Sometimes I think our imagination and our creativity
are gifts from God that allow us to, beyond logic, grasp
His nature.

In the story above the Bible records just how creative we can be.

One man who had been invited said he had just
bought a field and had to go inspect it.

Another man who turned down the invitation had to
go check out five yoke of oxen he had just purchased.

The last one had the best excuse of all: He had just
gotten married and could not come.

We can be as creative as the people in this parable,
can't we? We can come up with a hundred and one
reasons why it just is not possible to change our eating
habits. We hem and haw and put off the decision to get
our eating under control and get on with our lives.

God has a beautiful banquet called life waiting for
us. It is all ready. It has been prepared for us to enjoy.
Isn't it about time we stopped making excuses and
started living?

_____

*Lord, help me to be honest with myself and with You. Help me to
recognize my excuses for what they are. Give me the strength to
come to Your feast.*

*I know that there is nothing better for them
than to rejoice, and to do good in their
lives, and also that every man should
eat and drink and enjoy the good of
all his labor—it is the gift of God.*
—ECCL. 3:12–13

As their children grow older, American families eat fewer meals around the dinner table. There are so many things to do and places to go that meal time is a quick rush between other activities. Add to that a dual income household where both parents work, and you have something just short of bedlam.

Breakfast together is out too. Even if everyone is up at the same time, they are rushing about so that no one is at the breakfast table together.

Lunch is a brown paper sack for the kids. Mom and Dad will grab something at the office.

Dinnertime should be a chance for the family to come together and catch up on the day. Too often, everyone is supposed to fend for themselves because Mom and Dad are too tired to cook. Instead of a time of sharing, we hear, "Will you kids keep it down? I'm trying to watch the news!"

Have you lost the tradition of the evening meal? If you have, it is not too late to recapture it. Special effort and planning may be required. Family members may balk at having to be in the same room with each other, but be patient. Make it a special time.

---

*Father, my family is so precious. Thank You for giving them to me.
Bring us closer together.*

All my close friends abhor me,
And those whom I love have turned
*   against me.*   —JOB 19:19

Job knew what it meant to be deserted and taunted by friends. They not only left him alone, but also they rubbed salt in his wounds.

My eight-year-old niece, Danielle, was singing a song the last time I saw her, and I asked her to repeat it for me:

There's only one of me on the planet earth,
I'm learning to be, my way,
My own best friend, as I've found out
There's no one else like me.

Friends come and friends go. But that little song expresses a simple and profound truth: My own best friend is me. If I treat myself right, I learn self-confidence. If I am concerned enough about myself to eat right and exercise, then I am my own best friend.

Do you like yourself? Are you happy to be just with you, or do you need to surround yourself with others?

God said that to love others, it is important to first love ourselves. If you do not love yourself, you need to seek the help you need to recapture that love. You have just left it somewhere along the way. All you need to do is go back and pick it up. It is probably right where you left it. Go look.

Father, loving myself is so hard. Help me as I learn.

> *And have no fellowship with the unfruitful*
> *works of darkness, but rather expose them.*
> *For it is shameful even to speak of those things*
> *which are done by them in secret.*
> —EPH. 5:11–12

Do you hear the words of darkness in that passage? Isn't that exactly how you have felt when you abused your body with food? It is a shameful secret you do not want exposed. But the *reasons* for "works of darkness" usually derive from abuse you suffered in the past. That abuse may be sexual, physical, or mental. It can be the abuse of abandonment, of loneliness, of fear. If it happens early enough in our childhood, we bury it deep, denying its existence because that is the only way we can cope with the pain.

Often, we are adults before we realize life does not have to be this way, and we attempt to dig inside ourselves to find why. The sad truth is, in order to thwart the works of darkness, it is necessary to expose the secrets. Allowing them to stay hidden retains their power over us. When we expose them, we can see them for what they really are and ourselves for who we really are.

It seems as if many of us compound those secrets by our own shameful eating disorders rather than reveal the dark truths. Isn't it time to break the cycle? Isn't it time to get the past out in the open? Expose it to the light of reason and truth.

Father, I know You see everything. Help me to have the strength to uncover the secrets of my past.

*Then they said to one another, "Look, this
dreamer is coming!"*   —GEN. 37:19

I have watched the health of a family I know go down-
hill steadily. The mother started out neat and trim as a
bride, but after the birth of her fourth child, she was
fifty pounds overweight. The oldest daughter is forty
pounds overweight. A son, twenty-one years old,
weighs fifty pounds more than he should.

What is going on? Why are these people becoming
unhealthy? The answer, unfortunately, is an overde-
manding husband and father. When he and his bride
were first married, he bought a farm. He has added
more and more land, and in order to make the farm
work, he put his wife and children into the fields working long hours.

The father's dream has turned into the family's
nightmare. He is obsessed with keeping the farm going, no matter what the costs. He runs the family with
such a tight hand that none of his children or his wife
have ever protested their forced labor. Instead of telling him to "stuff it," they stuff themselves with food.

Perhaps you are living someone else's dream but it is
a nightmare to you. You are entitled to your own life,
you know. Did this person ever ask you whether or not
it was your dream too?

Today, determine to live your own life. It is all right
to have your own dream. What are your dreams? Go
for it!

Father, thank You for dreams. Help us to strive to fulfill our dreams.

You are my hiding place;
You shall preserve me from trouble;
You shall surround me with songs
    of deliverance.   —PS. 32:7

There are so many times in my life when I have just wanted to run to some place safe and hide. When I was a child I had a special room. As an adult I wanted a place, not to live out my dreams, but to cover my head and say to the world, "Go away!"

I never found a physical place in which to hide. What I found instead was a refuge in food, lots of it. In my car or at home—as long as it was private—my hiding place would become candy, ice cream, cakes, pizza, whatever I desired.

Instead of an escape, food became my prison. It became a monster I could not control. I locked the door, drew the blinds, turned off the phone, to be alone with my food. It almost destroyed me.

I have been set free from that prison and my Savior was Jesus. I have learned to turn to God for my hiding place now. God has filled my world with songs of deliverance.

If He can do that for me, He can do that for you. I am not a special case. The motivation for my deliverance is the love He has for me.

If you are locked in a prison, don't give up. Someone is working for your release. Watch for that door to open, just a little bit, and then run for freedom.

God, I praise You for reaching me in my prison and showing me the path to life.

*A man who has friends must
himself be friendly,
But there is a friend who sticks
closer than a brother."*
—PROV. 18:24

A self-controlled and structured life does not come by accident. It comes through purpose and skillful planning. For most of us it's necessary to plan out our time in order to be more productive and enjoy life. Without planning we can't seem to get anything done!

A happy life cannot be planned without emphasizing spiritual growth. Time for the study and meditation of God's Word and for prayer puts our lives in perspective, and realigns our priorities.

A happy life also includes a large dose of other people. We are social beings and need the interaction with others. Included in this interaction with people should be fellowship with other like-minded individuals. We need to be able to talk and share with one another about our spiritual trials.

Too often we do not plan for ourselves. In order to be happy and productive, we have to take time out for us. Taking the time to plan to eat right and to get the proper amount of exercise helps keep our bodies and our minds running smoothly. Take a walk. Ride a bike. Plan some kind of physical activity for your day.

We are creatures of habit. Too often, unless we are careful, they are bad habits. Today, commit to taking care of yourself and planning your days better.

Father, be with me as I plan my day. Give me wisdom to glorify You.

> *Shall we indeed accept good from God,*
> *and shall we not accept adversity?*
> —JOB 2:10

A friend I know dropped by the house the other day. I was even more alarmed when I saw tears in his eyes. Before I could even say, "What's wrong?" he began to sob uncontrollably.

He told me his wife and their three children had just left him. He couldn't understand it. He thought everything was going fine. There'd been a few stormy moments, but nothing to lead up to this.

I listened, and I found out about what he called "storms." They had been in such bad shape financially that they had to refinance their house to avoid bankruptcy. His mother had suffered a near-fatal heart attack. His aunt died; two grandmothers died. Everywhere he turned it seemed there was death.

He told me that six months ago his thirteen-year-old daughter had run away. While his father was visiting him recently, his uncle, whom they had both loved, passed away.

There are times when tragedy after tragedy hits us, and we wonder how we are ever going to make it. This world is full of death, sadness, illness, and pain. But we have been promised help and support, love and understanding, from a God who has been here, and suffered just like we have. Let Him comfort you in your grief.

Lord, sometimes I just don't think I can go on. Hold on to me then.

*And I was afraid, and went and
hid your talent in the ground.*
—MATT. 25:25

It is a common situation today: a need arises, a special
kind of need that requires a special talent or gift to
address it. And the one person who could fill that need
is too occupied by how they look or their lack of perfection, and the need goes unfilled.

God gives everyone a gift. Some people have gifts
that are more noticeable than others. What is yours?
Once you find your gift, will you share it or hide it?

If your gift is teaching, then teach.

If your gift is listening, then listen.

If your gift is compassion, be kind to others.

If your gift is helping, then help where you can.

If your gift is comforting, then put your arms around
the hurting.

If your gift is drawing, then create.

If your gift is decorating, bring joy to someone's
home.

If your gift is praying, we need more of you in the
world.

If your gift is serving, don't be afraid to serve.

Goes does not want us to hide the talent He gave us.
In Matthew, when the man hid his one talent, the Lord
was angry and took that man's talent away.

Find your talent. Show your talent. Thank God for
the talent He gave you.

*Father, thank You for the gifts You've given to me. Use my gifts to
show the world that You love us.*

> *Charm is deceitful and beauty is vain,*
> *But a woman who fears the Lord,*
> *she shall be praised."*
>
> —PROV. 31:30

Lois is a new friend of mine. She is retired and lives in an apartment designed for the elderly. My husband and I were invited over to her place for dinner. She greeted us in the lobby in a bright red shirt and a red bandana in her snow-white hair.

After taking us through the lobby, she opened the door to her apartment. My breath was taken away. Inside her small one-room apartment was a miniature garden. There were plants and flowers everywhere. Bright red tulips intertwined on her bedspread, couch, tablecloth, and chair upholstery. Everything was coordinated with red and white accents, and looked like a picture out of a home decorating magazine.

She had just moved in a week before. I was not prepared for the visual treat that awaited me beyond her door. Lois showed her love of life, and her love of self, by the beautiful way she decorated her room. Dark wood or somber colors would not suit Lois.

Lois's room reflects Lois. She has not given up on life because she retired. Her room is bursting with life. I wanted to gather up the room and embrace it, for it captured the essence of Lois's enthusiastic attitude.

Thank You, God, for people like Lois, who continue to show what love of life is all about.

*The Lord is my strength and my
    shield;
My heart trusted in Him, and I am
    helped;
Therefore my heart greatly rejoices,
And with my song I will praise Him.*
    —PS. 28:7

When my husband and I walked into Lois's small apartment, we were met with a wonder of beauty. She also fixed us a wonderful, nutritious meal.

Lois has arthritis and many other health problems but she refuses to dwell on her aches and pains. Her beautiful home is proof of that. I marvel at her. Lois's room says to those who enter it, Come in. You are so welcome and I am very proud of my home.

Lois's home took me back to my twenties, when I was in the midst of my bulimia. I did not care what my apartment looked like. I could not have cared less about flowered bedspreads or wicker furniture. My apartment reflected how I felt about me. It was dreary and messed up most of the time.

Can you relate to my response to Lois? Look at your home. Is it bright and cheerful, or is it drab and depressing? Does your home project an invitation to friends, or does it keep people away? Now that I am healthier emotionally, my house is filled with bright colors. My kitchen is baby blue, pink and white. I have flowers all over my fireplace.

It took time for me to enjoy decorating. If you do not care about your surroundings, ask yourself why.

Father, in all areas of my life I desire to reflect You and Your love.

> *No one has seen God at any time. If*
> *we love one another, God abides in us,*
> *and His love has been perfected in us.*
> —1 JOHN 4:12

A wooden plaque in my kitchen reads, "Home is where love surrounds us." I believe God created the home for that very reason.

David and I have "adopted" a lot of our neighborhood kids. Many days after school, they will knock on my door, come into my kitchen, and we will sit and talk, eat cookies, and drink milk. One day I found myself in my kitchen with five kids around my table. Lavinia, a beautiful thirteen-year-old, said, "Whenever we're together outside we don't get along. But whenever we're in your house, we do. It's like a house of love." Lavinia made my day.

I have had to mourn the losses of my childhood and the losses of my addiction, but I can make up for the things I missed by creating the very things I deserved as a child. Maybe my mom and dad did not have the time to fulfill a lot of my needs. As an adult, I can meet some of them.

It is wonderful to know I can fulfill a need for someone because I have been there. The children in my neighborhood, like all children, long to be loved and accepted. I can give a little to them by simply inviting them into my kitchen.

Maybe your childhood was not "a home surrounded by love," but yours can be now. The choice is yours.

Father, show me how to love the people around me like You love them.

O my God, I trust in You;
Let me not be ashamed;
Let not my enemies triumph over
me.
Indeed, let no one who waits on
You be ashamed;
Let those be ashamed who deal
treacherously without cause.
—PS. 25:2–3

A university student, struggling with bulimia, approached me crying. She had lived with the shame of a lie all her life. When she was five, her mother had miscarried and had told her, "The baby died because of you. You are such a bad girl, the baby died."

She could not get over the guilt her mother's accusation had caused and she carried the shame with her wherever she went. In order to assuage her guilt, this girl had turned to bulimia. The purging symbolically cleansed her of the guilt. It also numbed her to her shame.

When we are young, we believe what our parents tell us. As adults, we must confront what they told us and discern the truth.

Today, look back and examine what you have been told. Accept the truth and reject the lies. Above all, you need to go on.

Father, You tell us to honor our mother and father. But, Father, sometimes our parents have not treated us the way You would want them to. Help us to love them anyway.

Show me Your ways, O Lord;
Teach me Your paths.
Lead me in Your truth and teach me.
—PS. 25:4–5

When I met Rachel, her posture was stooped and shame and guilt were written all over her. At a wedding celebration when she was fourteen, a friend of the family asked her to go with him for a walk. When he had her away from everyone, he raped her. He said if she told anyone she would be sorry.

This young man was a friend of the family, loved by everyone. She could not understand what had happened to her, and she felt it must have been her fault. For four years she carried around the shame and guilt. Food protected her from the pain.

I encouraged Rachel to imagine that he sat before her in a chair, and to tell him how she felt. Timidly she said, "You shouldn't have done what you did to me."

"Speak up," I told her. "Tell him how you really feel."

Her pain and her rage slowly emerged. "I trusted you!" she yelled. "You raped me and you're walking around smiling, fooling everyone. I'm sick of it. You had no right to rape me! I'm going to tell on you."

Through therapy, Rachel was able to tell her parents what had happened. She was afraid they would blame her, but they did not. Her shame was lifted. Her confidence returned.

Are you carrying someone else's shame? If you are, you need to return it to its rightful owner.

Father, please take away my shame. Fill me with Your hope.

*But You, O Lord, are a God full of
compassion, and gracious,
Longsuffering and abundant in
mercy and truth.* —PS. 86:15

Televsion makes the holidays look so picture perfect: turkey perfectly cooked, a table full of gorgeous goodies, and the hostess who looks like she has not just spent the last thirty-six hours getting food ready.

You have done some changing in the past year; you guess that everyone else has too, but no such luck.

Aunt Bess still complains about everything.

Dad still drinks more than his share.

Mom still runs around serving everyone else and never stops long enough to talk to you.

Grandmother still blames everyone for her problems.

Brother still yells at his kids.

In most families, the role you played as a child will be the one you are called upon to play as an adult. Although you may have changed, the family may have stayed the same. We need to put aside our unreal expectations of others.

With tables full of delicious food, it is too easy to drown our disappointment over our families in a mountain of mashed potatoes. Commit to love your family and not expect more than they can give.

Father, being with family can be so difficult. Help me to be patient and forgiving.

> *Let nothing be done through selfish ambition*
> *or conceit, but in lowliness of mind let*
> *each esteem others better than himself. Let*
> *each of you look out not only for his own*
> *interests, but also for the interests of*
> *others.*
> —PHIL. 2:3–4

Does meeting your needs mean you have to hurt someone's feelings?

Is everyone else more valuable than you are?

Do you always do what others want, and leave your own needs for later?

If you answered "yes" to any of these, try this one. Do you use food to make yourself feel better?

Reexamine why you feel the way you do. Do you think that is the way God wants it? Scripture says we are to think of others as better than ourselves, but it does not mean we think absolutely nothing of ourselves. Read the second part of this passage from Philippians: Look to your own interests as well as the interests of others. Doing one does not preclude doing the other.

God has never expected you to be everyone else's doormat. How are you going to be any good to anyone else if you are no good to yourself?

If food is your way of feeling better, how long does that good feeling last? Food is not the answer. Taking care of yourself and loving yourself is the answer. From that you gain the strength and security to reach out and help other people.

Father, give me a strong love so I can love others.

> *And Hannah answered and said, "No, my lord, I am a woman of sorrowful spirit.*
> —1 SAM. 1:15

When I was a little girl, my dad used to tell a story: A little girl was approached by a family friend. He asked her, "Are you happy?" "No, I'm not happy. Mommy never lets me have candy when I want it. I'll be happy when I'm older and can do what I want."

When she was a teenager, the friend asked her again, "Are you happy?" "No. Mom has such dumb rules. I'll be happy when I turn eighteen and I can make my own rules."

At eighteen she moved out of the house, got married, and had children. The friend again asked, "Are you happy?" "Happy? With a husband who's gone all the time and two screaming kids? I'll be happy when these kids grow up and I can have some peace."

The friend waited for some time, and when the woman was old, he asked her again. "No, I'm not happy. My kids and grandchildren never visit me. I'll be happy when they let me know they're alive."

As an adult, I appreciate just how true this story is. The girl was always looking for her happiness somewhere in the future, never in the present. She ended up unhappy, lonely, and bitter.

Happiness is an attitude: "No matter where I am, I will rejoice because God loves me."

Father, teach me to rejoice in Your love and Your grace.

> *And do not be conformed to this world, but*
> *be transformed by the renewing of your mind,*
> *that you may prove what is that good and*
> *acceptable and perfect will of God.*
> —ROM. 12:2

We can change the script of our life. We can rewrite what is wrong with us. We can sing a new song. We can create a beautiful picture.

In an art therapy session, I was told to draw a picture of how I felt about life. I painted huge black broken hearts with tears falling from them. It was a depressing picture, but that is how I felt. My heart was broken. It was like a puzzle, and I needed to find the pieces and put it back together. I did not like that picture, and I learned I could create a new one.

I could dwell on the past, or I could confront it, relive it, understand it, and forgive it. I could be angry at those who had hurt me for the rest of my life, or I could express my anger and go on. I could continue to be sick with my bulimia, or I could deal with the reasons why. I could stay numbed to everything, or I could open up to emotions and feelings.

I decided to write a new song for my life. I decided to start the book of my life with a clean sheet of paper. That is how God works. Each time we say, "God, forgive me," He gives us a clean, white sheet of paper to start again.

Whatever we have done, whatever we have been through, there is great hope in knowing we can paint a new picture any time we desire to change.

Father, thank You for cleaning my slate so I can start over.

*He who gets wisdom loves his own
soul;
He who keeps understanding will
find good.*   —PROV. 19:8

Ann is a good friend of mine. She has a gift of accepting people right where they are. She did not come about this gift by accident. In high school, Ann was overweight, and to make matters worse, she had a twin sister who was thin. It was as if a thin version of herself walked around reminding everyone how fat she was.

The summer after her junior year the weight came off. When she began her senior year, she went from being the "fat" twin to being the "busty" twin. People who had not given her much thought before suddenly wanted to be her friend.

"I wanted to laugh in their faces," she told me. "I, the inside me, hadn't changed at all." Instead of succumbing to the pressure to adopt new friends and habits, Ann chose to stay who she was.

Ann says, "I don't look much at what a person looks like. That's subject to change without notice. What I look for is who the person is on the inside. When I was fat I wanted people to see beyond that and look at who I really was.

Do you have trouble accepting yourself because of your outside packaging? Inner beauty is what really matters; the rest is "subject to change."

*Father, forgive me when I fall short and judge people's appearances.
Help me to look into other people's hearts instead.*

And they clothed Him with purple; and
they twisted a crown of thorns, put
it on His head.   —MARK 15:17

Life is like licking honey off a thorn." I saw that on a billboard once and those words have stuck with me. It is a odd statement, but a true one. God gives us the gift of life. Life is precious and to be cherished. The essence of life should be sweet like honey. But because of our weakness and our sin, our problems and pain, the thorns appear under that honey.

When I think of thorns, I think of Jesus on the day He died for me. The soldiers placed a crown of thorns on His head to mock Him. Jesus, our Lord, could have called down angels from heaven, or He could have sent fire down to destroy those who were mocking Him. Instead, He chose to die for them.

The message He brought of redemption from sin was sweet news to this bitter world. But even Jesus had to contend with thorns.

If you are careful, you can probably suck honey off a thorn without getting hurt. But just one false move and that thorn rams home, stabbing painfully.

I look forward to the day in heaven when my honey will not come with a thorn. There my Lord will not be wearing a crown of thorns, but His rightful crown of glory. Until that day, I will be as careful as I can, and look to Jesus for my example. He did not let thorns stop Him from doing what He needed to do.

Father, help me to cherish the sweetness of life and give me courage as I encounter the thorns.

And I saw a new heaven and a new earth.
—REV. 21:1

The question was asked at a luncheon I went to the other day, "What's heaven going to be like?" Loudly a woman responded, "No more diets!" Everyone laughed.

Then I pictured God meeting me at the pearly gates, and saying to me, "Welcome, Cynthia. I want you to know that there are no celery sticks or protein drinks up here. Heaven is very different from what you're used to so I've made up a list of things you should eat during your eternal stay here:

"First: every day, you will need a hot fudge sundae.

"Second: over there are the banquet tables. Eat whatever you want. We don't have calories up here.

"Third: make sure to pick up a chocolate bar. You'll need all the energy you can get.

"And Cynthia, no more exercising. You did enough of that on earth for twenty people. Here in heaven, glorifying my name will be enough."

I know my Father in heaven laughs at thoughts like this. But I look forward to heaven because I will be set free from my earthly body and its concerns. The old rules will not apply.

A woman I know says she has asked God to exchange her size fourteen body for a size six when she gets to heaven. But in heaven, we will not worry about what size we are. Praise God!

Father, I thank You that You have a place like heaven waiting for us, and a new body to replace this one. Thank You for all You give to me, Father, both here and now and in heaven.

About the Author

Cynthia Rowland McClure is a former award-winning television reporter and is a professional lecturer on eating disorders, related addictions, and the dysfunctional family. Cynthia is also author of *The Monster Within* and *The Courage to Go On: Life after Addiction*.

The author lives with her husband, David, and son, Micah, in Pomona, California.